CRAFT OBSESSION

CRAFT OBSESSION

The Social Rhetorics of Beer

JEFF RICE

Southern Illinois University Press   Carbondale

Southern Illinois University Press
www.siupress.com

Copyright © 2016 by the Board of Trustees,
Southern Illinois University
All rights reserved
Printed in the United States of America

19 18 17 16   4 3 2 1

Cover illustration: Russian River sampler, 2010; photo by author

Library of Congress Cataloging-in-Publication Data

Names: Rice, Jeff (Jeff R.), author.
Title: Craft obsession : the social rhetorics of beer / Jeff Rice.
Description: Carbondale : Southern Illinois University Press, [2016]
   | Includes bibliographical references and index.
Identifiers: LCCN 2016012117 | ISBN 9780809335282 (pbk. : alk.
   paper) | ISBN 9780809335299 (e-book)
Subjects: LCSH: Drinking customs—Anecdotes. | Beer—Blogs.
   | Social exchange. | Social networks. | Digital storytelling.
   | Narration (Rhetoric) | Rice, Jeff (Jeff R.)—Anecdotes. |
   Rhetoricians—United States—Anecdotes.
Classification: LCC GT2890 R53 2016 | DDC 641.2/3—dc23 LC
   record available at https://lccn.loc.gov/2016012117

Printed on recycled paper. ♻

To Vered, Judah, and Jenny

When the kids turn twenty-one, we're going on a serious beer trip.

CONTENTS

Preface   ix
Acknowledgments   xv

Introduction: Craft Parenting   1
1. Craft Introductions   20
2. Craft Interruptions   41
3. Craft Networks   72
4. Craft Terroir   98
5. Craft Delivery   127
6. Craft Tracings   155
7. Craft Sharing   179
8. Craft Obsession   206
Epilogue: Father-Son Stories   231

Notes   241
Works Cited   247
Index   269

PREFACE

This book tells a social media story about craft beer. *Craft beer* designates thousands of small breweries across the country that produce less than six million barrels annually and use adjuncts only for purposes of flavor (as opposed to the economic reasons large conglomerates embrace rice and corn). As of 2014 there were 3,418 craft breweries in the United States ("Number of Breweries"). Craft beer is a growing movement, as the *Wall Street Journal* reports:

> Craft sales jumped 14% to 5.1 million barrels in the first half of 2011 after rising 11% last year, putting them on course to log their fastest annual growth rate since 1996, according to the Brewers Association. The Boulder, Colo.–based industry-trade group defines a craft brewery as "small, independent and traditional" and counted 1,740 of them as of the end of June, with another 725 in planning stages. (Esterl)

Notable craft beer breweries include Stone, Dogfish Head, Schlafly, New Belgium, Three Floyds, and Cigar City. In the last few years, craft beer has made its way into popular culture and not just onto the store shelf. The 1970s TV show *Laverne and Shirley* used beer (Shotz) as the backdrop to fairly familiar plotlines of mishaps and adventures. Since then, the 1980s show *Northern Exposure* featured Alaskan Brewing neon signs in Holling's bar; the character Andy in Showtime's *Weeds* drank Stone IPA in more than one episode; in *Parks and Recreation* the characters drank Upland Dragonfly; in *The Walking Dead* various Atlanta-area craft breweries made appearances in the background; Dogfish Head and its charismatic founder, Sam Calagione, were the focus of Discovery's short-lived *Brew Masters* reality show; and Dark Horse Brewing is the star of History Channel's *Dark Horse Nation*. As a rhetorical term, image, and object, craft circulates across media outlets. Beer writer Ken Weaver describes craft as one such rhetorical marker:

PREFACE

> "Craft" serves as a placeholder for other things. It's how we talk. "Craft" can stand in place of "small," "flavorful," "good," "local," "independent," "traditional," "not-macro," and countless things beyond that. When we choose to buy "craft" beer, it's a modest show of support for those values (or at least our best attempts at doing so). ("The Future of Craft")

The story I will tell in this book is about craft beer, but it is also about rhetoric and, in particular, the rhetoric of social media. The story I will tell is about craft beer, rhetoric, and social media's intersection.

The rhetoric of craft beer exemplifies a growing national obsession with artisanal goods (breads, pastas, cheeses, olive oils, cured meats, etc.). From faux artisanal products such as Domino's "Artisan Pizza" to the growth of regional farmers' markets nationwide, craft is a quotidian, artisanal experience. We experience craft in supermarkets, outdoor events, festivals, restaurants, and often at home. Craft recaptures William Morris's nineteenth-century vision of the Arts and Crafts movement's rejection of modern production in favor of artisanal making. Unlike Morris's vision of "curing the evils that exist in the relationship between Art and Commerce" (*Art and Socialism* 4) craft's status is not exceptional in that it does not erase mass production, as Morris would have desired. Craft has become social and media based.

This book does not delineate craft as either artisan or as mass produced. Instead, I approach craft as rhetorical. In a series of "craft" chapters, *Craft Obsession* explores craft beer as a series of rhetorical moments informed by social media. Unlike other books on social media, *Craft Obsession* does not differentiate between platforms (Twitter, Facebook, Instagram, etc.) and instead focuses on rhetorics, or modes of expression, that shape various consumer and public interests, including craft beer. These rhetorics, I contend, stem from social media and influence how we construct meaning. Craft is a network of influences, and in that network we encounter the following rhetorics:

- anecdotes/beginnings
- interruptions
- repetitions
- participation
- networks
- delivery
- assumptions
- sharing
- obsession

PREFACE

Each chapter demonstrates these rhetorics, often overlapping them as each is introduced and explained. There is no one definition of craft in this book, but rather I explore a number of features of a network called craft, a network that leads to an overall feeling of obsession. The age of social media prompts new ways to explore obsessions and passions—whether found in consumer culture or elsewhere. These obsessions are identified in the industry I discuss, in those who buy craft beer, in those who write about craft beer, and in me. The content of this book, then, is meant to be both academic and personal. I hope both academic readers concerned with rhetoric and social media and readers of beer-related texts find this book useful in its specific approach to craft beer and social media. For me to express and explore a craft obsession, I must draw upon all available resources, as they are part of the same network—the professional and the personal, the academic, the media, and the beer based. Media theory and rhetorical theory inform how I approach craft, but so, too, does the craft beer world: YouTube video channels, blog posts, beer reviews, message board discussions, professional beer writing, personal moments, and online imagery.

Like my previous books—*The Rhetoric of Cool* and *Digital Detroit*—*Craft Obsession* tells a story via isolated rhetorical moments. Like those books as well, I use one subject—in this case, craft beer—to tell the story of another subject—in this case, the rhetorics of social media. Walter Benjamin associated storytelling with craft, noting that "the traces of the storyteller cling to the story the way the handprints of the potter cling to the clay vessel" and that "it cannot come as a surprise that [the storyteller] felt bonds with craftsmanship, but faced industrial technology as a stranger" (92). Benjamin concludes by networking the storyteller to materialism:

> One can go and ask oneself whether the relationship of the storyteller to his material, human life, is not in itself a craftsman's relationship, whether it is not his very task to fashion the raw material of experience, his own and that of others in a solid, useful, and unique way. (108)

The story I tell in this book is that of the industrial and the handmade, the personal and the technological. Craft, as the Arts and Crafts movement argued, fashions a world outside industrialization, favoring the handmade and the artist over the impersonal, mass-produced object. Relationships, craft claims, come from the artist, not the machine, objects associated with the machine, or the machine's by-product of consumption. Howard

Risatti writes, "In understanding something about the machine we come to understand how the handmade craft object stands against it, how the craft object stands in support of the individual's unique existence in the world" (48). But craft, as well, is the machine—from the assembly line to the computer. This type of story, craft versus the industrial, is a common one. It is familiar. It is repeated often. As a repetition, it is a contagion, a social media gesture at making familiarity dominant. Yet, this story lacks detailed focus through its emphasis on the generic. Details, as I will show, are social media based as well. The familiar will not be the story I tell in this book, but it will appear as part of social media's rhetorical complexity.

Craft exists as aesthetic and as practice and involves an emerging culture of artisanal and handmade work framed *within* a new media environment, not against it. This work reveals how "things fashion one another" in ways the Arts and Crafts movement did not anticipate, for craft, today, is also technology as much as it is the handmade. As Malcolm McCullough writes in *Abstracting Craft*,

> Any return to traditional artisanry becomes all the more unlikely. A century ago, in the time of Ruskin and Morris, work may have seemed only recently displaced—and perhaps recoverable. But today the separation is so great that traditional methods seldom survive as anything more than a personal recreation or a form of protest. Truly practical craft, practiced as a livelihood, is reserved for esoteric production, where cost is no object or where the main impetus is not the product, but the process. (48)

In craft beer, livelihood, of course, does matter. But within social media, livelihood yields to other forms of craft expression where the process of generating content, creating audience, and delivering content takes new forms. That process is an aesthetic.

In what could easily be dismissed as a commercial contradiction (projecting identity while simultaneously rejecting said identity), this aesthetic, as Adam Sachs mocks in *Details* magazine, has made everything both craft based and artisanal:

> What's new is the astonishing ubiquity of the aesthetic. Small-scale has hit it big. Farmer's markets sell artisanal cheeses—and so does Costco. Suits available in midwestern malls have machine-made details that mimic the hand stitching once found only on a Neapolitan tailor's eccentrically rolled lapel.

PREFACE

To fret over whether an object is or is not craft is to express concern over artistry and the kinds of pleasures and aesthetics artistry evokes so that the object does nothing (but the artist, alone, does *something*). Craft for some, however, is not artistry. "Use artisan and artisanal to denote craftsman and good craftsmanship, not artistry," Michael Ruhlman warns. Whatever the craft or artisanal aesthetic might be, then, it need not be an artist-based practice. It need not be classified as "good" (rescue from the ills of mass culture or bad pizza) or "bad" (pompous and pretentious). Craft can be the space where objects interact with humans and other objects to produce a network of relationships. These networked relationships allow for new kinds of storytelling regarding the social media environments we work within. As Richard Sennett writes, "People can learn about themselves through the things they make, that material culture matters" (8).

In the introduction, I begin the story of craft obsession with a proposed genre *I make*, the parental beer tale, which shifts social media studies from the grand narrative to the small story and detail. Chapters 1 and 2 expand my first parental anecdote by focusing on repeated anecdotes, beginnings and interruptions in craft beer. These repetitions and interruptions are essential to what I call a craft identity, a network of interactions across various distributed narratives. Chapters 3 and 4 expand the discussion by focusing on the specific network aligned with Russian River's Pliny the Elder (whose repetitions produce an identity) and the assumptions generated by networked terroir, as aggregations shape terroir's meanings. Chapters 5 and 6 develop the network as a mode of delivery, a complex method of delivering the idea of craft beer across distributed spaces, including beer release days. Chapters 7 and 8 conclude the book with detailed examinations of the concept of sharing. From image sharing to experience sharing to beer trading, participation and involvement challenge conventions regarding sharing's operations. Finally, in an epilogue, sharing becomes extremely personal as the parental beer tale I begin with—in order to introduce craft obsession's sharing—parallels a different parental beer tale devoid of such sharing.

This book is my craft knowledge, my craft story, my crafting of a series of social media gestures that will allow me to understand an obsession. Craft is too large a story to be limited to one area of expression or knowledge. To explore craft obsession, I must, in other words, fully explore my craft obsession, a state that captures all I encounter in the world of craft, rhetoric, writing, and social media.

ACKNOWLEDGMENTS

No acknowledgment is complete without recognizing Pliny the Elder, the beer, not the person. I love you, Pliny.

I wrote some of this book in my home office during the summer of 2013 and while on teaching leave from the University of Kentucky during fall 2013. I also wrote sections of this book while enjoying a beer at The Beer Trappe, Lexington Beerworks, West Sixth Brewing, and Country Boy Brewing in my home city of Lexington, Kentucky.

Portions of this book were written with support granted by the University of Missouri and the University of Kentucky.

I thank DePaul University, Northern Iowa University, the University of Central Florida, and the 2014 Summer Institute of the International Writing Centers Association for inviting me to speak about craft at their campuses and event. Other portions of this book were delivered as talks at the Rhetoric Society of America conference and at the Conference on College Composition and Communication.

I thank Bradley Dilger, Kevin Patterson, Nate Kreuter, and Geoffrey Carter for feedback on early versions of the manuscript. I also thank Amy Young and Thomas Rickert for additional feedback on the manuscript's first draft.

To my broventure beer traveling companions—Bradley Dilger and Thomas Rickert—this book could not have been written without our various trips together. Nor would I have attended Dark Lord Day without Thomas and our early morning drives up to Munster from West Lafayette.

In 1998 Bradley took me to a homebrewers' get-together in Micanopy, Florida. On the way, we stopped at a local convenience store off of south Thirteenth Street in Gainesville to buy beer to bring. This moment, picking out 500-milliliter bottles of Tuchor, and other beers I had never heard of, may be my first real craft beer moment. I wish I could remember what bottles were shared at the event. Of course, I had no idea what I was drinking anyway. I didn't know yet that craft existed.

ACKNOWLEDGMENTS

I thank Julie Johnson for online conversations and for sharing with me the first issues of *All about Beer* magazine. I also thank Stan Hieronymus, Tari Fahrendorf, Roger Baylor, Jeremy Cowan, and Garrett Oliver, who joined her as speakers at Craft Writing: Beer, the Digital, and Craft Culture, a one-day symposium I organized at the University of Kentucky on February 15, 2014.

And I thank my local craft friends whom I share beers with every other month or so, the Coalition of Craft Beer Lovers of Lexington. They share with me much beer knowledge, and, of course, beers.

Not a day goes by that I don't thank my wife, Jenny Rice, who shares beers with me, who devotes part of every trip to visiting a brewpub or bottle shop, who sent me my first mail-order package of beer (from John's Grocery in Iowa) and whom I am always in awe of. She is a sounding board for my ideas and thoughts, but she also is the person I drink beer with the most, after 8:00 P.M., when the kids are asleep and we have that small window to drink an IPA or two and watch some TV.

And who else would tweet something like this after I tweet one of my nightly beer reviews?

CRAFT OBSESSION

INTRODUCTION
Craft Parenting

Early in Quentin Tarantino's *Pulp Fiction*, Vincent is telling Jules a story about his time in Europe, a story now canonical among the film's fans. "You can walk into a movie theater in Amsterdam and buy a beer," Vincent recounts. "And I don't mean just like in no paper cup; I'm talking about a glass of beer. And in Paris, you can buy a beer at McDonald's." The story frames an experience that, to Vincent and Jules and maybe even to the viewer, seems odd, eccentric, exotic, and a bit out of place in the narrative. Beer makes the scene memorable in an otherwise unmemorable moment: two gangsters dressed in suits are driving in a car and talking. That scenario, by itself, is not out of the ordinary. What matters in this anecdote, as Vincent tells Jules, are "the little differences." In America, you can't buy a beer in McDonald's. In Amsterdam, you can. The detail or difference, the odd moment of being able to buy and drink beer in unexpected places like fast food restaurants, makes the story more compelling than a simple account of lunch. The scene stands out because of the unique beer detail, not the narrative of gangsters having a conversation.

The beer detail is an important part of certain stories, particularly those associated with the craft beer experience. While I've never had a beer in a fast food restaurant in Amsterdam, I'm interested in storytelling and "the little differences" that make storytelling occur. I'm not interested in making up stories or writing fiction. Instead, I am interested in how we frame events or interests or beliefs by way of stories. Despite Walter Benjamin's proclamation in 1936 that "the art of storytelling is coming to an end" (83), I discover stories all around me, stories, as this book shows, that involve beer. Sometimes we tell stories—about beer or other items—via details as in the *Pulp Fiction* example; sometimes we employ other media strategies. In the first book I wrote, I was interested in a specific story about 1963 and writing instruction. In my second book, I was interested in the stories we tell about cities like Detroit, Michigan. All along, though, I've been interested in two other stories: the story of craft beer and the story of social media. Social media are the new media art of storytelling.

INTRODUCTION

In an age of emerging technologies noticeable in the early twentieth century, Benjamin lamented the proliferation of information and the ability to communicate across nations, across timelines, across interests, what today we experience via the aggregation and dissemination of ideas via social media. "If the art of storytelling has become rare," Benjamin writes, "the dissemination of information has had a decisive share in this state of affairs" (89). Yet, the art of storytelling hasn't become rare. Via image, post, tag, update, comment, share, like, tweet, podcast, upload, and response, we create and read stories across various media. These stories affect taste, consumption, behavior, political affiliation, and other activities for the ways that they frame overall interests. Businesses have taken notice.

"Stories are going to fuel business, organizations and products in 2013," one news account proclaims, "and social media is going to play a big role in those stories" (Burns). Pandodaily—the tech startup blog—declared 2013 the year of the story. "Some of the most exciting startups in social media are the ones that help us make these small, fragmented pieces of content into richer stories," Pandodaily's Erin Griffith writes. "Every social media action we take contributes to what could be an incredible narrative." Facebook's Timeline upgrade was meant to turn individual profiles into stories (the time frame over which one has updated, posted, and commented) for both user and potential advertiser (user content stories, it is assumed, will fuel targeted consumption). Twitter's View Conversation shows the larger story taking place across tweets, a feature captured by apps such as Storify and turned into a narrative shared across various social media platforms. The computer is a primary vehicle for storytelling.

"Machines and narratives are not alike," Alex Galloway differs (71). They are not, and neither Twitter nor Facebook are narratives per se; we make narratives out of the platforms. The social media machine prompted by databases and content management systems generates stories, which drive the new media experience. One story I am fascinated with is that of craft beer, one of the fastest growing segments of the food and beverage industries, told across social media. Sometimes it is told as a story of marketing—how craft brewers utilize social media to reach and discover a customer base that otherwise would go unnoticed. Sometimes it is told as a story of economizing—how craft brewers, with no budget for advertising, take advantage of social media to generate a brand. Sometimes it is told as a story of pioneering—how craft brewers, despite the obstacles of consolidation, fizzy beer, and blandness returned to near pre-Prohibition levels to produce flavorful and well-produced (or even artisanal) beer.

INTRODUCTION

The craft beer story captures much of the familiarity we associate with narratives in general: conflict, estrangement, overcoming the odds, and success. The craft beer story is a unique one, and the obsessive customer base—those who actively purchase and consume craft beer—is the focus of this book. Most people who regularly consume craft beer have specific stories to tell: stories of first times, stories of sharing, stories of getting or missing out on special releases, stories of waiting in line, stories of finding a "whale," stories of aging beer, stories of trading, stories of travel, and so on. Within these larger stories there are details that, like the *Pulp Fiction* scene, complete what is otherwise a common narrative. Details, *Craft Obsession* argues, are the heart of social media.

I, for instance, could begin my craft beer story by narrating a common experience—moving to another state (for me, to Michigan in 2002)—with a detail or little difference—buying a bottle of Kalamazoo Stout at a corner grocery and discovering Bell's. Or I could tell the story of a friend sending me a beer-of-the-month present for my wedding, and from that gift of six beers every month, I discovered that beer could be shipped online. Or I could tell a 2007 story of trying to order Lagunitas online from Archer Liquors in Chicago and being told by the store's owner that the beers were past their prime; I should order something else. I could tell these stories because of their details, and I may do so, but I will likely tell other, more complex and social-media-shaped stories also based on details and little differences. These stories are anecdotal, are theoretical, and are media based. To tell the story of craft beer and social media is not an easy task. There is no linear narrative to tell, only one of interruptions and breaks. Because craft beer and social media represent obsessions for me, I feel the need to tell these stories. The craft beer obsession story, what I call *craft obsession*, is my story as well.

This book is as much my story as craft beer's story. In the tradition of storytelling, and because of that overlap, my storytelling must be personal as much as it should reflect the need to study and understand the relationship between craft beer and social media. My storytelling is my everyday consumption of craft beer and the impact of this consumption beyond spending money and drinking beer. My storytelling is about merging myths and the everyday, for craft beer has become mythic. Bryan Alexander identifies the mythic and the everyday as what "appeals to us as media consumers" (9). Grand stories (heroes, villains) and the banal (having a drink, eating) coincide as popular modes of narrative expression. Alexander comments that "we can also conceive of digital storytelling through examples of it in action, such as . . . a video clip about a mother-daughter relationship over time" (3). My mother does not drink beer. Most of my family does not drink beer either. To begin to tell the story of craft beer and social media, I, as Alexander suggests, turn to another familial narration.

In the tradition of storytelling, there is always a place not just for mother-daughter relationships, as Alexander points out, but for father-daughter stories as well. I make this comment to understand how I, someone who wants to tell a story about what I believe is a unique experience, must begin with a small detail that is familiar to other stories. My interest in craft beer is familiar as a narrative genre (I'm not the only one who drinks craft beer) but unique for its sharing (I'm an academic producing scholarship about craft beer and social media). The father-daughter tale, as opposed to the mother-daughter relationship Alexander highlights, is one place to begin my story, with the person who has been with my story about craft beer since the moment she was born.

The genre of the father-daughter story is extensive. It might be captured as a series of memories one turns to for comfort, as Paul Simon advises his daughter in the opening verse of the song "Father and Daughter." The father-daughter story might be told as the moment the relationship is challenged by life transitions, such as Jonathan Raban's essay "The Getaway Car," which describes Raban taking his child to college and the thoughts such a trip evokes. Or we might consider the like-minded tale of Spencer Tracy and Steve Martin giving away their daughters in different versions of the film *Father of the Bride*. Such stories often revolve around saying good-bye. A daughter moves away to attend college, a daughter gets married; the father is sad, the relationship withstands the challenge. If there is a generic father-daughter tale, it is likely the formula of "the girl who has grown up" and the father who misses his "baby." The genre is familiar for how it imagines family relationships as bonds that cannot break. The genre comforts fathers and daughters, telling us that we will never be apart.

If there is a genre that drives my own stories of my daughter, it does not match that of loss or of advice. I am driven by food- and beer-related thought more so than any of the above narratives I outline. If I were to have my own genre for father-daughter storytelling, it might be described as "parental beer tales" because of the moments my daughter and I have shared over craft beer. Out of all the tales told by fathers, the parental beer tale is the most obscure, whether told via social media or some other platform. In fact, I cannot name one parental beer tale other than my own. In the contemporary craft beer renaissance currently being experienced across America, there should be more parental beer tales to tell; there should be more narratives that juxtapose the pleasure of craft beer with the pleasure of being a father. If 2013 is indeed the year of the story, why would the parental beer tale not play a part in that yearlong event or in any other year? While this book is not concerned only with parental beer tales, it is concerned with such juxtapositions of craft with pleasure. It is concerned with familiar and nonfamiliar methods of storytelling. It is concerned with the overlap of narrative and social media. It is concerned with the academic and the personal.

My initial interest, then, is one of writing and fatherhood. Professionally, I have been concerned largely with questions that do not involve parenthood but that deal with digital writing, namely, how new media affect communicative practices. Whether in pedagogy or in scholarship, I trace and perform the logics of new media: appropriation, commutation, nonlinearity, juxtaposition, and visual writing. More recently, I have begun to reflect on the nature of parental storytelling. Like all parents, I want to tell stories about my children. This is a familiar position regarding the stories we tell about children and food, and I will not be the only one to write about eating meals or sharing food/beverage experiences with children. In her description of traveling with children, food writer Naomi Duguid describes herself as a "hardcore evangelist for kid travel" (11). Through Thailand and Laos, India and Bengal, Duguid took her children on food-related research trips. "Once a kid has taken charge of food or a dish," she notes, "your worries are over. He's taken possession of it for life" (14). In this kind of narrative, the mother (or maybe father) introduces food and culture to children so that later appreciation may develop. A linear narrative develops out of the experience: lack of knowledge, introduction, appreciation. On the other hand, the father-daughter narrative showcases a specific generic structure of loss or protection, and this structure, we might assume, is tied to print-based logics of linear progression. Daughter is born. Daughter grows up. Daughter moves on. In both instances, a progression occurs and is told to a readership. Even Calvin Trillin, whose work often defies such conventions, frames the food experience as such. His daughter, we are told in "Magic Bagel," moved away to San Francisco. Her return, Trillin surmises, can only be hastened if he rediscovers the pumpernickel bagel of her youth. A conclusion to the progression is needed. Similar to any interest I might share with this structure of storytelling, I question the ways new media, as well, shape my own desire to tell a parental story, one about my daughter and about beer. I don't, however, want that story to resemble linearity or progression.

INTRODUCTION

Early new media concerns with narrative (such as that of hypertext) focused largely on the nonlinear and interactive nature of new forms of expression. Readers who choose where to click on a given page, hypertext criticism told us, force narratives out of the confines of linear structure. Michael Joyce famously argued that interactive storytelling shifts power from author to reader as readers take control, via links, of the order in which stories are read. "The primacy of the text," he claimed, "must be marginalized" (194). Such proclamations influenced writers to question overall narrative genres of progression. "How will interactivity change the stories we tell in the future?" Jane Yellowlees Douglas asked (8). I, on the other hand, find my model not in the interactive gesture typically associated with one aspect of new media (hypertext) or in a rejection of the primacy of the text. Instead, for the parental beer tale, I look to another model: the fragment, the condensed version, the brief moment, the shared photograph, the daily encounter, the detail that we focus on in the contemporary practice we have come to call *social media*. Social media—which at times are simultaneously mythic and everyday—include blog posts, status updates, tweets, images, and feed headlines that, while interactive, are also short, brief encounters with a given moment. Social media are the primary focus for the parental beer story I want to present in this introduction and for those that will follow throughout this book. This book sketches out that story without hewing too closely to traditional genres of writing: history, criticism, review, analysis, travelogue, allegory, or another. Whatever genres I rely upon, I don't want them to be so familiar that they are circulations of already told stories—as father-daughter tales often are. That point holds true for those who read/write traditional beer stories as well as those who read/write traditional academic critiques. My approach is intended, as I believe social media do overall, to undermine or shift both.

Narrative depends on any number of gestures for conveying meaning: setting, tone, time period, and so on. The anecdote, for instance, typically plays an important role in constructing large-scale narratives by framing the daily event as monumental in importance. As Wallace Martin notes,

> Writers, as we learn form their notebooks and prefaces, often begin from an anecdote or scene that they find striking and then create an intricate web of character and circumstance that will "motivate" the scene or push it to a revealing conclusion. (65)

Gregory Ulmer, on the other hand, notes that in narrative (hypertext or otherwise), anecdotes provide the basis of invention strategies that writers engage with in order to tell a story. The anecdote, for Ulmer, bridges print narrative structure with the structure of an emerging digital form of narrative that Ulmer defines as the new media moment called "electracy" (a contemporary version of literacy practices). In electracy, the anecdote allows for invention. Ulmer's example is an André Breton anecdote; Breton tells the story of coming up with the sentence "there is a man cut in two at the window." Ulmer identifies the gesture as "the 'eureka anecdote,' marking the moment or flash of insight" (*Heuretics* 7). The Breton narrative is the large-scale gesture toward the invention of surrealism. In the examples I began with, the large-scale gesture or revelation is that the father will miss the daughter but accepts her need to move on. The anecdote of dropping a daughter off at college allows for this moment of insight. Like any narrative, the one I want to tell begins with an expected and familiar introductory moment as well, an anecdote that sets the tone of the story about my daughter and craft beer. The suggestion may be that by telling this story I can then tell a more significant story about craft beer and social media. Only, my daughter has not moved on, and there is no major revelation at stake. I have no grand gesture to make. I promise no moment of invention or insight. Instead, I have short, fragmented moments I want to share. Sharing without grand revelation, *Craft Obsession* claims, is another form of narrative.

To begin, then, I share an anecdote. When my daughter was two weeks old, she went to her first brewpub, Otto's in State College, Pennsylvania. I convinced my recovering wife that—now that pregnancy was over—we could finally venture out of her townhouse and into the world again. I also convinced her that our first stop should be beer oriented. As nervous first-time parents, we placed our daughter's car seat on the table at Otto's, ate our lunch, had a couple of beers, and watched our baby sleep during our meal, oblivious to the noise around her. An uneventful, everyday episode (lunch with newborn) became important and slightly mythic (craft beer as part of my daughter's life; we're parents!). What seems minor, the anecdote shows me, became transitional in our lives. I'm not sure that point is insightful, but it does frame the genre I want to develop.

So begins my story about two of my passions: my children and craft beer. Even if this anecdote sheds little light on how the two come together or what the rest of this book will be about, it allows me a vehicle for expressing my mutual passions. My daughter's first visit to Otto's led to many other craft beer trips. From Otto's, my daughter visited many more brewpubs as we made our move from Pennsylvania back to Detroit, where I, then, lived (Royal Oak Brewery, Woodward Avenue Brewers) and on to Columbia, Missouri (Flat Branch Brewing, Broadway Brewery), where we lived for four years, and on to Lexington, Kentucky (West Sixth Brewing, Country Boy Brewing, Blue Stallion, Ethereal), where we currently reside. In between, she has had lunch at Russian River, ordered ice cream at Bear Republic, taken the tour at New Glarus, sought shelter from a stifling heat at Free State, shared a sandwich at Three Floyds, experienced a bathroom accident at New Belgium, enjoyed dinner at Revolution, ate popcorn at Thr3e Wise Men, and, during a trip to Asheville, watched her brother knock over an India pale ale (IPA) at Lexington Avenue Brewers. Except for the mentioning of my daughter's first experience at a brewpub, these are not powerful anecdotes of our experiences together. They do not offer flashes of insight or powerful moments of invention. They do not set up a narrative about beer with grandiose promises. They are not anecdotes at all, merely recollections of the parallel loves I share. Craft, therefore, is for me not a grand analogy about what it means to be a father within food culture (i.e., the anecdote allows me such a moment of writerly invention), but instead, craft is a focal point for sharing brief recollections so that I might compose a new parental beer writing genre in order to share what I feel. That genre, I discover, is not grand in gesture (as media or rhetorical criticism may demand), but it is new media influenced because of how it depends on brief moments or images. This book writes such a genre so that writing, in general, considers how new media stories, such as the one I tell about craft beer, relate a series of moments, photographs, and memories. Because these items are distributed over various spaces, are shared, are motivated by online activity, and are networked, I call this type of new media story a social media one.

Craft Stories

Social implies media and families. Despite the country's persistent fear of alcohol consumption (Sunday sales, limitations in online retail, age restrictions), families have always been present, to some extent, in the public displays circulated by and for the beer world. In an 1871 *Harper's New Monthly Magazine* article on New York's Atlantic Garden beer garden, for instance, W. O. Stoddard observes, "On every side there are family groups, father, mother, and children, all merry, all sociable, all well-behaved and quiet" (678). In a late nineteenth-century advertisement for Schlitz titled "Family Beer," a visitor asks his host, "Does your whole family drink beer?" The host responds, "Just Schlitz—no other."[1]

Revolution Brewing, 2010

George Orwell, writing about the ideal imaginary pub he calls Moon Under Water, describes a family-oriented place for drinking: "Up at one end of the garden there are swings and a chute for the children." A 1955 Falstaff ad, "Bring on the Falstaff," showcases a family gathering around a Thanksgiving Day meal with beer. A 1940 Budweiser ad, "Their Hero Arrives," shows two children standing at a gate, waiting for daddy to come home. Whereas contemporary corporate beer culture (InBev, MillerCoors, Heineken) reaches out to young college kids eager to drink thirty cans of beer in one sitting and, thus, makes beer a forbidden fruit to children and adults alike, craft breweries often appeal to families, to food-oriented parents who don't want to enjoy the experience of craft without their children. Social media guru Arik Hanson advises craft breweries to organize "middle-age parents" in order to be profitable, but in fact many breweries already do ("Are Craft Breweries"). In the mass-produced beer world, children are not wanted. In the craft beer world, children belong. Craft is relationship based.

A father does not need to be reminded how much his children belong in his life. While I yearn for a genre of writing that juxtaposes fatherhood, beer, and having a daughter, I also recognize the limitations of such a desire against the broader genre of beer writing, a genre that resembles other genres related to travel and food. These genres are dominated by reviews (positive and negative experiences shared) and travel narratives (getting in the car, getting to a destination, experiencing the destination, generalizing that the trip represents something major in life), and tasting (elevating the experience's status). Such limitations occur when a dominant genre is met by a newer, less familiar, and fairly experimental one. What holds true for other forms of storytelling holds true for beer narratives as well.

Familiar beer narratives not only follow conventional patterns but typically do not include children. Beer writers such as Pete Brown, Brian Yaeger, and pioneer author Jack Erickson never mention children in their tales of sailing around the world with a keg of IPA, locating the ideal beer bars in America, or discovering craft beer establishments nationally as tourist destinations. Famous beer hunter Michael Jackson, as well, traveled alone in his books and TV series. We might remember him wandering alone through a San Francisco festival during his California pilgrimage, but we don't remember him doing so with his stepdaughter. When writers tell family stories, they opt for the grand gesture of the anecdote as the flash-of-insight moment, telling stories of their fathers offering them that first beer while working in the yard, at a ball game, or sitting in front of the television. The first beer, the anecdotes show, opened the door for later appreciation. DadCentric.com's Jason Avant tells one such story of first trying beer. "My dad wasn't a regular beer drinker," he writes,

> but he certainly enjoyed a cold Bud after a few hours of moving the lawn under the blazing Nebraska summer sun. One day I mustered up the courage to ask him. He looked at me, considered the possible outcomes (not the last of which: my mom yelling, "what the hell are you doing, giving him a beer?") and passed the can. (88)

This, too, is how I was introduced to beer. My dad, a nonregular beer drinker, passed me a Heineken. We were working in the yard. The cold beer quenched my teenage thirst. It felt rebellious and comforting to try a beer with my dad. The story is the same as Avant's story (and this story will return in chapter 1). This is how we often introduce our children to beer. This is also how we introduce ourselves to our children and food, through similar, repeatable stories. A first-time experience is a repeatable, conventional genre. My story is Avant's story. And his story is someone else's as well. These stories are meant for longevity, to withstand some metaphoric "test of time" as they provide the familiar as comfort, regardless of the ways little details differ or resemble one another in the narratives.

The stories, as true as they may be, are mass produced and generic. They are not the products of craft.

Craft beer is a response to generic food culture. While I, too, find generic tales comforting, I also search out the nongeneric when sharing beer with my daughter. I have introduced my daughter to beer, not by giving her a beer to drink (I haven't; she's only seven), but by sharing a part of my life with her that circulates around my obsession with craft beer. I share my daily, less generic experiences: my details. When we travel, we always make arrangements to visit a brewpub or brewery in addition to a zoo, aquarium, or children's museum. When we take day outings to Cincinnati or Louisville from our home in Lexington (or to St. Louis when we lived in Missouri), we start with a kid activity, have lunch, and do something related to beer (visit a brewpub, take a brewery tour, go beer shopping). Beer has provided us with a social bond that my daughter's collection of Disney princesses or my life as an academic cannot. While beer stories or travel narratives may involve canonical ideas like "the first time" one tried a particular style or a pilgrimage to a famous brewpub or brewery, they don't yet explore parents bonding with their children over lambics, IPAs, and saisons during an afternoon. Like any narrative of parental bonding, the father-daughter narrative can be one based on beer. It does not have to settle for a generic retelling of familiarity.

In our travels we have found the craft experience to be a family-oriented one. Brewpubs often have balloons or crayons for our kids when we visit. Even some bars, such as Petaluma Taps in Petaluma, California, have kids' menus. I remember my daughter ordering kids' chicken fingers at the Falling Rock bar in Denver. I remember the hostess at Great Dane in Madison handing my daughter a pink balloon. I remember my daughter playing outside at Avery Brewing while I took the short tour. I remember my daughter playing with dolls while I drank a sour beer in Wicked Weed's basement bar. Memories like these are the basis of a new type of story we might start telling about craft beer hunters (those obsessed, beer-minded people, like me, who are always searching for new beers) and our children. These stories won't be generic or mass produced. They won't be as grandiose as a "pretext to gain a view of America through the prism of a beer glass," as Ken Wells writes of the beer traveling experience in *Travels with Barley* (7). Nor will these stories conclude with a *Dead Poets Society* homage to beer travel and adventure, as Brian Yaeger's *Red, White, and Brew: An American Beer Odyssey* concludes in dramatic form when he notes, "The point is, break out of your comfort zone" (234). Nor will these stories align beer with the very foundation of democracy as Jack Erickson's narrative does in *Brewery Adventures in the Big East*: "The craft brewing tradition started almost 400 years ago when the first colonists set foot here and began building a new life. They came for freedom and brought their Old World brewing traditions with them" (3). Instead of such hyperbolic promises or analogies, parental beers stories offer a medium for showing excitement over something mundane and quotidian such as eating a meal or having a drink. These stories show why such means of excitement are important when children share mundane experiences as well, even if that sharing is only being together for the hour or two spent in dad's obsessive pleasure in craft. These stories shed some light on excitement over the common and ordinary, but they don't necessarily promise flashes of insight or moments of large-scale narrative invention. "It is certainly when I divulge my private life that I expose myself most," Roland Barthes proclaimed (*Roland Barthes* 82). It is also certainly when I divulge my private beer life that I expose my family emotions most as well. Like most forms of social media, the parental beer tale is an exposure. A photographic exposure controls light. A parental beer exposure allows some light onto the mundane and banal details of an experience, making the moment anything but. This "anything but" moment I call craft obsession.

Great Dane brewpub, Madison, Wisconsin, 2008

INTRODUCTION

Obsession

Obsessive is a key term in the craft experience. The story of father-daughter bonding over craft beer experiences is the exposed story of a father's obsession. Craft, as Richard Sennett writes, is tied to obsession: "We are more likely to fail as craftsman, I argue, due to our inability to organize obsession than because of our lack of ability" (11). I am an obsessive father. I trade for beer (on the online site Ratebeer's trade forums, with friends in other states; on Google+ with members of my beer circle). I purchase beer on travels (there is always a prized beer shop in each city I visit, which promises treasures not distributed in my home state of Kentucky). I design family travels around craft beer (pairing a kid's activity with lunch at a brewpub dictates which cities we visit over which others). I return from a family trip with over $100 of beer in the trunk, a box of another $100 worth of beer from a recent trade waiting on the door step, and panic over missing a release that just happened the day I arrive home in Lexington. Obsessed individuals don't want to keep their stories to themselves. They want to organize and share their experiences and beer achievements. Otherwise, excitement—no matter how mundane—is an individual experience and, as such, has limited meaning in the long term regarding the building of relationships (thus, Vincent tells Jules about his trip abroad). Online, there are thousands of beer blogs devoted to sharing beer-drinking stories. Beer drinkers share their excitement by videoing themselves drinking beer and posting the results. On forums, raters list the attributes they discover in the beers they consume (grass, malt, bitter, pine, grapefruit, biscuit) in order to share their experiences. On Twitter, beer drinkers engage each other and members of the craft industry over their excitement. On Facebook, a photographic parade of acquisitions and drinking moments appears in my news feed. Publishing, too, has taken notice of beer obsession as new titles dealing with craft beer appear each year, from guidebooks to brewer memoirs. Sharing is central to the craft experience, whether in beer or elsewhere in the experience of consuming food. The obsessed individual, like me, needs to tap into that narrative of sharing.

Sharing. Travel. These are characteristics of the parental beer genre borrowed from other parental and food-oriented stories. We travel. We share. We obsess. The parental beer-tale genre is symbolic of our current age of social media where information travels at such speeds that it must be shared or missed entirely. The vehicles for sharing in social media are many: Facebook status updates, tweets, e-mail forwards, Yelp reviews, Instagram photos, and blog posts. These are the contemporary vehicles for sharing. When I imagine a parental beer genre of storytelling, I imagine it always as a product of digital culture where fragmented moments of sharing are captured on our laptops and phones as much as in our memories. Just as the tweet or the blog post need not capture an entire narrative (such as the first time I drank a beer, the moment of parting, the epiphany of bonding), neither should the parental beer tale aspire to such. The parental beer tale is not bound to a linear progression of storytelling. Thus, *Craft Obsession*'s organization is not linear. I move within ideas, hoping that these ideas can assist toward an understanding of social media's influence on craft beer and obsession.

My stories are not linear. Nor are they monumental. I cannot recount the entire story of pizza and a beer sampler at Russian River, but I can visualize the moment of looking across the table at my daughter, who was eating and still tired from the flight and long drive from the San Francisco airport. The fragment sticks with me more than a grand narrative about Sonoma County, terroir, or food culture would ever do. I cannot recount every detail about my daughter using the restroom at Bruisin' Ale's beer store in Asheville, North Carolina, the door wide open so that she was visible to all in line, but the fragment sticks with me more than the prototypical tale about visiting grandparents that I could easily spin out of the trip as a whole. Even in this introduction, I merely list snapshots of moments with my daughter because what I want to share is not the experience of grandiose metaphor (i.e., sharing beer adventures with my daughter is like . . .). What I share is the gastronomical equivalent of 140 characters, an Instagram image snapped in a moment of thinking, or a status update shared with others over my profile. I capture the brevity of a given craft moment because craft is a brief experience (find the beer, drink the beer). Craft beer is often brief in production (small batches) and distribution (limited quantities). Brevity, as popular culture often tells us as well, is both the blessing and curse of being a parent (crises may pass quickly; children's time in our lives feels brief and too quick). Brevity is a digital experience. What is online today may be gone tomorrow. My daughter and I only experience digital experiences: our adventures are mapped online; our memories are captured by iPhones and digital devices; our photos are shared via Flickr and Instagram; fifteen-second home movies shot with a phone end up on our Apple TV. We digitally check in to locations we visit. The digital was designed for ease of sharing (upload, tag, send) in brief moments. It models a new type of food/beer writing genre. It models a new type of obsessive writing in general.

INTRODUCTION

Russian River sampler, 2010

That model involves the brief moment of sharing. Our culture is a culture of sharing. "Eating puts us in touch with all that we share with the other animals," Michael Pollan claims, "and all that sets us apart" (10). In food culture, sharing has meant banquets, feasts, hospitality in foreign countries, celebratory moments, artisanal production, get-togethers. Specific food, on the other hand, conjures up the image of sharing. People share beers. People share bread. "People who bake bread are generous," Dana Bowen writes in one *Saveur* editorial (8). Sharing is a generous experience; sharing is the *being with* experience. If there exists a grand concept in parental beer tales, it might be that of *being with*. Sharing these moments in narrative showcases the feeling of *being with*. We do that via social media, and I do that via craft beer. I do that via the parental beer tale that unfolds in this introduction.

Being with is being with your daughter in Against the Grain in Louisville with a large beer sampler on the table and a big pile of smoked brisket on the plate. Being with is being with your daughter in Goose Island, having a sandwich, still giddy with stories about the Chicago zoo we visited minutes earlier. These being-with moments are not self-centered moments the way that digital media often are labeled as narcissistic for how they frame brief moments of experience. These are new versions of the family experience where the photograph is not bound to an everlasting memory

Goose Island, 2010

(as an anecdote might insist) but instead speaks to a fragmented moment that happened so one could *be with one's child*. One is *with* another, even if the moment is temporary and fleeting.

Craft Production / Mass Production

In response to what I have presented here, a reader of this book's introduction might question the value of a narrative genre if its focus is brief, fragmented, uneventful moments of sharing. A father-daughter tale should revolve around a strong anecdote and promise a larger life lesson than sitting in a brewpub or getting a balloon or even feeling *as if you are with someone*. The tale should be grand in gesture and in content. As I discuss in chapter 1, Jean François Lyotard argued that the age of the grand narrative—the overarching stories told to make sense of experience—is over. In an age of database logic (the fragmented bits of information brought together in temporary moments), he wrote, we make sense of ourselves and our surroundings through small stories. Small replaces large. The brief replaces the everlasting. The banal replaces the grand. The detail drives narrative. I, too, make sense of my relationships with craft beer and my daughter via small, fragmented stories. Just as the excitement of a beer experience may be mundane and quotidian, so, too, is the story created

INTRODUCTION

to share that mundane and quotidian sense of excitement. I move against the generic preference for exaggerated tales of being with children in favor of this other form of expression whose focus is the fragmented moment. When Steve Martin's character George Banks walks his daughter down the aisle in *Father of the Bride*, the scene embraces the grand gesture of hyperbole: floral displays, large church, lit candles, and, of course, the panicked father. The equivalent food or beer tale, we assume, should mirror that type of gesture. As I have discovered, with craft, it shouldn't. Hyperbole, too, is present in the craft beer world: special release days, one-off beers, hyped styles, caged-and-corked bottles designed to mirror wine. What I'm trying to capture is not the sense of exaggeration that artisanal food production depends on to promote its unique status in a world of mass-produced goods. I'm trying to capture the small story. I intend for this book to be a series of small stories, each teasing out aspects of social media and craft beer in ways grand narratives fail to account for. One such story, as I propose here in the introduction and will conclude with in the final two chapters, is sharing. The other stories that follow will include social media practices of sharing (returned to in the final chapter), contagions (repetitions), anecdotes, aggregation, and rhetorical delivery. These practices, I contend, make up social media rhetorics, and as such, they help us understand specific obsessive cultural practices, such as craft beer.

In the age of digital reproduction, we not only experience the everyday sense of sharing, but we, as well, depend on the ever-present experience of mass production to make sense of our lives. Mass production—from Hollywood remakes to Disney theme parks—frames most of our common narratives, as well, about fathers and daughters (Disney characters are always involved in father-daughter issues; George Banks gives away his daughter in a mass production of a wedding). A good father should be taking his daughter to Dollywood or Disney World, not Schlafly or Moylan's. While many of us embrace the anti-mass-production narratives of food associated with *Fast Food Nation* or *Super Size Me*, and while many of us resist the mass production represented in these stories, mass production still exists in our lives. Despite my craft sharing, my daughter still has Cinderella and Sleeping Beauty dolls. She adores Hello Kitty. She loves *Arthur* pasta (boxed pasta and dehydrated cheese patterned after the character from the Public Broadcasting Service show of the same name). Craft is my attempt, if for a brief moment, to intervene in the mass-production narrative she is already exposed to and that will likely never vanish from her life (since, after all, it has never vanished from mine). I don't expect

INTRODUCTION

Three Floyds brewpub, 2011

to overturn the mass-production narrative. I don't expect to end grand narratives of beer. I only hope to offer brief interventions. Craft is an intervention in mass production the way social media often are as well. It is not, as the Arts and Crafts movement argued, an overturning.

Mass production, as any cliché cultural studies argument attests, is a grand narrative based on exaggeration (whether directed toward a mouse in a tuxedo or a tale of a princess whose father's death leaves her in the arms of an evil stepmother). Craft is a limited story based on a single moment or activity: an afternoon in a brewpub, a kids' menu hamburger, an imperial stout sitting on the table, a spilled IPA, a brother's baby bottle juxtaposed against a little girl's brewpub lunch. Craft is the way small stories get reproduced as well into databases of brief memories, not as grand gestures or hyperbolic retellings of fathers and daughters in familiar generic patterns. Craft delivers small moments of consumption and pleasure. In lieu of the monumental anecdote, there is merely the being-with moment. When we link or network these moments, we discover craft obsession.

Still, I don't ignore anecdotes. Even in my parental beer tale, I turn, in the end, away from the series of fragments that make up my narrative and conclude this introduction with an anecdote. One day a couple of years ago, my daughter, playing in our finished basement, turned away from her plastic kitchen that occupies a great deal of her imaginary time. She has a remarkable imagination sparked, at times, by her parents' eating habits. Either in that kitchen or in various children's museums nationwide, she plays "restaurant." "Hi!" she might declare. "What would you like to order?" Pretending that a copy of the book *Snow White* is a menu, she demands that you find something to eat. On this particular day, however, she turned her attention away from the fake cans of beans, the plastic french fries, and the tiny box of green beans that make up a portion of her toy food. Instead, she picked up a plastic bottle likely designed by its manufacturer to be soda. Instead of announcing what restaurant we were in or what the special for the day was, she held out the bottle to me as evidence of where we were now in her imaginary world. "Hi!" she said. "Welcome to beer shop. Would you like an IPA?" "Would you like an IPA?" is our moment of connection, a beer-based question that socially links us to common experiences and sharing. This book is not about parental beer tales. This brief introductory gesture at something I call the parental beer tale sets the tone for what will follow by tapping into familiar and nonfamiliar methods of scholarly writing. I call this method and this subject *Craft Obsession*.

Country Boy Brewing, 2012

CHAPTER 1
Craft Introductions

> Please allow me to introduce myself.
> —Mick Jagger, "Sympathy for the Devil"

Unfortunately, I begin with an anecdote. I write "unfortunately" because anecdotes have become a fallback gesture for introductory narratives. To introduce *Craft Obsession*, like many other writers, I turn first to an anecdote. When faced with how to begin, the writer often relies on the anecdote as a framing mechanism for a larger, supposedly more important, narrative. The anecdote, in turn, introduces the narrative in order to solicit interest, capture attention, or simply set the tone and setting of the overall story. To begin my story, I should begin with an anecdote about drinking beer. After all, this would be the expected introductory gesture. My anecdote could be learning about craft beer at a homebrewers get-together in Micanopy, Florida, around 1998. My anecdote could be the first night of my job visit at the University of Missouri, where soon-to-be colleagues took me to dinner at Flat Branch Pub and Brewing. My anecdote could be about my (not yet) wife having a bottle of Arrogant Bastard in the fridge for me when I'd visit her circa 2003 in Austin, Texas. My anecdote could be how, at sixteen years old, I thought Moosehead was an exotic beer. I'd buy a six-pack from the Farm Stores drive-through on Dixie Highway in Miami; the store did not card.

I won't begin with these anecdotes because I don't imagine these stories as the beginning of my overall story titled *Craft Obsession*. While he has no anecdote to begin with, John Porter begins his 1975 book *All about Beer* by noting, "I have often wondered why most books have an introduction." Porter then questions the whole notion of a beginning:

> I mean why not just get right to the thing the reader bought the book for in the first place? Maybe I do know why: it's an acceptable place for the author to talk about himself and some of his reasons for writing the book. (xi)

George Orwell has no anecdote for the imaginary pub he describes in "The Moon Under Water." Beer writer Martyn Cornell, though, tells an anecdote when, after reading a newspaper story, he speculates whether the English bar the Plough, mentioned in Orwell's story, resembles the ideal pub Orwell describes:

> I knew the Plough—itself closed now, woe—from when I was chairman of North Herts Camra all of 30 years ago (and Colin Valentine was probably still drinking Irn Bru). It was one of dozens of little pubs that served the quiet, isolated villages of North Herts, a part of England that is astonishingly rural, despite being only 30 miles from central London, and you could still get dark mild there, albeit from Greene King's Biggleswade brewery. ("The Woman Who Served")

This beginning, posed as coincidence of place, establishes for Cornell an ordering of English beer culture where a pint of mild connects George Orwell to a Plough server to other notable people who may have had a mild at the Plough (Dylan Thomas, Motörhead's Lemmy Kilmister). As a beginning, the anecdote arranges a beer narrative for Cornell regarding life in England. American author Henry Miller, as well, uses the anecdote to order his life in Brooklyn, turning to beer in order to nostalgically remember the comfort of all-male evenings at friend Ed Bauries's house: "We had plenty of beer to drink and a whole big house at our disposal, for it was in the summertime, when his folks were away, that we held our gatherings" (*Tropic of Capricorn* 300). In a classic instance of Miller's endless lists of pleasure, he orders his memory of family gatherings via an anecdote of things, a long list of things that includes beer. A partial section of the list explores "[a]ll kinds of nuts, walnuts, buttered nuts, almonds, pecans, hickory nuts, pecans, with lager beer and bottled beer" (*Black Spring* 104). Beer orders. Beer arranges stories. The beer anecdote can arrange my own story as well.

Not all anecdotes, however, neatly arrange like these examples I highlight. Some anecdotes work in reverse. Kenneth Burke imagines a book whose justification for offering a specific beginning (such as an anecdote) could only be uncovered by writing it backwards, "adding one beginning before another, as though the book had been elicited by a relentless cross-examiner." Burke demonstrates that examination accordingly:

> Q. And why did you begin with this?
> A: For such-and-such reason, that logically preceded it.
> Q: And why was this reason logically prior?
> A. For such-and-such other reason, logically prior to that—etc.
> (*Grammar of Motives* 338)

For every reason to offer an introductory anecdote, Burke suggests, another likely reason precedes it. The question of *why* to begin one way as opposed to another, therefore, remains in question. This, I suggest, is a social media dilemma as well.

Anecdotes familiarize stories for readers; they frame stories by sharing the simple point that if it happened to me, it has likely happened to you. The anecdote, Barry Brummett writes, "is a dramatic form which underlines the content, or the specific vocabulary of discourse" (162–63). Anecdotes, Brummett argues, "represent well what happens in the media because the *media* are anecdotal" (162). Stories, as a media form, are by nature anecdotal. Other media, we might assume, are anecdotal as well, from videos to websites to essays to social media applications. Beer, too, offers a medium for the anecdote. I begin with a craft beer anecdote because the story I want to tell is a craft-beer-oriented one found within social media, and social media, as well, are anecdotal. By beginning with one such anecdote, I don't assume that another anecdote does not precede it; that is, I don't assume my anecdote is, in fact, my beginning. I assume that by telling this anecdote I will say something about myself, my identity, and the identity of the product I consume. Writing to poet Malcolm Cowley in 1917, Kenneth Burke connected beer to his own identity as a rhetorician and philosopher: "But I find that reading philosophy is a much better preparation for writing novels than reading novels is. And it lends more dignity to my beer" (Jay 37). Like Burke, but in a reverse of his narrative gesture, I find that beer lends more dignity to my writing about social media and my writing about myself. With my own craft anecdote shared here, I will say something that the reader (particularly the reader interested in craft beer) will relate to and then generalize from. I briefly shared this anecdote in the introduction.

When I was a child, my anecdote begins, my father shared a Heineken with me while we worked in the yard on a sweltering afternoon in Miami, Florida. I rely on this anecdote to create a familiar situation for the reader that will establish a comfortable tone from which the overall narrative can be told, and from which the reader might identify with my beginning. This anecdote will underline the overall vocabulary of my bigger story, as Brummett claims for anecdotes in general. And this anecdote, following Burke, lends dignity to my story because it situates my story within a memory. Memories, as recalled years later, add credibility to current experiences by building up important narratives to tell. When James Beard begins his canonical 1964 cookbook, *Delights and Prejudices*, he connects such larger stories regarding food and childhood to the notion of taste memory. Anecdotal beginnings, we can say, are tied to memories of taste, such as that of a Heineken on a hot Miami afternoon when working in the yard with one's father, or some other assumed important moment in one's life. The anecdote, for Beard, begins with the literary figure Marcel Proust, whose memory, narrated in *Remembrance of Things Past*, was sparked by a small cake, and not a cold lager:

> When Proust recollected the precise taste sensation of the little scalloped *madeleine* cakes served at tea by his aunt, it led him into his monumental remembrance of things past. When I recollect the taste sensations of my childhood, they lead me to more cakes, more tastes: the great razor clams, the succulent Dungeness crab, the salmon, crawfish, mussels and trout of the Oregon coast; the black bottom pie served in a famous Portland restaurant; the Welsh rabbit of our Chinese cook; the white asparagus my mother canned; and the array of good dishes prepared by the two of them in that most memorable of kitchens. (1)

The bigger story, for Beard, stemming from these dramatic and detailed Northwest sensations is gastronomy and a life devoted to cooking. With my Miami anecdote, there are no similar recollections of cuisine or South Florida lifestyle. The Heineken does not remind me of Miami, the weather, local foods, the beach, or anything at all. Instead of such a grand claim to memory and storytelling as Beard makes, I realize that my bigger story is one of social media and what Tony Sampson calls "contagion," imitation gestures facilitated by social media and networks. My anecdote, it seems, is not just mine. It's been imitated many times before me. I'll elaborate on this point shortly.

Describing social media's rhetorical repetition, Sampson chooses *contagion* over more familiar terms for online imitation because "*meme* and *the viral* (the marketing buzzwords of the network age) have been conjured up from an assortment of crude renderings of evolutionary theory" and business interests (2). "These viral atmospheres," he writes, "are increasingly evident in the opportunities online consumers have to share their intimacies, obsessions, and desires with producers" (58). Unlike Sampson's negative approach to the social media contagion (whose basis in capitalism bothers Sampson), I find the contagion useful for understanding how stories are shared as such intimacies, obsessions, and desires, whether via a madeleine or a beer. Sampson rejects the contagion's impact on how consumers "are mostly unaware that they are part and parcel of a process of consumption at all, despite being prompted by a continuous stream of automated assists prompted to be from friends that further exploit the desire to attract more friends" (Sampson 32). With or without the negative "consumption" label, friends prompt friends to share interests, stories, and, it seems, anecdotes. Sharing is a social media concern. Thus, I began by sharing parental beer tales. I will conclude this book with a similar gesture.

Sometimes friends share via beer. When Don Draper, in *Mad Men*'s "A Night to Remember" episode, convinces his wife, Betty, to buy Heineken from the grocery store (without her realizing it) for an upcoming dinner party, he, too, plays into this sense of contagion (albeit, pre-Internet) by encouraging information sharing that contagions support. The repetitive act of buying a lager that *Mad Men* frames as 1960s advertising will eventually make its way to any given teenager sharing a Heineken with his dad on a hot day. As with me, the dad convinces the son (without him realizing it) to share a beer on a hot Miami day as part of a long-standing media tradition of Heineken memories. As one 1984 Heineken ad states, "I'll have a Heineken and so will my friends" (Adclassix). The beer moment is a shared and repeated moment. Sampson critiques advertising for helping facilitate this repetition; social media facilitate sharing as a rhetorical gesture of expression. Don captures Betty as an imitated middle-class housewife whose consumption patterns—noted in Heineken marketing—can be replicated and shared. The father captures the son as well when an anecdote is told. In this book, other moments will be captured as shared repetitions.

The anecdote captures other anecdotes. It turns out that when I offer this simple Heineken anecdote from my childhood and share it in the first few pages of this chapter, I begin by imitating a number of stories that precede me (stories outside *Mad Men*'s fictive universe). Imitation, Sampson writes, "instills the feelings that we are the originators of our own thoughts, beliefs, and actions" (49). We feel we are the originators of concepts or gestures even as we repeat ideas, memes, beliefs, and so on that precede our own gestures. Imitations are contagions. They spread gestures as much as they spread ideas. Beard spreads the Proustian gesture to introduce cooking in the 1960s. I am beginning with a Heineken gesture. Contagions mark, as Roland Bathes notes, beginnings for those who repeat and allow them to spread. "Such an introduction can only repeat itself," Barthes writes, "without ever introducing anything" (*Pleasure of the Text* 18). Social media, such as Facebook or Twitter, help facilitate this process of repetitive beginnings (though it occurs elsewhere as well in a general media culture). Sampson summarizes:

> Inventions stemming from desire are then contagiously passed on, point to point, via radiating ideas, fascinations, passionate interests, beliefs, and any other suitable social media for imitation, feeding into a continuum of invention and further adaptations of the entire social field. (25)

Such was Jean François Lyotard's theory that grand narratives—the large-scale beliefs we accept as natural (democracy, capitalism, Marxism, etc.)—are merely repetitions:

> A collectivity that takes narrative as its key form of competence has no need to remember its past. It finds the raw material for its social bond not only in the meaning of the narratives it recounts, but also in the act of reciting them. (22)

A narrative of taste memory, for instance, could be one such recitation; the narrative assumes that all tastes connect childhood experiences. Taste memory is grander than the objects being tasted and consumed.

For Lyotard, however, the age of database culture (what we currently understand via social media sites as well as any content management site that functions by way of a database) undermines the grand narrative by producing little stories, or what Lyotard called "the quintessential form of imaginative invention" (60). Lyotard framed the grand narrative as a story being disrupted by smaller stories. Drinking a cold mass-produced lager on a hot afternoon could be one recited grand narrative of experience waiting to be disrupted by any number of smaller stories. These stories, such as having a beer with one's daughter at various brewpubs and breweries around the country, seem inconsequential or, in the case of my beginning, as not a part of the anecdote's overall purpose. Yet, social media teach that the supposedly inconsequential—the tweet, status update, shared image—is, in fact, the focal point of an emerging rhetoric. Contagions, as alternatives to a grand narrative approach toward understanding social media, allow for an examination of the supposedly inconsequential in order to more fully understand one aspect of digital communication. Whatever may seem inconsequential is the focal point of the craft narrative I am telling in parts. Anecdotes begin the process.

Anecdotes, like the one I begin with, are contagions; they help spread grand narratives—even in the age of database culture—but they also allow for the telling of small stories. In craft beer, the anecdote is a popular way to begin a story; it is a rhetorical gesture relied on by numerous writers so that the specific experience of beer consumption is read as a fairly universal experience and not as an imitated fascination, interest, or belief. Craft beer anecdotes, like my own, often focus on first times we consumed beer, Heineken or otherwise. "I was eleven years old," Ken Wells begins *Travels with Barley*, "sitting on the front porch steps next to my father on a summer's day, when I took my first sip of beer" (1). "Some people remember their first beer as the one their dad popped open on a summer day sitting on the porch," Brian Yaeger opens *Red, White, and Brew*, "but I recollect sharing mine with Punky Brewster" (1). Bob Skilnik begins his narrative of Chicago beer history similarly:

> As a kid growing up in the predominately Irish neighborhood of Bridgeport during the 1950s and early '60s, there were two distinctive smells I'll always remember, the putrid fumes of the nearby Chicago Stockyards and the balancing sweet malt aroma from our two neighborhood breweries. (ix)

A young Garrett Oliver, on his first trip to London, drinks a beer and thinks, "'What is this stuff?' The bitterness ran across my tongue, assisted by only the faintest prickle of carbonation. Then it exploded in layers of flavor—hay, earth, newly mowed grass, orange marmalade, and baking bread" (*Brewmaster's Table* x). Lost Abbey's Tomme Arthur, in his foreword to *Farmhouse Ales*, reminisces that as a child "I remember three constants: a lawn mower that rarely ran well, the sweet smell of freshly mown grass, and a swig of dad's lager at the end of the day" (viii). "When I was a kid," Lew Bryson begins his guide to Pennsylvania breweries, "my father had often let me have sips of his beer with dinner" (xv). Chef and restaurateur David Chang, bemoaning craft beer in general, attributes his love of lousy, cheap beer to a lager on a hot summer day: "I remember watching my grandfather mow the lawn on a ninety-degree day in Virginia, and as soon as he finished, he'd ask me to fetch him a can of ice-cold beer" (Chang).

In 2009 *All about Beer* magazine posed a question to readers and writers, "What is your dad's favorite beer?" Writer Lisa Morrison responds, "My dad's beer was Busch. He would let me have sips of it whenever I wanted. And I liked it! I remember enjoying the way the bubbles tickled my tongue." And in reply to the same question, reader Nicholas Porochnia answers, "My dad would crack open a can of Budweiser, and pour me about 1/5 of a plastic cup so we could enjoy the time together" (Barbera).

An October 2013 thread on Beer Advocate asks for the "First Beer You Ever Tried" ("First Beer"). While the responses don't repeat narratives of mowing the lawn or summer, many do situate that moment with a father or grandfather, a can of Budweiser or other macro, and being young. Each repetition is a rhetorical act of sharing.

These anecdotes frame craft beer as a shared experience whose introduction (father, yard, taste, youth) should be familiar to those interested in this particular subject matter. The imitation circulates as a network—a loosely tied group of like-minded stories—of familiarity. That circulation is a contagion for how it picks up the stories that precede one another but that are basically the same. There is no financial motive for this repetition—the basis of Sampson's critique of social media or Don Draper's encouragement of his wife's beer shopping. There is, though, a suggested or vested interest in sharing. I will touch on more of these events throughout this book, but for my own introduction, the anecdote begins this examination of repetitive sharing. As Brummett argues, "Thus, the representational anecdote is useful for studying widely used symbolic strategies in many different media, because it sifts out those discourses which offer the same formal symbolic equipment to an audience" (163).

If there exists a symbol for the craft beer anecdote, it is the anecdote as entrance point to the larger, supposedly more important, narrative at stake, the belief that a grand narrative should follow. Drawing from Burke, Brummett notes that such anecdotes are not only representational but they generate patterns (what Sampson calls "imitation") and thus equip individuals for living. Anecdotes "are strategies for dealing with situations," Burke claims (*Philosophy of Literary Form* 296). They help us understand the narratives we tell or feel a part of. Anecdotes help foster belonging or, within the focus of this book, the socialness of social media. Burke says, "People find a certain social relationship recurring so frequently that they must 'have a word for it'" (*Philosophy of Literary Form* 293). That word can be *anecdotal*. As such, anecdotes single out "a pattern of experience that is sufficiently representative of our social structure, that recurs sufficiently, often *mutandis mutatis*, for people to 'need a word for it' and to adopt an attitude towards it" (*Philosophy of Literary Form* 300).

As these first anecdotes I retell demonstrate, in craft beer one pattern of experience might be "the first time." First times, the imitated anecdote demonstrates, lead to a type of equipment for living, a progression or movement from initial innocence (what is a beer?) to more sophisticated tastes (tastes that allow the author currently to write about beer in a reflective, more learned manner). First times are equipment of living. The first time organizes an initial moment so that the experiences that follow are better understood. A beer, therefore, becomes more than a beer. It becomes an experience—father-son relationship, yard work, path toward finer taste. As Burke writes, anecdotes suggest such logical ordering from beginning to end and thus provide for the reader or audience a sense of linearity (and overall order) that readers and writers typically attribute to narratives:

> No aim could be more rational than the desire to find a philosophic language whose order would correspond with the order of things as they are and must be—somewhat as the sequence of letters in a phonetic alphabet corresponds with the sequence of verbal sounds of which these letters are the signs. (*Grammar of Motives* 74)

No story, of course, is so simply ordered that its construction and telling might follow the "sequence of letters" in an alphabet. "We see the representational anecdote," Bryan Crable notes, "as a concern with the complications that surround the inception of any project: Where does one begin?" (320). Where does one begin? We would think, "At the beginning. Let me tell an anecdote to establish that supposed beginning. The first time I had a beer . . ." Sequence becomes naturalized; we believe it should be as such. There is a grand narrative, therefore, to anecdote telling, one often recited through various writers' work. One begins. One follows up that beginning with a larger narrative. One does not question the ordering. Thus, I begin with my own unfortunate anecdote. I have assumed it is the only logical way to begin. But there are, as well, small stories to tell.

Roland Barthes challenges such assumptions regarding anecdotes and beginnings in his pseudoautobiography, *Roland Barthes*. "He is not very good at getting to the heart of things," at one point Barthes says about himself and the complexity involved in showing a project's inception or in sharing one's anecdotes for some larger purpose (127). For Barthes, narratives are complicated by refusals to locate beginnings. Instead of relying on an assumed sequence, Barthes argues, such narratives approach their topic via fragments, figures, stereotypes, and other gestures that Barthes bundles under the terms "pleasure" or *jouissance* (terms that resist representation or grand narrative gestures and instead indicate a feeling or movement toward something, as in Barthes's concept of the "Neutral"). This bundling is summarized by Barthes's question: "What is the meaning of a pure series of interruptions?" (94). Barthes extends this question by reminding the reader that his "autobiography" is nothing more than a series of beginnings as interruptions: "To write beginnings, he tends to multiply this pleasure: that is why he writes fragments: so many fragments, so many beginnings" (94). Instead of beginnings, Barthes offers interrupted fragments. The fragment offers the basis of an interrupted, anecdotal narrative. The fragment is the small story.

Where does one begin, I ask, when telling a story about craft beer and social media, two items not typically coupled in the same uninterrupted beginning and whose focus, in popular discourse, is often grand in scope? Where does one begin, I ask, when there are so many beginnings to start with? "Where should we start?" Bruno Latour asks about the narratives we tell about various phenomena. "As always, it is best to begin in the middle of things, in *medias res*" (*Reassembling* 27). Following Barthes and Brummett, I might begin this project by considering a series of fragmented interruptions, knowing that it can be too difficult to get "to the heart of things" when one is telling beginnings. My stories about craft beer are fragments, bits and pieces of experience, observations, tastes, objects, moments, other people, the middle of things, and, of course, beginnings. I am on social media every day. Facebook is open in my browser. Twitter continuously updates. Pictures fill my Instagram account. I drink a beer every day. These moments should be inconsequential, but, like a repeated anecdote (or even repeated discussion of repetition), they are not. Each everyday moment interrupts and complements the next. The rhetorical implications for these shared interruptions are what is at stake in any understanding of social media and the obsessions they might help generate. Social media, as I will show throughout this book, function by interrupted beginnings, networks of fragments and beginnings, rhetorical gestures that start and stop in imitative manners, gestures that lack grand conclusions. To get to the heart of social media, if at all possible, I must interrupt my story about craft beer. I must interrupt the first time I had a Heineken. I must stop this grand examination and focus on a small story.

An Anecdotal Beginning

I unfortunately begin with an anecdote, an anecdote that reflects a first time, but not the first time of drinking with my father (as the previous examples demonstrate). Instead, I have another anecdote to tell, one that interrupts the first. Like Barthes, Burke challenges the notion of a beginning and ending as a linear path from anecdote to conclusion. "A beginning," he writes, "should 'implicitly contain' its ending—and an ending should be the explicit culmination of all that flowed from the beginning.

But also, there was some kind of almost mystic reversibility here, and the hint of infinite regress" (*Grammar of Motives* 338). No doubt, I would hope my anecdote allows for its own ending (via hint or allusion) even though I will interrupt this anecdote periodically as I tell my story. My anecdote, which interrupts my previous anecdote, is as such: It started with a beer rating. One beer rating. And that one beer rating changed my understanding of beer and social media.

On August 8, 2005, I entered a rating of Weyerbacher's Merry Monk in the RateBeer database after having a beer with my wife at Zeno's, a craft beer bar in State College, Pennsylvania, located across the street from the Penn State campus, where my wife was an assistant professor of English at the time. Almost a year earlier, on October 16, 2004, I had joined the online message-board community called RateBeer, my first real interaction with social media apart from a small weblog I ran on a Graymatter platform. RateBeer is a social media site that allows for information sharing among those interested in craft beer. The site includes a message board, internal e-mail, buddy systems, rating mechanisms for beer and beer-oriented places, and other online features. Founded in 2000, RateBeer claims thousands of members from over sixty countries. RateBeer centralizes one part of the online beer community (other sites, such as Beer Advocate, offer similar services). It allows users (with or without paid pro accounts that offer additional features) to keep track of beers that they have consumed through a rating database system, trade beers with other members, rate places they have visited, read editorials and commentary, follow one another's writings and ratings, and engage in beer-related conversation on a threaded message board.

RateBeer taps into the ratings system logic like many other social media sites such as Yelp or Amazon do. One purpose for these sites is to share taste. For some writers, such as *Scientific American*'s Michael Moyer, ratings—on beer, food, or consumer sites—are inaccurate measurements of taste: "People tend not to review things they find merely satisfactory. They evangelize what they love and trash things they hate. These feelings lead to a lot of one- and five-star reviews of the same product" (26). RateBeer and its system of ratings is one of many social networking sites that cater to taste, though that taste is hardly limited to extreme responses of either one or five stars. Ratings allow for contagion-styled idea sharing because of how they repeat experiences and information across a network of users. Dogfish Head's Sam Calagione describes the importance of sites like RateBeer to craft brewing:

> Literally dozens of busy web sites specialize on the craft beer segment; chat rooms abound where beer and breweries are discussed, and detailed rating systems for judging and ranking beers by categories of style and region are shared online. Some of the most popular and best organized are Beeradvocate.com, beertown.org, RateBeer.com, and realbeer.com. Anyone who wants a broad, informed impression of the brewing industry would learn a lot by visiting these four sites. (106)

Writing for the website Beerpulse, Jacob McKean, maker of Modern Times beer, considers ratings' overall effect on the beer industry as a way of sharing taste and knowledge:

> Also, let's take a moment to consider how remarkable it is that anyone is passionate enough about what we make to write lengthy, detailed reviews of it. There is simply no denying that beer ratings websites have played a crucial role in popularizing craft beer and putting our industry on the cusp of mainstream success. A brewery like mine can plausibly enter the industry with a marketing budget of zero in large part due to the efforts of passionate beer geeks who spread the good word about good beer.

Pinterest, Google+, Facebook, and Twitter all allow for the sharing of taste and interests as well; RateBeer centralizes one particular taste, however, into its social media space whose focus, unlike, for instance, Google+, is clearly defined as the central focus of the site's interests and desires. While other sites attract passionate beer geeks who spread the good word about craft, RateBeer is designed *specifically* for these folks. In Google+, one can be a part of a beer circle of individuals sharing beer experiences, but the entire site is not devoted to beer as RateBeer is. RateBeer, with all of its features, is mostly a shared rating site. Those of us who belong to RateBeer—for the most part—share our ratings and tasting experiences. We do so, following Mark Dredge's understanding of the phenomenon, because we possess the desire and need to rate beer and share those ratings:

> I want to see exactly what I drink over a year, I want to be able to track my drinking, I want to see the beers I loved and the ones I didn't, I want to see the variety of beer I drink, the quality of beers. Basically, I want to be able to look back at the end of the year and see my drinking from a quantitative view-point, rather than just a qualitative one from memory and pencil scribbles in a note book. ("I Rate Beer")

While such a process may feel individually oriented ("I want to . . ."), it also is a social one for how it places ratings in a shared space so that users may connect over tastes or interests. "I want to . . ." is not the leading directive when rating; sharing is. The ratings, as experiential anecdotes, are public and designed to be read by others. I may want to see the beers I loved or the ones I didn't, but I also want to see the beers others loved and didn't. And I want others to see what I love or didn't. Or as one beer blogger writes, ratings and like-minded social media gestures to connect with beer culture are social in nature: "Though seemingly just a beverage, beer is a vehicle for human contact, collaboration, and innovation. Each follower is a potential new friend, networking opportunity, educator, etc." (Schimke). Ratings educate. Standing in a store, bottle in hand, rushing to make a purchase before one of my kids knocks something over, pulling up RateBeer on my phone, I look up the ratings of a beer to check what others think (or if I have already tried the beer) before I make my purchase. In that way, RateBeer allows for permission marketing (what I will return to in the final chapter) where one online endorsement or rejection affects another's action. Ratings create followers. Interests in one style or brewery can cause another rater to follow one's activity. In this way, ratings play into what Eric K. Clemons calls the four Ps of online social networking: Personal, Participatory, Plausible or believable, and Possibility of physical transition. Ratings are personal (for me), participatory (shared), plausible (the belief in what someone has consumed or experienced), and pose physical transition (a shared rating can prompt a physical consumption at a later point in time).

Ratings, as well, offer the opportunity to engage with writing in brief, concise ways as opposed to grand gestures of explanation, interpretation, and analysis—forms of writing that often dominate rhetorical discussions regarding food culture and that are academics' most familiar forms of writing. In ratings' fragmented moments of expression, shared "small stories" are easier to navigate and move among than an extended discussion of cultural implications of consumption. Thus, via ratings, we can connect more easily at the level of the everyday.

Public writings offer examples of this process. In his "Beer Samizdat Manifesto," blogger Jay Hilman writes about beer accordingly. The desire to write about beer (rating or otherwise) comes to one as part of the natural, daily process of connectivity:

> Stringing together a few words about beer is so goddamned *easy* that even a ham-handed chimp can do it; or in my case, a workin'

man tryin' to raise a family & put food on the table & who doesn't have as much time as he'd like to write long essays about *whatnot* on the internet.

Avoiding the whatnot of long essays on beer, ratings tap into the overall online culture of everyday reviews. On YouTube, on Facebook, and on other sites, craft beer drinkers leave reviews for others to read. On my Really Simple Syndication (RSS) feed of beer blogs, there is no shortage of daily reviews of beer being consumed across the country. These reviews become small stories aggregated and shared across various delivery networks. Whereas we might identify the everyday as a site of interest or study in academic discourse (following Michel de Certeau or Walter Benjamin), small, fragmented writings connected to experiences and one another across social media networks are typically not emphasized for their rhetorical importance. The October 16, 2004, RateBeer rating I am leading up to (and the anecdote I am interrupting) is one such small story, an everyday moment of writing whose supposed inconsequential status connects to other stories in this book. The rating's sharing, though, proved problematic for me when I eventually understood how it connected or did not connect to other reviews.

Aside from RateBeer, I discover beer ratings from blogs aggregated on my RSS feed. I find that on August 24, 2009, the *Barley Blog* reviewed Pliny the Elder as "floral, piney, and lightly spicy" ("Pliny, Homebrew Stouts"). On May 25, 2012, the New Brew Thursday crew videotaped their review of Three Floyds Zombie Dust, identifying the beer as influenced by West Coast IPAs ("May 24"). While I rate on RateBeer, I've avoided writing beer reviews on my beer blog, *Make Mine Potato*, despite a promise in a September 2007 post (after my first online order arrived) to "post some reviews shortly" (Rice). Those reviews never came. When beer weblogs review beers, they rate, but they do not connect to other ratings the way an online database like RateBeer does. Many people, no doubt, watch New Brew Thursday or read the *Barley Blog*, and many people have tasted both Pliny the Elder and Zombie Dust, but the posted reviews are not in the same circulated system of sharing and connecting that a database such as RateBeer offers. With random reviews or rates not stored in some kind of network or database, Pliny the Elder and Zombie Dust are left unconnected and outside a craft network. On the other hand, when the reviews or ratings are in databases, the connection can surmount beer itself. Reviews become ticks. Numbers. Achievements. Status. Obsession. Lists. For that reason, ratings are sometimes mocked, as in a *Salty Dog* comic strip written by Bill Coleman for the beer publication the *Ale Street News*. In the strip, two dogs debate ratings as one professes to being a member of Beer Advocate. "I have to rate only 68 more beers (about a week's worth) to raise my status to Grand Imperial Wizard," one dog proclaims (Coleman). Ratings, in this case, project the status of nerd (the wizard title is imaginary), a way to score "brownie points" with other nerds, as the other dog says. And while the ticks and rates that create an ethos of being a nerd exist on RateBeer, ratings (most of the time) do a bit more than merely project such a status.

Instead of reducing ratings or reviews to nerdy status, we can consider their insights and revelations that extend beyond the beer itself into anecdote-style stories about taste and place. When I rate, I may also be telling an interrupted small story about where I am or where I have been. For instance, video ratings and reviews reveal knowledge about location in ways RateBeer ratings do not: in a video review, we may see the reviewer's bathroom, kitchen, family room, bedroom, or whatever part of the house the reviewer records in. The rating, in this case, also becomes voyeurism. The rating becomes insight not only into how someone thinks as opposed to how others think (as a RateBeer or Beer Advocate beer rating does), but it becomes insight into how someone *lives*. Ratings, like an anecdote, are a type of equipment for living. Ratings reveal the everyday as a way to be in this world.

For instance, my anecdotal recollections regarding video ratings and reviews tell me that I know video reviewer Ryan Reschan has an old barrel in his dining room that he props bottles on ("A Response"). I think that the series of white filing boxes behind Chad9976, in his reviews, are comic books ("Chad Reviews Stuff"). I know what the host's kitchen at Beer Geek Nation looks like. Ratings, in these sporadic moments, connect me to the banal living conditions of people I may never meet in real life regardless of the similarity or differences in our shared rating experiences. These types of ratings give me material insight the way that a story of a first time trying beer might. Despite this knowledge, I'm not connected to these posted video ratings, by review or by place, the way I am connected to reviews on RateBeer. My knowing, though, indicates involvement. I'm *involved* in the environment and in the people who post such reviews the way I might hope readers can be partly involved in my Miami childhood via a specific anecdotal story about my first beer experience on a hot summer day. If someone were to read *Make Mine Potato*, the blog's contents might not reveal material insight (i.e., my physical surroundings) beyond the kind of toaster oven I own (when it is posed with beers I drink) or what my kitchen counter looks like, but the blog's contents might reveal more profound insight into my daily life (travels, time with my kids, religious holidays I observe, conversations with my wife) so that others feel involved as well. Online ratings are location bound in that sense as well—the aspect of daily living—but they also aggregate what one owns or lives among as one lists daily consumption.

The BeerGraphs website asks how connectivity is tied to location, though not to people's living rooms or kitchens. By studying Untappd check-ins (a mobile service where users can record beer ratings), Matt Murphy's study of state-to-state beer drinking discovers that "the ratings for in-state beers were higher than those for out-of-state beers" while, simultaneously, "check-ins more than 2000 miles from the brewery actually had the highest rating of any distance group" (Murphy). Sharing is tied to the places one lives or the places one visits. Thus, I may be inclined to feel connected to a brewery from my state and even tell a rating-based story about that connection, but I still will rate a brewery from a faraway state higher. Regardless of my location, though, I will rate higher if I am knowledgeable about the conventions of social connectivity, to which the activity of rating belongs and which my forthcoming first-time beer-rating anecdote (I am still interrupting myself with background and context) will complicate. "People want to be connected to the products they have," Larry Bell of Bell's Brewery says. "They are tired of buying from faceless corporations [when] there is no connection to our lives." Ratings connect and influence via location but also via the feeling of association with location (as Untappd might allow for and which I will, in a later chapter, tie to terroir). My ratings are not influenced by who has rated the same beer before me; my ratings are influenced by the time I have spent writing down my thoughts for each beer I have consumed and my desire to connect those thoughts to others. I call that period of time *knowledge*. Knowledge involves a writerly connection—the rating I've written or someone else has written. If I am not knowledgeable, I may rate an out-of-state brewery—such as Weyerbacher—lower than other breweries, particularly since Weyerbacher was only 574 miles from where I lived at the time.

When I wrote that first Weyerbacher rating, I engaged social media similar to how Dredge and Hilman did; I was trying to connect and share. Like stringing together a series of anecdotes as a narrative, I connect beers to one another via ratings; I connect beers to other users via ratings; I connect to the beer in question via ratings. Later when my laptop is at hand, I log in to RateBeer and record my impressions. I allow everyday experiences to guide writing moments of connection. My impressions are also recorded by RateBeer as an RSS feed so that those who follow me can connect to my experience. My impressions are also tweeted by a button on the Ratebeer ratings page that allows me to share directly to Twitter and Facebook (where I do not share my ratings because of other kinds of connections I am trying to establish). Experience and connectivity are an ongoing process. They are also selective processes.

These ratings I record on RateBeer are not important because of how or what I write (using "grassy," "floral," "grapefruit," "pine," or "barnyard" to describe what I am drinking, whether in critique or in praise) but for how they maintain general connectivity across the community itself. "What does it really mean to be connected?" Steven Shaviro asks. "What does it mean to be a node in the network?" (28). I don't claim that ratings provide an answer to these questions or resolve my experience as a rating node among thousands of other nodes. Ratings I make highlight the rating and me as two such nodes in a craft network of experience. Without ratings,

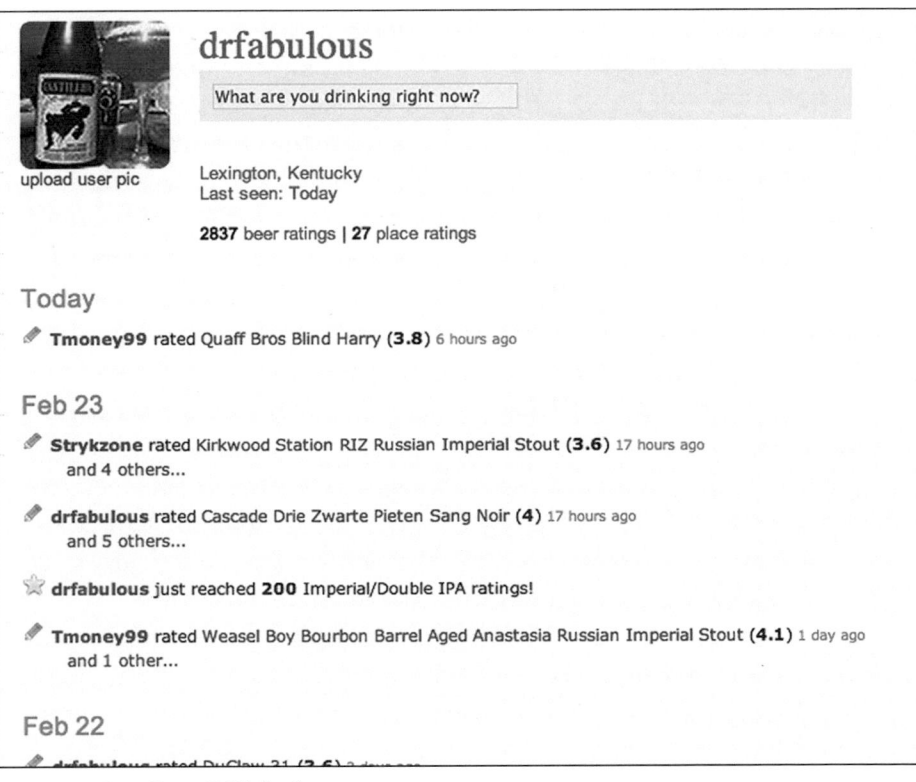

RateBeer RSS feed

I will forget my consumption and my place in a given network. Without ratings, a big piece of my overall beer network will vanish, and my overall beer experience will be altered dramatically. I won't be, I believe, a craft beer drinker without ratings.

As my Weyerbacher anecdote promises (but is still being interrupted), I was introduced to social media and craft beer via a beer rating. For Beer Advocate's Todd Alström, ratings also came with an introduction to craft beer, somewhat in the way that lagers have introduced many to craft beer. Alström reminisces about himself and his brother on a Beer Advocate thread:

> When Todd came back to the US, he wrote his first beer review on a napkin. Soon after he landed a gig creating websites just before the big Internet boom. At the same time the "microbrew revolution" of the 90's was in full-swing, and the bros signed-up for the revolution and began tasting beers on a daily basis. To record their personal beer notes and adventures, Todd created a website: BrewGuide.[1]

A rating was not my introduction to drinking craft beer. Ratings, however, became an added node to the craft network I joined and helped build for myself. For some time, I did not rate.

My earliest memories of craft beer—drinking Stone Arrogant Bastard and Flying Dog Gonzo Imperial Porter in Gainesville, Florida, or buying my first Bell's (Kalamazoo Stout) at a corner store off Woodward Avenue in Ferndale, Michigan, were not accompanied by follow-up ratings. Much of that initial beer connectivity I engaged with is now lost to me. When I would spend Fridays at Woodward Avenue Brewers, Royal Oak Brewery, or Black Lotus, I did not sit with rating notebook at hand. Instead of ratings, I have only vague, anecdotal recollections. I remember searching the shelves at Merchant's old store in Royal Oak, Michigan, confused over which bottle of Rogue to buy. I remember having Dogfish Head 60 Minute for the first time, loving it, and when returning to find it no longer there being told, "We only get it now and then." I remember the bottles of Tucher I consumed as being exotic (German wheat beer as exotic?). I remember returning my Jolly Pumpkin Maracaibo bottle to Holiday Market two times because I swore the beer had gone bad (when, in fact, Jolly Pumpkin had just begun to barrel-age their beers). But these memories do not provide the connectivity that ratings do. These memories are not social but individual moments, nodes left out of a network of meaning. These moments are noncontagion anecdotes, small everyday experiences interrupting the real story of ratings I want to tell.

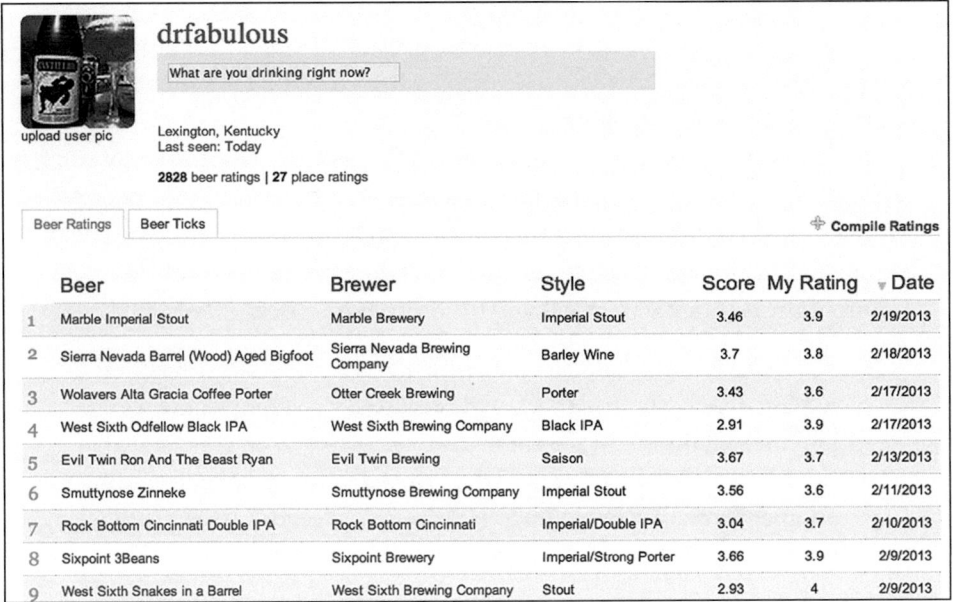

RateBeer ratings from February 2013

When I am rating, I am also engaging in social media in a way similar to Clay Shirky's fascination with user-generated information or Axle Bruns's concept of the prosumer, an agent within "collaborative, user-led content creation" (6). By offering a rating, I contribute to existing content and collaborate in a social space. My rating, as anecdote, helps shape that space (as one of many ratings that will generate a cumulative rating or identity for the beer in the space). What makes ratings possible are the numerous ratings; altogether they produce not just an average score, but they also produce a general assumption about a given beer based on collective contributions. These collective contributions are mythic in stature; they are hyped (as in Shirky's writings or in Steve Johnson's *Future Perfect*) as progress in a world of changing content creation (i.e., collectives produce content or make decisions better than individuals can). Each rater on RateBeer is a creator of user content, and as many of the overhyped stories of social media proclaim, each contribution generated by user content supposedly makes the world a better place. Or maybe not. As the creator of one particular piece of user content, I was not kind in my individualized evaluation. When I entered that first rating in State College, Pennsylvania, I had no sense of shared craft beer taste. Even though I had been a member of RateBeer for a year, I had yet to rate a beer. I had minimal understanding about being a member of a social media community. I was not part of the collective. I did not put my rating anecdote to good social usage.

With this interrupted explanation and background supplied, I feel as if I can share the anecdote about rating a Weyerbacher beer for the first time. The rating I entered reads, "Had this one at Zeno's in State College, PA. From a bottle, it poured flat. Not even close to Belgian style. Watery, hint of Budweiser and rancidness. A complete let down." When I compare my unkind review (.5 out of 5) against reviews I have more recently entered or even against other ratings of this particular Pennsylvania brewed beer, I question my 2005 judgment and understanding of social connectivity. I *know* I did not like the beer when I first consumed it. I *know* that it displeased me. But my knowledge, obviously, was limited despite Shirky's claim that in social media spaces like RateBeer (and in Shirky's example of Wikipedia), "the desire to make a meaningful contribution" generates an overall shared knowledge (*Here Comes Everybody* 132). I desired to make an overall meaningful contribution and even be a part of what James Surowiecki calls "the wisdom of crowds." "If you can assemble a diverse group of people who possess varying degrees of knowledge and insight, you're better off entrusting it with major decisions rather than leaving them in the hands of one or two people," Surowiecki argues (31). I desired to be, and found myself, among a diverse group of people, but with hindsight I am displeased with the results of this first crowd experience. I am surprised I rated the beer so low. Surprise provides me a place to interrupt this anecdote. I am still surprised. "Beyond the concept of network," Latour writes, "there is always that movement, and that surprise" (*An Inquiry* 33). Could the beer really have been that bad? (When I look back on the crowd, other ratings by other drinkers suggest that my gut feeling was way off and that, no, this beer is in fact good and widely liked). Why was I so eager to dismiss a moment of drinking a beer? Why was I so sure of myself? Why was I so confident? Why is this my introduction to one aspect of craft beer as opposed to the more nostalgic (and imitated) gesture of the first time? Why is this my representational anecdote? Why is there no grand narrative (no larger life-learning lesson) here?

Ignorant of the rhetoric of rating, the practice of evaluating consumption, and the feeling of rating, how could *I have known* how to situate that knowledge? Not yet a participant in a social networking space and the various activities that compose that space and its culture, how could I have known how to temper, evaluate, and compare shared knowledge? I obviously did not. Participation consists of shared experiences that help us understand what we know and how we know it. While participation demands little prior knowledge regarding *how* to participate (i.e., we don't need to study participation in order to be able to do it), the memory of one specific moment of participation makes a lack of knowledge regrettable. I regret this rating when I remember it. "After the difficulty of scoring and ranking comes the problem of treasured memories," beer writer Michael Jackson writes ("Farewell, Father . . . It's Beer War"). I am also not the first member of RateBeer to question his or her initial ratings. There is, thus, some aspect of contagion, after all, to my failed rating. An October 2013 thread, "Post Your First Ever Review and Critique It," offers MagicDave6's recollection of his first rating: "I was a complete idiot back then" (Magic-Dave6). And LinusStick remembers, "I go back and read those early ratings and crack up at the phases I went through" (LinusStick). AdamJackson similarly remarks,

> I kind of wanna re-rate my first 100 beers. I was insane. Also, I used to post whole paragraphs. I've gotten really lazy about my reviews. Should really focus on adding more details. Now it's just a single line. I'm a bad ticker. (AdamJackson)

Because of what I feel capable of writing today and because of how I now understand shared communal knowledge and taste, like some of these reflections I regret my novice efforts. Rating a beer is not the only experience to showcase this inability, of course, but it's an experience that has since influenced much of my understanding of online writing, online rhetorics, social media, and beer. If I have an introduction to craft beer that I can share and one that is indicative of one aspect of craft beer's introductions, I prefer not to begin with a grand tale of the specific first craft beer that inspired me to pursue this interest (Arrogant Bastard? Dead Guy? Was it something else?). Instead, I begin with the problematic review I posted in a social media space because of how it speaks to an initial desire to share that is felt by many social media users. This beginning also speaks to the interruption that Barthes aligns with narrative beginnings. My current interests, and how I might situate those interests within a larger rhetorical moment, are interrupted by this beginning. I can't begin without this interruption. Let me, then, begin the next chapter with another interruption.

CHAPTER 2
Craft Interruptions

> The best way to ask for beer is to sing out Ubik. Made from select hops, choice water, slow-aged for perfect flavor, Ubik is the nation's number-one choice in beer. Made only in Cleveland.
> —Philip K. Dick, *Ubik*

The rating, as a marker of social media involvement, suggests confidence. *I feel as if what I contribute to this social space is productive and valuable.* Why I felt confident and compelled after that Weyerbacher moment to post a review, I do not remember. Why I currently feel compelled to continue rating the beers I consume after beginning this practice on such a sour note, I do not know. Why I feel compelled to write a book whose beginnings focus on the question of beer and ratings rather than a larger narrative regarding beer and America, I still do not know. For some reason, I feel that I can. I am confident.

Social media depend on confidence. Craft beer narratives do as well. My introductory gesture to craft beer, noted in the Weyerbacher review, lacks the self-confidence and direction that many craft beer narratives maintain—even as they operate within the same contagion network. Confidence expresses ethos, or more specifically, *proairesis*, choice based on ethos. Social media hyperbole is often based on such confidence. "When new technology appears," Clay Shirky exclaims, "previously impossible things start occurring. If enough of those impossible things are important and happen in a bundle, quickly, the change becomes a revolution" (*Here Comes Everybody* 107). Shirky's confidence turns a communicative moment into a revolution. That claim, no matter what effect the technology has on communication, is exaggeration. Revolution is often a topos of exaggeration. The exaggeration, in this case, extends Shirky's ethos as one who writes about social media. Choosing exaggeration as a focus will make Shirky believable for a significant part of his audience (some critics aside) because of how he makes social media grand in gesture. Grand narratives (regardless of content) project writerly confidence. Small stories interrupting one another may not.

That I don't review beers on my weblog, for instance, might be interpreted by craft beer enthusiasts as a noncredible (I do not participate in the grand narrative act of reviewing) and thus nonconfident gesture since I am not participating in an accepted space for expression, one in which the speaker or writer demonstrates great confidence in sharing opinions of taste. That I don't begin with a story of traveling throughout the country searching out the best or most interesting beer available, too, might be interpreted as such. Such contagion—imitated—narrative gestures as the review or the travel story evoke proairesis (the choices project ethos). Proairesis creates confidence. Confidence allows the listener or reader to believe in a given story.

As in social media visions such as Shirky's, the confident beer story is also familiar in the world of beer storytelling, where grand narratives play dominant roles. Confidence, in these stories, interrupts other interventions (such as my own writing in this book) since only the dominant story is granted ethos. In such stories, we are sometimes told, beer begat everything that we hold precious and true. Jeffrey Kahn, for instance, narrates the story of human civilization as one based on beer:

> We needed something that would suppress the rigid social codes that kept our clans safe and alive. We needed something that, on occasion, would let us break free from our biological herd imperative—or at least let us suppress our angst when we did.
>
> We needed beer.

Tom Standage repeats the same story in *A History of the World in Six Glasses*: "Beer is a liquid relic from human prehistory and its origins are closely intertwined with the origins of civilization itself" (10–11). Tapping into this contagion of confidence, Dina Spector gives a contribution to *Business Insider* the title "How Beer Created Civilization." If beer is the basis of civilization, then it is *the* most important thing of all time (thus, confidence is projected in the narrative in order to strengthen it). I don't typically write in such a manner. Not writing in this manner hurts my beer-writing ethos. My anecdotes so far do not showcase beer as *the* most important thing to me, let alone civilization. I love beer. But is it *the* most important thing of all time? Is craft beer more important than my children? My job? The printing press? The Internet? Medicine? The environment? Is craft beer or is my daughter the focus of my parental beer tale? Still, and not sure yet of my own response, I am not without confidence as I move through anecdotes. My projected confidence promises a narrative far more significant than what the anecdote initially appears to represent (i.e., sharing a beer with one's father or misrating a beer) yet falls short of identifying the beginning of civilization. With confidence, in other words, I include an embarrassing anecdote. (I should have known better than to rate Weyerbacher a .5, but I'm confident enough today, after over five thousand ratings, to own up to such error.) Why I present the embarrassing anecdote, though, remains a secret since, no matter how confidently I present it, I am undermining my ethos. Michel Maffesoli points to network interactions as a rhetoric of secrecy. "Step by step," Maffesoli writes about networks, "one can see a mystical network being built" (83). Out of this mystical network, Maffesoli notes, "the theme of secrecy is surely a preferred way of understanding the social context before us" (90). Stupidity and confidence may be equally difficult to understand as each builds a given user-generated network.

As I work through this secrecy, I interrupt my small story about rating with a series of grand narratives. In one of the first popularized discussions of beer, Michael Jackson's *Playboy* essay "Beer Chic" concludes with a nod toward a grand narrative of beer. "The pleasure" of beer, Jackson writes, is in "gaining the experience: the encounters with the unexpected, the possibility of triumph or disaster, the pursuit of the elusive, the constant lessons, the bittersweet memories that linger" (166). Triumph, disaster, life lessons, bittersweet memories are confidence keywords as much as civilization is in another context. These keywords project the writer's authorial stance as more than just someone who enjoys a good beer. These keywords proclaim: this is someone who knows about life. And someone who knows about life and beer, we might think, should be heard. When beer writer Pete Brown begins his tale *Three Sheets to the Wind*, he projects anecdotal/narrative confidence in order to demonstrate ethos as well. The phrase "fancy a pint?" he tells us, will

> lead to an awful lot more than just a second of third. This is a pint that will have far-reaching consequences, a pint that will change my life, a pint that will cost me a lot more than the price of a late cab home. (3)

Jack Erickson begins *Brewery Adventures in the Big East* with such confidence by declaring in grandiose fashion, "America is a nation proud of its history." To this he adds, "Beer is the most American of all beverages" (1). And in *The Great Beer Trek*'s early pages, Stephen Morris declares, "I began to perceive, not surprisingly, that the entire country, if not the world, revolved around beer." He continues, "On an entirely unfrivolous [sic] level, I realized that by understanding a nation's beer drinking habits, one could understand the nation" (4). The movie *Beer Culture* begins with a declaration: "Craft beer is a metaphor for the American dream" (*Beer Culture*). Tom Acitelli tells us that craft beer changed "the American palate forever" (xv). "American's Northwest beckons like a new frontier," Michael Jackson proclaimed in his "California Pilgrimage" episode ("California Pilgrimage Part 1"). Dreams. The nation. The frontier. These are all confident gestures; they are attempts to translate the experience of beer into some grandiose and larger-than-beer-itself narrative. These gestures want to make beer unsecretive by revealing its true, larger than life, story.

Such beginnings offer grand narrative approaches to consumption; they pose a moment's interruption (the experience of a beer) with a larger gesture that is supposed to surpass the interruption's significance (the pint will cost me more than its price, the most American of all beverages, understanding a nation). The product, the story tells us, stands for values, morals, the human spirit. I, on the other hand, begin without a sense of confidence (even if I once believed otherwise): I misrated a beer. I was too arrogant. I was ignorant of what I was consuming. This misrating's connection to confident narratives of craft beer represents a mystical and mythical network of craft relationships. Why two moments connect in a craft network, as I will note later with beer-release days, is mythical. Secretive. Sharing is not as conclusive as some social media theorists claim.

From the time I recorded that first negative rating until the time I began writing this book (three years later), I had rated over 2,800 beers (I am now past 6,000). Whatever occurred during that early evening at Zeno's, I have since learned how to participate in a social media space (indicated by a desire to continue to record consumption). I now post daily ratings on RateBeer, tweet those ratings on Twitter, post pictures of these beers on Google+ (which I share with almost five hundred people in a beer circle), occasionally refer to craft beer on Facebook, and blog about my drinking. I call this activity *participation*. Participation as sharing activates what Marshall McLuhan deemed involvement: that is, the "total situation, and not a single level of information movement" (*Understanding Media* 39). The total situation extends from the physical (being in the same room sharing beer, for instance) to other types of experiences. I physically participate (I log in, I write, I click appropriate buttons). I emotionally and affectively participate as well so that I can experience involvement, not only in the sense of being in shared spaces or sharing consumption, but in knowing (knowing others' tastes, actions, behaviors, beliefs, consumption). Clay Shirky posits involvement as the basis of digital sharing, such as sharing information, updates, or files. For Shirky, though, what I experienced in my initial desire to share a rating was an emotional impulse already present in me; the website only facilitated what most of us want to do—share and be involved: "Motivation, energy, and talent for action are all present in those sorts of groups [like RateBeer]—what was not present, until recently, was the ability to coordinate easily" (*Here Comes Everybody* 159). When a site such as RateBeer coordinates, therefore, shared knowledge and involvement are naturally foregrounded. "Shared awareness," writes Shirky, "allows otherwise uncoordinated groups to begin to work together more quickly and effectively" (*Here Comes Everybody* 163).

My father shared a beer with me once, too. But that physical sharing was limited as an act of participation or involvement. It occurred. It ended. It was forgotten until imitation—the contagion effect of sharing stories via printed and digital media—recirculated it as an anecdote. The network, then, facilitates larger sharing moments such as anecdotes or confidence narratives. "Those who find that the content is salient to them," Karine Nahon and Jeff Hemsley write, "resonate with their views, or just interesting, share it with others and create an interest network. Some will share and create response content" (113). Contagions exist because of interest and response networks.

Social media offer a highly complex series of participatory and shared spaces, and, in turn, these acts generate stories—including the anecdotes that may precede them—not bound to one specific space or even one specific anecdotal beginning. Henry Jenkins posed the term *transmedia* as a way to explain narrative movement through various spaces for commercial purposes (fan fiction on websites, video games, books, and a film all telling a single story such as Jenkins's example of *The Matrix*). To follow a new-media-based narrative, Jenkins wrote, one follows all the media spaces as one narrative and not as disjointed media spaces. Otherwise, the overall narrative is not complete. In a transmedia space, a given story integrates "multiple texts to create a narrative so large that it cannot be contained within a single space" (*Convergence Culture* 95). In a transmedia space, a beginning—such as an anecdote—may be difficult to locate (its position secretive) among all the participants in a given interest or response network.

"We are seeing the emergence of new story structures, which create complexity by expanding the range of narrative possibility rather than pursuing a single path with a beginning, middle, and end," writes Jenkins (119). A beginning may be distributed across multiple spaces and not only exist at the start of a story. It is difficult to get at the heart of things, as Barthes warns, when narratives of a first time and confidence narratives are not beginnings but rather spaces among a transmedia story. Jenkins's concept reflects all storytelling, not just those stories occurring across video games, books, and movies, as Jenkins writes. Transmedia storytelling can be understood as a digital approach, but one that is not dependent on a specific platform or medium or even commercial endeavor. Instead, a networked approach recognizes that no narrative can exist in one space; narratives are built out of various activities and social spaces; their telling occurs according to how each networked space is engaged by author and audience.

A craft beer story would always be transmedia based, even if not recognized as such for its given author's anecdotal beginnings. To relate an anecdote about sharing a beer with one's father, therefore, may not be a true beginning gesture as it denies the multiple spaces that the anecdote was created within (as contagion theory illustrates). My experience was felt before I accepted that Heineken. Even if I didn't realize it, my experience was felt in books, in magazine accounts, in advertising, in travel stories, and then, when I was older, on the Web or a *Mad Men* episode. The beer-sharing anecdote, for sure, is a beginning since many of us start with its retelling, but maybe it is one closer to Barthes's concept of not getting to the heart of things. Networked beginnings don't start at one known and obvious point; they are engaged with, across various media spaces in known and unknown ways. My notion of the networked beginning, influenced by Bruno Latour, is not that such beginnings are fabricated; they already exist. As Latour argues throughout his extensive tracing of networks, networks are not created; they already are out there. My anecdote, like the others I cite, is one networked-media beginning among many; it is already caught in a series of networked (transmedia) stories and accounts. It interrupts the spaces of similar stories, and it interrupts my own ability here to begin over again this book's first two chapters with an anecdote in order to tell a more significant story about craft beer and social media. I am in a network.

Networked Beginnings

In a network, there is no heart, no center, no grand theme that explains the overall narrative, no tale of triumph or disaster. The story of craft beer, told in numerous books and magazine articles, on message boards, in conversations, on social media sites, in movies, might be read as a series of networked, or transmedia, tellings rather than as a space where one has to get to the heart of things (as one would have to do in an origin story, definitional story, thesis-driven story, argument, and so on). Craft beer, for instance, is not just the introductory story of one's first time or the confident narrative of grandiose gestures (as my previous examples demonstrate), but in this transmedia space it is also the introductory story of a revolution against the dominance of tasteless, mass-produced beer often exemplified in the hated, yet ubiquitous, fizzy lager (Miller, Budweiser, Pabst, Heineken).

The *revolution*, one retelling indicates, is another anecdotal interruption in the overall network of beginning stories. Craft beer writing often turns to the revolution or battle tale (reciting it often) to frame its larger narrative. Revolution is a repeated topos (or contagion) that functions as an expected grand narrative of explanation. For instance, William Least Heat-Moon, following Jack Kerouac's aside in *On the Road* that there must be an ideal bar in America, describes his 1987 quest for "genuine brew" as one of warfare:

> It was plain that the corporate warfare between the two largest American brewers had helped move some beer drinkers not away from one big brewer to another but rather away from industrial brewing altogether and toward an openness to try the beers of handcrafters who are working with only the four basic ingredients. (77)

Beer writer Andy Crouch argues that this battle is between the new and the established: "The craft beer revolution has always been about one beer, a single experience that shatters decades of programming from big brewery advertising and changes the way people perceive beer" (*Great American* 15). Crouch, a longtime presence in beer writing, is a strong proponent of telling this revolution/battle story. Elsewhere, Crouch describes craft brewers as "the industry's front line warriors" ("Death of the Flagship" 18). For Crouch, there is "the truth that craft brewers are not competitors so much as compatriots in the revolution of better beer" ("Celebrating the Success of Craft Beer").

"The revolution has arrived," Joshua Bernstein introduces *Brewed Awakening* (xi). "By 1980, four of every five American beers were manufactured by just six companies," Don Russell points out as the reason why the revolution was necessary (25). That time period, Stone Brewing's Greg Koch and Steve Wagner adds, was "the Dark Ages of brewing in the United States" (26). In that time period, Fred Eckhardt points out, brewery trade journals didn't "even call it beer anymore, they refer to it as 'malt beverage'" (*Treatise on Lager Beers* 2). In 1978 William Carlsen wrote in the *New York Times*, "It is difficult to find an ale brewed in America today" (C1). And in 1971 Fred Ferretti lamented the decline of New York brewing as symbolic of all brewing in America, where "brewing of beer is becoming more automated, more impersonal, more mechanical. Nowadays, it's all done with corn adjuncts or ground rice, corn syrup and different strains of European and domestic hops." He concluded with a bit of exasperation: "With uniform taste, comes a lack of adventure" (A8).

Out of this destitute time, we learn, came the revolution. "We've all played a part in the American craft brewing revolution that forever changed the beer industry," Ken Grossman writes in the acknowledgments to *Beyond the Pale*, the story of Sierra Nevada (xviii). Charles Papazian, credited with introducing homebrewing to American culture in the 1980s, advises homebrewers, when making a Belgian-style dubbel, to "start a revolution!" (*Complete Joy of Homebrewing* 141). The documentary *Beer Pioneers* frames its history of craft beer in its subtitle as "revolution" (*Beer Pioneers*). Maureen Ogle describes Michael Jackson's writing as providing "insight into and information about the craft-brewing revolution" (*Ambitious Brew* 318).

This revolution continues today. Brooklyn Brewery's president, Steve Hindy, describes the revolutionary aspect of craft's growth in a *CNN* op-ed: "America's small brewers have been on a roll in the past decade, claiming more than 6% of the U.S. beer market since the craft brewing revolution began in the early '80s." "Beer is having a big moment, a revolution of sorts," an ABC News report begins (Zinczenko and McClellan). A 2012 *Businessweek* article on beer poses the current battle between conglomerates and craft as "The Plot to *Destroy* America's Beer" (Leonard, emphasis mine). One Michigan craft beer retailer blogs, "In the world of craft beer, home-, micro-, and craft breweries challenge giants like Anheuser-Busch InBev and MillerCoors. These challenges are more than battles over market shares. These are challenges over cultural acceptance, distinction, and legitimacy more broadly" (Siciliano). Owner of Lagunitas, Tony Magee, has tweeted that beer conglomerates InBev and MillerCoors have an "imperial demeanor."[1] And on a blog post now deleted, Magee writes, "I see Craft brewing as a sort of American-style civil uprising. A peoples [sic] revolt, ostensibly about the flavors, or lack thereof, in mainstream commercial American lagers—but ultimately more about the shriveling of other culturally connective tissues" ("The Most Prolific"). "Call me a revolutionary," Ron Jeffries of Jolly Pumpkin states in the "I Am a Craft Brewer" video. Revolution Brewing takes this word as the basis of its name. Urban Chestnut Brewing offers a Revolution and Reverence series of beers. New Glarus brews Organic Revolution. The revolution, these stories and brands relate, is one of taste. New Albanian's owner, Roger Baylor, writes, "We're experiencing a 'craft' beer revolution, our peers comprise 'Craft' Beer Nation, and it's all about fresh, local 'craft' alternatives. It's hard to define, but we persist in thinking that we know it when we taste it" ("Wednesday Weekly: To the 'Craft' of the Matter"). Stone Brewing's Greg Koch proclaims, "I must fully admit that I feel a bit of a revolutionary" (qtd. in Kaplan 26). "For the longest time we didn't have choices," *Beer Advocate*'s Alström brothers say in Anat Baron's documentary *Beer Wars*. "This is the battle ground, and the holy grail is your wallet," Anat Baron narrates in the film. "On one side is corporate America doing everything it can to win at all cost. On the other side are small brewers who are challenging the status quo," writes Brian Palmer; "a cadre of dissatisfied consumers launched a beer revolution." Dinah Eng, in a *CNN Money* 2013 profile of Samuel Adams, describes the brewery's founder, Jim Koch, as "beating the drum for its craft revolution." Eng quotes Koch describing the history of the brewery: "Samuel Adams was a brewer and a patriot and a revolutionary, so we named the beer after him. I wanted to create a beer revolution in the United States in the same way Samuel Adams created a political revolution."

Sometimes the revolutionary terms are reversed so that Goliath feels a part of the movement. A 2012 *STL Today* (website of the *St. Louis Post-Dispatch*) story quotes Lee Dolan, vice president for sales and marketing at MillerCoors's craft subsidiary Tenth and Blake, as saying, "There's a revolution going on in beer and we're glad to be a part of it" (Logan). "The narrative that craft brewers were held down by larger brewers is an old and well-worn story," writes Harry Schuhmacher. "But, as with most narratives, it's more complicated than a simple David and Goliath story" ("Change We Can Believe In" 71). Craft beer is an "us against them" story, a story about a fight, a story about a continuing battle, a story of the power of artisanal production in a dominating mass-produced world, a story of overcoming all obstacles. It is a story about a struggle that, we might add, ends in a Stone pint glass's printed declaration: "Fizzy yellow beer is for wussies." The strong have survived. The fizzy are weak.

Craft is the story of Jack McAuliffe's 1976 founding of New Albion in Sonoma, California, as the nation's first modern craft brewery—an act that causes CraftBeer.com to proclaim McAuliffe as "the man who started a revolution" (Hall). Fred Eckhardt describes McAuliffe's role as an early David accordingly:

> He brewed in 50-gallon batches and sold his first brew in 1977. His capacity was six U.S.-barrels per month (186 gallons). His small "micro" brewery achieved modest success and the beer was very good, but production proved inadequate and, in 1983, the tiny brewery finally closed. McAuliffe's real contribution was to make others believe that small breweries could be a success (even if his wasn't). His effort encouraged many others, especially among the nation's burgeoning homebrewer population. ("Craft Beer: State of the Union 2010")

In the *New York Times* Eric Asimov describes those early days of craft beer similarly:

> Nowadays, American brewers are among the most creative in the world, in the vanguard of pushing and transforming established styles of beer. But those pioneering craft brewers did not need to reach so far. At a time of only anemic mass-market lagers, the idea of making full-flavored, real beers in dormant traditional styles was indeed revolutionary.

"The year 1980," Eckhardt writes elsewhere, "was pretty much the real beginning of what has become the craft beer revolution here in this country" ("Craft Beer Revolution, 30 Years On").

These stories function as interrupted beginnings, narratives posing an introductory moment (revolution) as contagion. These stories are imitated and repeated across various craft beer networks as common interests (the battle against the conglomerate) and generate common responses. Those who repeat these stories represent the storytellers and an identity built out of anecdotes and interruptions, moments that stretch from first times to grand revolutionary gestures. To understand our current place in a world of consumption, these stories state, you have to understand the battles we've won, the ways we've surmounted obstacles and how we have overcome the odds. "Revolutionary writings," Barthes writes, "have always scantily and poorly represented the daily finality of the revolution, the way it suggests *we shall live tomorrow*" (*Roland Barthes* 77). These writings attempt to get at the grand gestures of a projected future—the ways we will live tomorrow in the world of craft beer's eventual dominance over the bad conglomerate. "The word Revolution," William Morris wrote when he was fashioning his concept of craft, "has a terrible sound in most people's ears" ("How We Live" 3). If it does have such a terrible sound in the rhetoric of craft beer, it is because the repetition of the term minimizes its overall effect. Following Barthes, the gesture can be limiting for imagining a perfected future—as all revolutions eventually describe for themselves—a moment when the good overcome the bad.

For me, a craft beer drinker without such aspirations, these stories remain as interruptions. I am sympathetic to the narrative (and a believer in the narrative), but I recognize it is a repeated (contagion) story. Revolution is not craft beer's identity (as the narratives project) but only a part of that identity. No identity is so pure as to be *one thing*, revolution or otherwise, without interruption. Identities are networks of interruptions. Identities, like a craft beer anecdote, belong within a larger mesh of moments, ideas, people, places, sayings, and so on. Identities do not strive for the moment we shall live tomorrow, only for how they may continue to mesh items together.

Stories, Kathleen Stewart notes, "mark the space of a searching or scanning" (30). If I accept the narrative of revolution as is, I might as well accept the narrative of a first time as is or the narrative of grand gesture as is. Contagions—imitation gestures—interrupt; they don't stand for the whole. In my own interruption, I scan or search for another story that reflects the transmedia and contagion effects that digital media have on such activity. I am also searching for an identity that networks an industry's identity with my own so that I may share this connection as a social experience. I call this identity a *craft identity* for its basis in the logic of craft beer (consumption shaping a sense of who I am) as well as in social media (the failed RateBeer experience that marks my initiation into shared participation). The basis of a transmedia identity is that the various items that shape being (who I am) come from disparate sites and generate conflicting, almost mythic, secretive meanings. They don't begin, and they don't end. But they are anecdotal.

Craft Identity

I put on hold this discussion of revolution and confidence with another, final anecdote in order to interrupt all that I have shared thus far so that I can explore the question of a craft identity in this chapter (and describe craft networked identity in the next two chapters). The craft identity began in the introduction with my effort to fashion a parental beer tale; it has moved throughout all of the anecdotes in chapter 1 and in this chapter's interrupted tales of revolution; and it will continue throughout the book's content in which this identity is explored through various social media rhetorical strategies. The craft identity I've shared so far has focused largely on "first times" or "us versus them" binaries. This identity, as craft frames it, serves, following Burke, to treat the anecdote as *"part of the whole* rather than a *reduction of the mental to the physical"* (*Grammar of Motives* 326). The first time is a part of the larger experience of everyday consumption (initial reaction to a beer becomes one moment in a larger series of important moments). The battle of us versus them marks the continuing struggle for market share and awareness (we began as Davids to Goliath; now we are growing stronger). As Burke also argues, "An anecdote about *what one may become* is hardly the most direct way of discussing *what one is"* (*Grammar of Motives* 331). The introductory anecdotes I pose so far don't reflect a sense of identity, but rather they suggest what something may be (foreshadow of future tastes, victor in the battle for recognition), or what one wants to be. That suggestion, though, may be problematic if we assume it is the basis of narrative structure (how a story has been or could be told).

Burke observes likewise in his initial reading of Richard Wright's *Native Son*. Burke, however, changes this initial reading after learning more about the history of the novel's authoring, realizing that the narrative's beginning was added last and discovering, as well, that the ideological affirmation was not initially part of the story. While the narrative appears to have a specific structure, Burke notes, the anecdote does not serve within that structure as we assume it should. Burke's example is hardly an anomaly. It exists in centuries-old beer stories as well. Samuel Pepys writes in his April 18, 1662, diary entry, "This morning sending the boy down into the cellar for some beer I followed him with a cane and did there beat him for his staying of awards and other faults" (221). We might assume that this minor incident, retold as anecdote, is part of a larger structure of seventeenth-century family abuse, which we can linearly trace. Or we may read the diary entry as an anecdotal interruption whose ordering is not clear among the diary's fragmented entries since it appears and vanishes without further reference to beer or abuse.

I turn to another interrupted anecdote in continuing to craft an identity, an identity that networks across all of my interruptions and generates its own transmedia story. For some time now my family has circulated the story that my grandfather's "uncle" was Sam Lazar, a notorious Philadelphia-based Prohibition bootlegger. In this narrative Lazar becomes the star of a circulated fantasy that is not unfamiliar (or foreign to its own contagion narrative) to many contemporary stories whose focus romanticizes a portion of America's once infamous, but now affectionate, history of selling illegal alcohol or participating in organized crime. By telling this anecdote, my family aligns itself with the legends of other Jewish bootleggers such as Meyer Lansky, whose notable representation circulates within much of media fiction as a series of imitations and as circulated Miami Beach jokes. There is the one my father likes to tell about Lansky going unrecognized while standing in line at a local delicatessen. (In the joke, Lansky politely lets a woman order before him; the woman fails to recognize the mobster as she receives her pastrami.) This anecdote contributes to a familial contagion where organized crime offers familial structure. When I was a child, I often heard my father introduce himself to strangers as "a tail gunner in the Mafia" or as being on the run because of mob ties. In reality, he sold insurance. "Thus the anecdote is in a sense a *summation*," Burke writes, "containing implicitly what the system that is developed from it contains explicitly" (*Grammar of Motives* 60). A portion of our family identity—no matter how far removed it is from organized crime in its present reality of suburban, middle-class, Jewish status—is summed up as gangster, criminal, and oriented around alcohol, or beer to be precise. Implicit in this Sam Lazar anecdote is a beer identity. Beer identity represents toughness. Rich Cohen describes his fascination with "tough Jews" similarly, in which storytelling centralizes "tough guy" identification: "The Jewish gangster stories told each morning by my father and his friends are really the remnants of old neighborhood stories, legends that have been passed from clubrooms and street corners to boardrooms and delis and on to suburban towns" (20).

Stories offer myths. In my family, Sam Lazar is a mythology told in our very specific Miami suburban life in Kendall (shared romantically with Meyer Lansky, who lived in nearby Miami Beach). Barthes's concern with mythologies was that they naturalize representations that are, in fact, coded. Barthes rejected the process of decoding popular representations in order to become aware of such coded practices (and, in turn, to resist these practices). Barthes did not search for a way to overcome myth. His fragmented exploration of toys, Garbo's face, wrestling, and other popular representations is not meant as a critical gesture of interpretation or explanation where a consumer suddenly becomes aware of the coded representations she consumes (and, in turn, stops consuming). For instance, when MillerCoors advertises its Coors Light brand as "Ice Cold When the Label Turns Blue," the brewer depends on an audience believing the mythology that cold beer is the ideal type of beer. Through circulated ads and restaurant practice, this belief becomes naturalized as *the* representation of beer (and thus it becomes commonplace for sports bars and pizza joints to serve beer in frosty mugs). To decode the myth would be to declare that cold beer, in fact, hides bad taste or poor quality. Drinkers would then "awake" and stop ordering beer in frosty mugs. They don't, of course, stop doing so.

Barthes writes, "A more attentive reading of the myth will in no way increase its power of its ineffectiveness: a myth is at the same time imperfectible and unquestionable; time or knowledge will not make it better or worse" (*Mythologies* 130). Instead of criticism ("time or knowledge"), Barthes argued for mythologizing anew; that is, respond to myth by making another one: "The best weapon against myth is perhaps to mythify it in its turn, and to produce an artificial myth; and this reconstituted myth will in fact be a mythology" (*Mythologies* 135). Barthes's notion of mythologizing the myth creates an alternative practice for framing dominant narratives or, more specifically, narrative beginnings. Instead of critiquing a previous representation so that an alternative may be read as a new start (the typical way to begin with representations), Barthes opts instead for a productive, yet fragmented, gesture that reworks what already exists. Personal anecdotes and the stories they tell are fragmented attempts at mythologizing the myths that produce dominant or grand meanings. Prohibition, for example, as the tale of a repressed American society, might serve as one alcohol-driven grand narrative whose decoding will reveal larger cultural anxieties or taboos still felt in contemporary America. Such is the typical way to write about Prohibition, an approach I am not interested in advancing. By saying that Sam Lazar was my grandfather's uncle, I will interrupt that anticipated critical narrative with an anecdote and, eventually, a "re-mythology." In lieu of repeating traditional critiques, I am looking to rework the myth.

The Sam Lazar anecdote begins with the grand gesture of Ancestry.com, a massive database of genealogy, as my father writes in an e-mail to me about his usage of the website and discovery of this distant relative:

> I found two references to his [Lazar] being a friend of a major Philadelphia mobster, involved in three alcohol companies plus gambling and other things. He was mentioned in Wikipedia as being present at a major mob meeting in Atlantic city in 1929. All the big names you have heard of were there, Italians and Jews. He was mentioned as a Jewish Mob Boss in Philadelphia.

The biography *Capone: The Life and World of Al Capone* lists Lazar among other mobsters who attended an Atlantic City meeting at the President Hotel in 1929. Its listing gives some basis to the anecdote's mythology by providing a representation to accompany the anecdote:

> Cutting across all the old ethnic and national divisions, there gathered around the table not only Italians and Sicilians, but also Jews, Irish, and Slavs, more than thirty gangsters in all. From Chicago came Frank McErlane, and Joe Saltis; the Caponeites, Jake Guzik, Frank Nitti and Frank Rio; from Philadelphia, Max "Boo Boo" Hoff, Sam Lazar and Charles Schwartz. (Kobler 258)

A reference in Steven Riess's *Sports and the American Jew* notes, "Several future bootleggers started off in gambling, such as Max 'Boo Hoo' Hoff and Sam Lazar, who originally ran a string of South Philadelphia gambling houses" (50). Internal Revenue Service records, as well, identify a Sam Lazar of Philadelphia, whose operations were located on Delaware Avenue and Green Street, as receiving alcohol shipments. A 1928 *New York Times* article reports that "fugitive warrants for Charles Schwartz and Samuel Lazar, alleged associates of Max (Boo Boo) Hoff, reputed Philadelphia 'bootleg king' were issued," although the two's whereabouts were unknown ("Philadelphia Trio Held in Liquor Plot").

Lazar supposedly raised my grandfather, whose parents died in the influenza epidemic of the early 1920s. Lazar's "uncle" status is, as well, mythological since we do not know if he was a blood relative or merely an "uncle," as in a family friend who took on parental responsibilities. Although Lazar was supposedly wealthy, my grandfather was not; what little success he earned was lost on a failed New Jersey chicken farm in the 1950s. Whatever happened to all of the bootlegging profits is lost to us.

Within this mythology, I don't need to prove that Lazar is a relative or even a historical figure. These suggested moments, when networked with my family's anecdote, offer the myth of the myth, as Barthes describes it, or the secrecy of the network, as Maffesoli claims. At the center of this myth, Philadelphia and beer, I rediscover my initial misrating, which occurred elsewhere in Pennsylvania, in State College (birthplace of my daughter). Weyerbacher, the object of my misplaced scorn, is an hour-and-a-half drive from Philadelphia. Philadelphia, as beer historians often retell, is the center of an American beer heritage, one that George Ehret, writing in 1891, noted. Even as colonial brewing waned leading up to the American Revolution, Philadelphia still brewed beer:

> Here and there, widely scattered over an immense extent of territory, a few brew-houses whose product had acquired an uncommon reputation—like the porters and ales of Philadelphia—remained in operation; but their output was infinitesimal as compared with the quantities of other inebriating liquors produced and consumed in the country. (28)

Such a scenario sounds like the Prohibition Lazar operated within. If I were to offer a marker of whatever this type of identity I want to mythologize as craft might be, so that its representation is identifiable, locatable, and a part of Philadelphia cultural history, it could be a location on a Pennsylvania map, a space surrounded by an imaginary and mythical triangle that connects bootlegging to me and rating beer by way of State College to Eaton (Weyerbacher) to Philadelphia, where my grandparents were raised.

The mythic triangle (or imagined social network) I discover allows a craft identity to emerge, one not evident in the initial anecdotes (small stories) I have told. This myth may also accompany a star, the ultimate marker of my identity (and Sam Lazar's). For, if I complete the triangle, I am left with half of a Jewish star, the Star of David or Magen David. The star, I also realize, marks another beginning, the beginning of brewing methods and identity. The Zoigl-Star is a six-pointed star (made up of a hexagram of two overlapping triangles) resembling and confusing an identification with the Jewish Star of David. In the Middle Ages, brewers used the star as representative of the mythical elements of water, earth, and fire and the material ingredients of water, malt, and hops—all which are essential to brewing. The Zoigl-Star, also known as the Brewer's Star, highlights a mythology of brewing, showcasing components of an object (beer) as beyond the material by representing the conceptual (elements of brewing). In the Middle Ages, brewers hung the star from their windows or doorways when beer was ready for consumption. The cosmic mythology represented in the star (as in my Pennsylvania map) is three, not the more dominant philosophical four, as Graham Harman relates. Harman finds four to be a principal number in philosophy:

> Along with the four elements of Empedocles, Plato's divided line, and Aristotle's four causes, we find Scotus Eriugena's quadruple scheme of creation, Bacon's four idols, Kant's four groups of categories, Heidegger's *Geviert*, Greimas' semiotic square, and McLuhan's tetradic laws of media. (79)

The mythological three, on the other hand, of water, malt, and hops is more indicative of a popular culture three that circulates as its own mythology of organization based on this number: Three Stooges, Three Little Pigs, Three Musketeers, *Three's Company*, Triple Hopped, and so on. In the star I find beer's mythology (tapping into the contagion of three) until yeast is added, and then four recovers. Beer is the network of the popular and the philosophical myth.

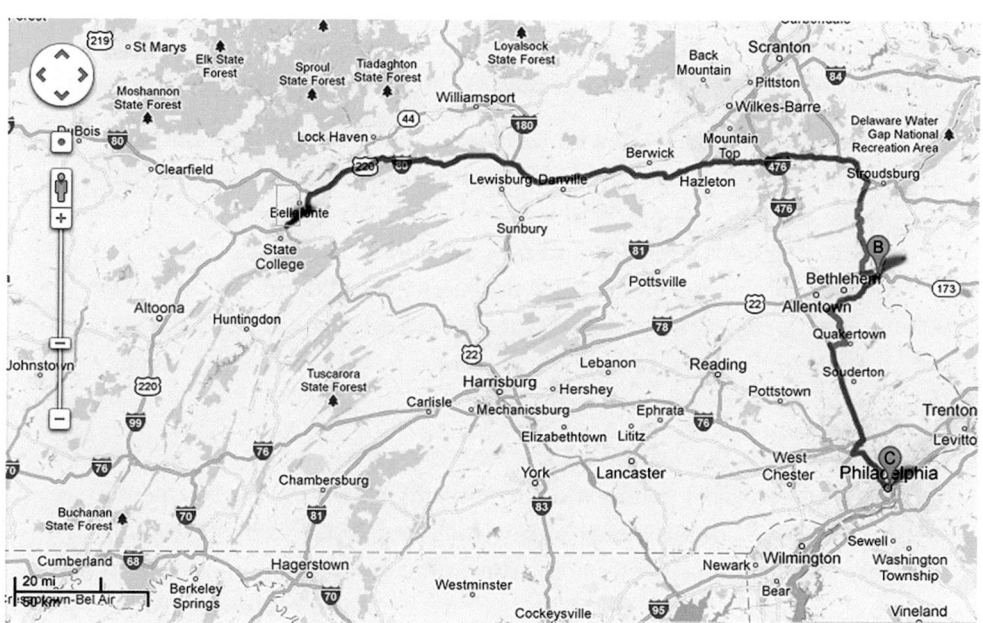

Potential mythic triangle of southeastern Pennsylvania showing a craft identity. Google Maps

The star is named for a German/Eastern Bavaria beer, Zoigl, a rarely produced amber or dark brown commercial beer (Snyder 56). Even in 2012, long after this tradition has largely faded from memory and the Zoigl-Star's usage has greatly diminished, beer writer Ronald Pattinson found the star while travelling in Neuhaus, Germany: "On the walk to my hotel I see that special sign. A white and a blue triangle combined into a beautiful, six-pointed star. Looks like somewhere is selling the beer today." According to Edo van Bree, fifteenth-century Neuhaus hosted a number of communal breweries called *Kommunbrauhaus*, and the Zoigl-Star would have been a common sight at the communal breweries:

> Why a Kommunbrauhaus? The Oberpfalz towns gave every civilian born in the town the right to brew beer and pour it to guests. Every civilian, except for the clergymen, the judges, the lawyers and the civil servants. Even now the cities own and maintain the Kommunbrauhäuser. Whoever wants to use it pays a small fee "Kesselgeld" and has to leave the place clean and tidy for the next brewer.

Matthias Trum's thesis for Technical University Munich, "Historical Depictions, Guild Signs, and Symbols of the Brewing and Malting Handcraft," devotes considerable space to the overlap of the communal Jewish and brewing meanings of the Zoigl-Star. After extensive analysis, he concludes that protection and communal origins in Bavaria join the two together:

> It appears possible that on the basis of above stated facts the hexagram was in those days in Franconia and northern Bavaria widely used symbol for protection and in this form used by everyone including both jews [sic] and brewers. The exiled jews of Nürnberg brought the star with them to Prague, where it became symbol of the jewish community and was then spread all over the world through letterpress. The brewing star remained however in south Germany and developed into a tapping sign.

I begin with the Zoigl-Star because of its resemblance to the Star of David and because I can locate it mythically on my Pennsylvania map as the whole that contains part of my imagined star. From communal anecdote to communal brewery to communal meaning to even communal mob gathering in Atlantic City, the star marks a site of introduction for me that I feel has interrupted all that I have written here regarding anecdotes, craft, media, and identity. These interruptions provide patterns, overlaps that write my interest in craft and social media. The logic of social media,

Zoigl-Star. Photo by Stan Hieronymus; reprinted with permission

Albert-László Barabási writes, marks the space of pattern formation and overlap. Barabási's own pattern quest finds himself in a mix of Hungarian history and networks, the Crusades and homeland security. This mix marks his identity. What Barabási calls "bursts," the pattern markers of predictability encountered across space or time, I call craft identity, the patterns that constitute any item or person's overall identity. Patterns—whatever they may indicate—lead to discovery. Barabási notes,

> By following the trail of these discoveries we will come to see the rhythms of life as evidence of a deeper order in human behavior that can be explored, predicted, and no doubt exploited. The insights to be gleaned require us to stop viewing our actions as discrete, random, isolated events. Instead they seem to be part of a magic web of dependencies, a story within a web of stories, displaying order where we suspected none and randomness where we least expect it. (*Bursts* 11)

The star is a social contagion. As a detail, it is also the basis of a small story. With these two features, it shapes a craft identity for me in bursts and patterns. Whatever may feel random, as I move through anecdotes, functions as a web of connected meaning. From the anecdote of a first time to the story of Sam Lazar, patterns (or bursts) construct a larger identity. My web of stories has found me moving from my first time drinking a craft beer to the Zoigl-Star, each story overlapping with the other. Barabási calls these moments—the star's reappearance or my first time drinking a Heineken—nodes. The node, as network theory shows, is the basic element connecting items within a network. Nodes connect and reconnect moments, many of which may feel disparate or unrelated. This is a phenomenon we sometimes attribute to serendipity or accident rather than to the power of the network as a vehicle for showcasing Latour's claim that "everything is data" (*Reassembling* 133). Data evoke ideas. Data connect. Data form patterns. "Striking similarities between events of rather different natures are often simply explained," Barabási notes. "These highly connected nodes were not there by accident, I soon learned, an insight that would help us discover the laws that govern the evolution of many real networks" (*Bursts* 119). A real network exists on a rating beer forum, in the stories craft beer tells about itself, and in family anecdotes about organized crime. A real network exists with all these moments (and others) functioning as nodes in the overall network.

One node-based law governing my anecdotal craft network is identity overlap. In my moment of overlap, I recognize myself, a Jew, within a triangle of beer patterns and connections. Up until this point, my identity has been limited to a similar first-time experience and the confident gesture. But as my mythic triangle demonstrates, ethnicity is present as well. The overlap of Jewish identity and beer is summed up by Jeremy Cowan, owner of Shmaltz Brewing, who, in in his memoir *Craft Beer Bar Mitzvah*, writes that his idea for the Jewish-themed HeBrew beer was based on overlap and hybridity:

> My original intention of the product was to reach those in the Jewish world called the "non-affiliated"—those who are Jewish by birth, who will define themselves as Jewish, but won't do much about it. They don't have the education, or the tools, or typically much desire to participate in the community. Quite often they have never had a particularly positive Jewish experience to justify any concern or curiosity for a more meaningful Jewish life. For them, identity has felt more a burden than a birthright. (11)

Beer and Jewishness overlap in order to produce identity so that one does not feel burdened by what one might be. In that sense, the anecdote's own sense of burden—of the promise of a larger, more meaningful story—is accommodated. Cowan accommodates the craft beer anecdote with the grand promise of identity formation: secular Jews finding identity in their Jewish-framed beer consumption. I discover that accommodation in overlap or in patterns that are finding their way here to ethnicity, not in traditional methods of storytelling that rely on beginnings and endings, but rather on small, connected stories. After all, my first-time beer experience had nothing to do with being Jewish.

Cowan and I also overlap via anecdotes. One such anecdote mentioned in Cowan's book is a marketing tour for retailers and restaurants that he took in Missouri to promote the distribution of his beer by Missouri Beverage. The punch line of Cowan's anecdote is that he eventually drives from Columbia, Missouri, to East St. Louis to bet on horse races and buy drugs: "What better way to enjoy race night, naturally, than to buy some crack cocaine in the ghetto of East St. Louis?" (207). My punch line is attending the Missouri Beverage event in Columbia (where we once lived) at the invitation of our friend who owned Sycamore restaurant. At the event, representatives poured samples of beer from the Missouri Beverage portfolio. When I stood in front of the Shmaltz table, Jeremy Cowan, to my complete surprise (he was the only owner present among all of the beer representatives), poured me a sample. We talked about bar mitzvahs briefly before I moved on to the next representative. Eventually, my own bar mitzvah picture would appear on the HeBrew Thirteenth Jewbelation anniversary bottle.

Me (third row down, second from left) on the HeBrew Thirteenth Jewbelation anniversary bottle

On the anniversary bottle, nestled among pictures of smiling kids in their tallit and kippot reading the Haftorah is a picture of me. A major tradition in American Jewish culture is to take a picture of the bar/bat mitzvah kid before the event, blow the photograph up to a large size, and have guests at the reception sign it. Prior to my "star-like" day of attention at the Kendall branch of Temple Israel, my dad took me into our backyard for my picture. I put on my flea market Rolling Stones shirt (with rock-and-roll pins attached) and picked up a ukulele as a substitute for the guitar I did not yet own. My dad stuck my copy of the record *Tattoo You* in a branch in the tree behind me. This moment returns to me when I read about the Missouri stopover in Cowan's memoir. This moment interrupts the narrative for me in ways that it won't for other readers. No one else can have this overlap; no one else can experience this moment of bar mitzvah/beer identification. Cowan's memoir revolves around anecdotes and how such overlapping anecdotes shape his sense of both beer and Jewish identity. I felt that overlap when I stood in front of Jeremy Cowan in Columbia, Missouri, discussing bar mitzvahs.

I feel that overlap in another anecdote that involves how Cowan came up with the byline "the chosen beer":

> Standing with the bathroom door slightly ajar, a couple feet from our bed, I was taking a leak, thinking of how Budweiser claims to be the "King of Beers," Miller is the "Champagne of Beers," and Coors calls itself the "Banquet Beer," however outdated that may sound. Shlong in hand, it came to me: We'll call our baby The Chosen Beer. It seemed so obvious. (14)

My obvious overlap with Cowan's bathroom story might be consuming beer and feeling the constant urge to urinate—a popular and often imitated gesture, prompted by the body, that most beer drinkers experience. As Barthes writes, the desire to find meaning in such an overlap might equate with the need to explain a pleasure such as urinating. Barthes's own fascination was with urinating in his garden and not wanting to explain its meaning. Some moments, like urination, don't require explanation; they are simply moments (however often repeated) that mean without interpretation (i.e., they don't stand for a greater idea or concept). Barthes wants to resist the desire to know "what that signifies" in favor of storytelling that "would report a thousand 'incidents' but would refuse ever to draw a line of meaning from them" (*Roland Barthes* 151). Even without the "meaning" of peeing and discovering a beer's tagline, Cowan's urination moment marks the iconic moment, the moment that stands out, whose role is mythical—meaning that the moment extends beyond the actual moment itself so that, like an anecdote, it stands for something greater than its initial representation. Urination granted Cowan the "aha" moment of understanding. Experiencing an aha moment is to experience the iconic moment of invention when the metaphoric lightbulb hovers over one's head. "One aspect of the story is the 'eureka anecdote,' marking the moment or flash of insight," writers Ulmer (*Heuretics* 7). Insight can come from tracing out overlaps in patterns instead of in the actual urination act. Insight, like the one I am having, comes from patterns that shape identity.

The technology of iconicity—exemplified not only in Cowan's anecdote but in the figure of a star I notice in Zoigl and the Magen David—unites me with a tradition (Eastern European brewing) that has no relationship to the culture I belong within (twenty-first-century new media). When I drink beer, I find no Zoigl-Star hanging over nearby breweries; instead I receive tweets and Facebook updates from local establishments that let me know what is now on tap. But the Star of David, the iconic marker of identity, I find everywhere in my life. It adorns PJ Library books my children receive in the mail. It is on a mezuzah on the doorjamb. It hangs from a necklace on my daughter's neck. The Star of David also indicates beer being ready for consumption. The star marks my identity in new and known ways. I have always known I am Jewish; I didn't know that the Star of David connects my ethnicity to beer (even if in a noncausal way). In that awareness of the star's iconic status, I experience a sense of eureka. "Aha," I say. I am craft beer.

The simplest (and maybe least satisfying way) to express this identity might be to proclaim that I am, then, a Jewish craft beer consumer (as an echo of the "I Am a Craft Beer Drinker" video meme). Writing in 1886, John Bickerdyke claims a Jewish history overlapping with beer, associating beer with biblical Judaism:

> In support of the theory that beer was known amongst the Jews, may be mentioned that the Rabbinical tradition that the Jews were free from leprosy during the captivity in Babylon by reason of their drinking "*siceram veprium*, id *est*, ex *lupulis confectam*," or *sicera* made with hops, which one would think could be no other than bitter beer. (26)

Stan Hieronymus finds the claim "unfounded" (*For the Love of Hops* 45). Still, even without strong historical connections to the history of beer and left with only this myth, I still recognize that Jews have been brewers; nineteenth-century Jewish American immigrants from Germany took up brewing in various midwestern and East Coast communities. Samuel

Liebermann, who founded what would become Rheingold Beer, was one such immigrant. More recently, in addition to Jeremy Cowan of Shmaltz, Ken Grossman of Sierra Nevada, Magic Hat founder Alan Newman, and Peter Zien of Alesmith represent Jewish brewers within the craft beer community. Representation, in anecdote or ethnicity, serves as a marker for larger communal connectivity and the logic of sharing. I feel connected to the beer community in ways mere drinking cannot support. "What's more offensive?" Cowan asks, that

> "I'm Jewish and really proud of it, and I'd like you to share that with me," or Coors Light having billboards in every single city, calling themselves the "official beer" and "proud supporters" of both sides of every blood-feud football rivalry? (191)

Craft offers a type of pride, but one that is shared. Cowan supports that "offensive" declaration of ethnic identity and beer consumption with mythological copy on the labels of his beer bottles.

These labels provide an iconic marker of beer identity, and they offer insight into the patterns of such identity. As the label of Jewbelation 8 (an anniversary beer brewed with 8 malts, 8 hops, and at 8 percent alcohol) proclaims, in part:

> 8 is a miraculous number in Jewish life. Chanukah, Passover, and Sukkot span 8 days. 8 humans survived the deluge on Noah's ark. Maimonides delineated 8 levels of *tzadakah* (charity). A *bris* (circumcision) comes on the day 8. King Solomon completed the First Temple in the 8th month of the 8th year . . . *Seinfeld* ran 8 years. Dylan has 8 Grammys. (217)

Or as the copy on the bottle of HeBrew 13, the bar mitzvah beer, declares:

> The Jewish calendar follows 13 lunar cycles. Apollo 13 failed to reach the moon after an explosion on April 13 (1970). July 4th falls 13 days after summer solstice. 13 stripes on our flag represent the 13 Colonies. The 13th Amendment abolished slavery.

Identity is also mythology. "I love numerology," Cowan writes, "which has long been a vibrant element of Jewish culture and tradition" (216). The numbers 8 or 13, in the case of Jewbelation, serve as a moment of surprise (such as the shock that Maimonides connects to *Seinfeld* or that Apollo 13 connects to the abolishment of slavery). Sam Lazar, who mythologically connects my identity to beer, beer ratings, and stories of beer revolution, is no accidental overlap but a type of triangle connecting various points along these networked anecdotes so that the result—surprise—is mirrored in the surprise I felt upon revisiting my initial review of Weyerbacher's Merry Monks. Identity, as Gregory Ulmer writes in *Avatar Emergency*, indicates a sense of shock or surprise. Ulmer ties this surprise to mythology and, in particular, to a formula resembling that of the anecdote: "The formula is simple to state: compose a set-up through exposition that creates in the audience a certain expectation, based on shared cultural background (habitus). This habitus constitutes your wisdom" (60).

Such as Ulmer describes is where I began: with the anecdote that sets up expectation (shared experience of drinking for the first time) with cultural background (the move from macro to micro beer experiences) so that wisdom (the story of craft beer) occurs. I have interrupted myself with the same interruption. I still have not told my story, and yet, via interruptions, I have begun it. I am caught in a craft beginning where mythology networks a variety of actors. This beginning will play out in later chapters where my identity shapes, is shaped by, and networks obsession. For now, I can say that my craft beginning is social for how it networks so many different forces. Part of the rhetoric of the social is sharing. I shared my personal photograph with Shmaltz Brewing for some reason I cannot fully explain. My father shared his Sam Lazar research with me. I share my ideas about drinking experiences via social media for some reason I cannot fully explain. "People make a series of socially embedded decisions when they choose to spread any media text," Jenkins, Ford, and Green write. "Is the content worth engaging with? Is it worth sharing with others?" (13). My experiences are shared with others and with each other for reasons I cannot fully explain (the myth or secret); that is, I cannot even answer the questions posed by Jenkins and coauthors in the affirmative when I share. I simply share as part of the larger mythology of meanings being shared across platforms, genres, and experiences. "Our technology," Marshall McLuhan and Quentin Fiore write about digital media and identity, "forces us to live mythically." They add, "Myth means putting on the audience, putting on one's environment" (*Medium* 114). I don't know if sharing my bar mitzvah photo with Shmaltz was putting on. That is, I don't know if my interruptions are a put-on regarding sharing (a joke or a punch line) or if they are putting me on the right track toward a craft identity (eureka). I know, though, that they guide me. I follow these interruptions as if they were virtual threads, status updates, and posts shared online. I follow their aggregation in my writing.

My photo of Cantillon Vigneronne

This beginning (or aggregation) is a series of interruptions or surprises. And I have another anecdote to frame this feeling of surprise. More recently, I encountered the Zoigl-Star as a surprise one evening while pouring a Cantillon Vigneronne. Cantillon holds a star-like position among beer enthusiasts for its limited production and limited distribution of sour and lambic beers. RateBeer trade forums are full of "in search of" (ISO) requests to trade for various Cantillon bottles. When I poured this bottle of Vigneronne, I admired the beer in the glass and then the dry, sparkling taste in my mouth. I also noticed the large Star of David on the bottle's label. The point of recognition in this moment (that's me) was countered by the quest for discovery. (Why is there a Star of David on a bottle of Cantillon when Jean Von Roy, brewer and owner, is not Jewish?) I did not yet know about the Zoigl-Star when I drank this beer and saw the star on the label. Surprise prompted me to discover, to share the anecdote and identify it in the larger network of beer experiences. My Cantillon surprise would not surprise nineteenth-century beer drinkers, some of whom would have found the star printed on bottles by brewers such as Hell Gate Brewery, whose George Ehret's Extra features a star on the label; Dubuque Star, which featured the star on its labels; and the William Peter

Brewing Company, which printed Zoigl-Stars on their bottles. And my Cantillon surprise should not shock contemporary craft drinkers who may still find the star on bottles or even on Three Floyds Dark Lord Day tickets (as the picture I include in my later discussion of Dark Lord Day shows). The Zoigl, too, is a contagion. And as my initial discussion of anecdotes shows about narrative and the ordering of narrative, I present the anecdote here in the wrong place; it probably should precede my previous explanation of the Zoigl-Star so that it leads to a larger story of identity and brewing. Infinite regress occurs.

    I might look at this Vigneronne moment as a sign, a marker of surprise that indicates identity as urinating provided identity insight for Cowan. It took the investigation I note here to realize the meaning of the overlap (historical, coincidental), and still, the meaning (no real relationship to Judaism) does not deny me the anecdote to share for the mere sharing of a sign. It's a sign! I can still declare and therefore feel a sense of discovery. This anecdote, though, of identifying with a beer label—and even with a Cantillon beer label—is, as well, not a novel recognition of "a sign," but instead is another contagion, a repeated narrative gesture that helps shape communal craft beginnings. Jeff Sparrow, who begins *Wild Brews* with an anecdote, notes his first time drinking Cantillon while in Europe:

> The bartender told me that if I wanted to try a very good beer, to drink this bottle, which he placed on the bar in front of me. The label featured a compelling drawing of a naked lady sitting on a fully clothed gentleman's lap. I was about to sample my first Cantillon Rosé de Gambrinus, and the complexity was beyond anything I had ever tasted. (2)

Here, too, the narrative begins with a Cantillon label whose sign (star or naked lady) marks the identity moment, the first time, the surprise experience, the moment of insight. Even as I yield to a sign that I believe to be unique (the star), I merely repeat others' interest in such moments (naked lady on a gentleman's lap).

    Signs are abundant in craft beer, from the iconic markers on labels to Cowan-styled aha moments. Sitting in Local Option on a cold Chicago October afternoon in 2013, I saw my reflection in the silver draught dispenser facing me; I noticed my wild, curly hair and thought: at forty-four, I'm looking a bit like Michael Jackson. It's a sign. Michael Jackson, writing in the brewing magazine *Zymurgy*, remembers a different type of sign:

> I have only once yielded to one of those signs that says: "Coldest beer in town." I had spent the day in a car that had no air-conditioning, crossing from Tennessee into Kentucky. The sign also said: "Last beer before dry county." (Papazian, *Zymurgy: Best Articles*, n. pag.)

As I write this book in Kentucky, where I live, I notice the overlaps of signs and experience as being transmedia based in small stories. Around me, dry counties crowd our blossoming craft beer scene in Lexington and Louisville. The mythical beer writer Jackson crossed, at least once, into Kentucky and into these counties near where I live. And in addition to this minor spatial overlap, the mythical beer writer Jackson shared my craft identity to some extent regarding ethnicity. As he writes, "My father was, again more by birth and culture than observance, Jewish" ("Blue Collar Brews"). Of course, I share this ethnic identity with many people globally, but the mythical, ethnic, and emotional connection to one of beer writing's most canonical figures as I attempt my own version of beer writing does offer a sense of surprise and pleasure. I identify with this connection no matter how superficial it may be. My experience is not cold (as in a cold beer or my lack of desire to decode the Miller Lite ad or as in the off-putting retort "so what that we are both Jewish") but is found in the mythic nature of craft identity. That myth involves signs. That myth also involves familial heritages: fathers, such as mine, who may have been Jewish by birth more than by culture (i.e., the opposite of Jackson's father). That myth is found in moments more extensive than the Jewish Mafia connections I trace here briefly. Despite these identifications—identifications in which I feel a pull to a canonical, half-Jewish beer writer—when I watch *The Beer Hunter* documentary about Jackson, I don't identify with his preference for "literary pubs." I, the former English professor, don't care about literary pubs (bars literary figures supposedly frequented). The literary pub sign of cultural lineage (to drink where a famous writer drank) affects me less than the accidental overlap in Jewish fathers I share with Jackson, an overlap that creates for me a far greater identification than drinking in the same pub that James Joyce once visited could ever do for me. These are all signs of identity, whether or not the signs are agreeable. Identity is not a homogenous experience; it is a contradictory one, and its signs offer anecdotal contradictions as well.

Urination is one additional such sign. Jackson, too, regards urination as essential to the father-son parental beer tale. As he remembers his father saying to him when he was a teenager interested in drinking, "You pay good money for beer, then piss it all away. Why does an intelligent Jewish boy behave like this?" ("Blue Collar Brews"). I interrupt Jackson with another anecdote. For our honeymoon (the mythic celebration of marriage), my wife and I vacationed in Belgium, where Cantillon is brewed. We planned, I suppose, on pissing away some of our wedding money drinking beer. Prior to our departure, my wife learned she was pregnant with our first child and would not be able to drink as much as me (or at all). One afternoon in Brussels, we went to Poechenellekelder, the well-known café across the street from the famous Manneken Pis fountain. One legend or myth surrounding the Manneken Pis involves

> Duke Godfrey III of Leuven. In 1142, the troops of this two-year-old lord were battling against the troops of the Berthouts, the lords of Grimbergen, in Ransbeke (now Neder-over-Heembeek). The troops put the infant lord in a basket and hung the basket in a tree to encourage them. From there, the boy urinated on the troops of the Berthouts, who eventually lost the battle. (*Brussels Sights*, n. pag.)

At Poechenellekelder I ordered a Cantillon Gueuze, and, to my wife's amusement (and disappointment since she could no longer drink on this trip), the bottle came in the traditional lambic straw basket. Without knowing the tradition of the basket, she expressed surprise ("What is that?"). A straw basket surprised her as silly (not matching the identity of drinking experiences in America where cold glasses dominate if they are even served along with a bottle). "Since the beers are bottle conditioned, they are nestled in baskets and handled gently and with reverence" (Jabbloner). The tilted basket allows for sediment in the bottle-conditioned beer to settle and not be poured into the glass. The basket is a serving vessel. The basket's mythology is an interesting one: when did servers decide to lay the bottle in straw? Why did this beer receive a basket for the ceremony of pouring and other beers do not? The Manneken Pis legend, not too removed from Jeremy Cowan's origin story of urination for HeBrew, is that of pissing from a basket. Orion, the offspring of three gods—Zeus, Poseidon, and Hermes—often found urinating on a bull hide, is also named Kandaon. "Orion is Kandaon," Robert Brown writes, "and Kandaon is a Semite" (280). Stan Hieronymus, citing a seventeenth-century doctor, notes that hops—a staple component of beer for preservation or aroma purposes, though mostly for preservation in a gueuze—were once believed to "provoke urine" (*For the Love of Hops* 47). There is no escaping urine in this craft identity, it seems.

We did not tour Cantillon during that trip, and the question persists: why—when in Brussels for the first and maybe only time in my life—did I not want to tour the most famous lambic brewery in the world, the one Webb, Pollard, and McGinn call the "easiest and most impressive of all Belgian breweries to visit" (34)? Such a question is not easy to answer. Anecdotes, interrupted or otherwise, do not solve the overall questions we are faced with when telling stories about beer. Why did we only discover Sam Lazar's Prohibition connection later in our lives? Why do I have the same first-time beer drinking narrative as others? Why have I not chosen the easiest of all tales to share about craft beer, that of history, tastings, guidebooks, and travels, as most of the beer books I purchase and that line my shelves do? As Meredith Canham-Nelson writes in her own introductory beer narrative, "It became clear that my beer education was not going to come at the hands of bartenders," so she traveled and wrote about those travels (6). I, too, have traveled (as I indicate in the introduction regarding my daughter's experiences with beer), but I have little to say about such ventures or how they might educate others. Does a visit at Wicked Weed in Asheville or Against the Grain in Louisville allow me insight into beer or taste or culture in ways other travels don't? Why am I, an educator, not educating? In stringing together the various anecdotes that make up this chapter and the previous one, I have not written much about my beer travels or even beer consumption, and I don't know

My bottle of Cantillon Gueuze in a traditional lambic straw basket

Poechenellekelder, where I ordered the Cantillon Gueuze

what I have taught regarding craft beer. I have instead merely interrupted myself by distributing my anecdotes over a network of moments, items, people, and places. I am calling those interruptions social for the ways they connect experiences.

Like the parental beer tale I yearn to tell, I rely upon the anecdote to frame the fragmented yet networked experiences that shape not only my craft identity but others' experiences as well. I assume these anecdotes emerge from the logic of social media, where repetition of stories and sharing of those stories occur. In the realm of contagion, I learn that any experience, such as the craft one I am drawn to, is not a singular event but rather a shared one. In this sharing, networks come together. In these networks, I discover my obsession (and, I assume, others discover their own obsessions). To get more fully at these networked experiences, in chapter 4 I begin my craft beer story again, this time with a specific tale of obsession: the release day. Release days, I discover, are networked moments; that is, they are not days at all. Like a craft identity, they are aggregations of interruptions, moments, experiences, people, and, of course, obsession. Before I do so, however, I must offer yet another interruption in chapter 3: the relationship between networks and craft beer. This relationship, an aggregation as well, is called *terroir*.

CHAPTER 3
Craft Networks

Grab a beer. It don't cost nothing. —Bluto, *Animal House*

In *Where Good Ideas Come From*, Steven Johnson notes that the historian Pliny the Elder's mythological status stems from the networking of two different concepts into a new idea, the wine press and the printing press: "[Pliny] took a machine designed to get people drunk and turned it into an engine for mass communication" (153). In this small network that Johnson highlights, communication and beer consumption juxtapose to form an insight (how to disseminate ideas to a mass public). My attempts to begin with an anecdote in the previous chapters owe something to Pliny's invention, for via print and online information I can trace a number of contagion anecdotes about drinking beer, confidence narratives, and revolution stories. When I understand these items as part of a network (i.e., how they come together), I understand craft identity better, particularly for its relationship to social media. The printing press precedes the social media application. The wine press precedes the beer assembly line. Moving through social media logics and sites, I am telling a story about social communication and beer, two items not normally discussed together. Part of that story, and not mentioned in the previous two chapters, is Russian River's Pliny the Elder.

Pliny the Elder is a double IPA brewed by Russian River, and it has been ranked the number two beer in the world by RateBeer ("RateBeer Best Top 50"). The rankings featured by RateBeer are aggregations of user input reformulated on a yearly basis from user ratings. From the 2013 RateBeer list, number three is Russian River's hoppier and rarer version of Pliny the Elder, Pliny the Younger. My RateBeer review of Pliny the Elder appeared in 2008, and it strikes me—despite its overtly positive reflection—as only a slight improvement over the initial Weyerbacher review that caused me discomfort since its composition three years prior and that I interrupted myself in order to discuss. According to my RateBeer profile, I recorded my first consumption of Russian River's Pliny the Elder on Saturday, August

16, 2008. There is nothing in my review to network it with other reviews. In my review I don't use the socially based language typically attributed to IPAs in RateBeer write-ups, an indication that I may not yet have been knowledgeable of such common parlance or that I was not yet a part of a contagion network. The discussion of Pliny the Elder on RateBeer and other social media platforms operates according to other contagion rhetorical effects, as similar language is deployed to describe the experience of this one highly desired beer.

The most imitated terms used in RateBeer reviews to describe Pliny the Elder are *grapefruit, pine, resin, hoppy,* and *floral*. If there are commonplace meanings attributed to the IPA or double IPA, these terms provide such meanings since they are stable markers used by beer drinkers to designate and understand the experience of consuming an IPA. Like all rhetorical markers, these terms anchor experience. Across social networks—blogs, video reviews, message boards, books, newspaper accounts—the experience becomes repeated as a continuing narrative of consumption. The experience is a repeated small story.

Andy Crouch describes Pliny as unleashing "a torrent of hop goodness, with blasts of evergreen and pine, grapefruit, and assorted citrus, and a tinge of resiny bitterness" (*Great American Craft Beer* 141). "Everything you'd expect from a great IPA was here, huge juicy lemons, limes and grapefruit, hints of guava and passion fruit and a whole pine forest of resinous wonderment," beer blogger Matt Curtis writes about his experience drinking Pliny. "I opened the abnormal 500 ml bottle and mistakenly thought I sliced open a tart grapefruit," the Perfectly Happy Man blogger writes. "It has that much of a tart grapefruit aroma and the taste is similar" ("Russian River Pliny the Elder."). Brewpublic's Angelo De Lesso videotapes himself drinking a Pliny the day it was bottled and notes the "big tropical fruit notes" (De Lesso). The video reviewers at the Beer Diaries identified "tropical fruits" and "grapefruit," as they simultaneously tasted Pliny the Elder in Canada and London via a Google Hangout (Zeschuk). Published tasting notes from a *Celebrator News* blind IPA tasting describe Pliny as having a "hop nose of citrusy orange, herbal aromas" ("Blind Beer Tasting"). *Business Insider*'s own construction of a RateBeer top twenty (borrowing algorithmic work from Stanford's Julian McAuley and Jure Leskovec that compares user ratings to expert communities) lists Pliny the Elder at number seven in the world and reports: "It's a blend of citrus, pine, and fresh hops, and has become something of a legend around the country for its balanced taste and dry finish" (Willett). *Draft Magazine* lists Pliny the Elder as one of eight essential beers to try before one can call one's self "a craft beer lover." The magazine also notes the beer's "citrusy, piney, hops" ("8 Essential"). When I entered into a trade for Pliny the Elder in May 2013, I acquired three freshly bottled bottles (less than a month old), and my reflections, again, even after consuming this beer many times previously, repeated these commonplaces: grapefruit, resin, pine, floral, citrus. Commonplaces not only circulate elsewhere; they often stay with us over time and drinking habits. They become internal lists drawn from in order to organize experiences. Commonplaces are essential components of craft networks. Pliny is one such network.

The myth of Pliny the Elder—and now commonplace narrative—internalized in a segment of craft beer narratives is that Russian River's Vinnie Cilurzo wanted to brew a bigger beer than the average IPA, so he "invented" the double IPA by doubling the hops and bringing up the malt bill ("Vinnie Cilurzo"). Cilurzo notes,

> I thought we should take our regular IPA recipe, double the hops on it, and the idea was not only would we get this super, over-the-top hoppy beer, but also that hops act as a natural preservative. Really. I didn't know any better, but that's still how we all operate. (qtd. in Koch and Allyn 31)

This mythic stature is repeated as an anchor for a networked and shared beer experience. The San Francisco band the Famous once recorded a tribute to the beer (Brooks, "New Pliny Elder the Video by the Famous.") "Drink it up and have no fear," they sing, "it's the Russian River beer." Arne Frantzell's comic strip *Trouble Brewing* in issue number 80 of *Beer Advocate* features two brewers on a sinking ship who can only stash five beers for the desert island they will land on. "You brought five Plinys?" one asks the other on the island. "What are we supposed to cellar?" ("Trouble Brewing #80"). Ben McFarland's short entry on Russian River in *The Oxford Companion to Beer* leaves out the beer's cultural connotations or any tasting notes and only states that "Russian River's most revered ales include 'Pliny the Elder,' an American 'Imperial IPA' with an IBU of 100 and 'Supplication,' a brown ale aged with sour cherries in Pinot Noir barrels inoculated with Brettanomyces yeast and Lactobacillus and Pediococcus bacteria" (705–6). *Zymurgy* magazine has named Pliny the Elder "The Best Commercial Beer in America" several years in a row. In his guide to 350 of the best beers known to man, Mark Dredge describes Pliny as "grapefruit pith in your gums" and tells an anecdote:

Those who have had it know just how good it is and those who haven't tried it yet dream about the day they can say the wonderful words: "a pint of Pliny, please." I'd landed in San Francisco a few hours earlier. I was lost, it was dark and raining, and I'd been awake for 24 hours, but I finally found the Toronado beer bar and said those words. Standing alone in this heaving, rocking bar, I won't forget that first mouthful of Pliny. (*Craft Beer World* 133)

Imbibe magazine lists Pliny as the best beer to "serve to your friend who claims to be a beer snob." The magazine's description of the beer includes "pine needle aroma" ("99 Bottles").

Pliny is a historical figure associated with beer. It is also a beer. It is also a series of references, tastes, opinions, and definitions. Pliny is also an anecdote. It is also a rating I entered into a database in 2008. Pliny, like the anecdotes I have moved through, is also a contagion. It is repeated as a reference point, among specific audiences, for craft. Pliny anchors conversations and tastings; it anchors rhetorical exchanges among craft beer enthusiasts. Pliny is a social media network of interactions and involvement.

Beer Boundaries

In *The Natural History*, Pliny the Elder wrote, "The People of the Western world have also their intoxicating drinks, made from corn steeped in water" (274). This passage, with its description of creating a rudimentary wort out of corn, is often interpreted to mean "beer." That interpretation, as it circulated from reader to reader to brewer to writer, eventually led to the naming of the famed Russian River double IPA. Vinnie Cilurzo

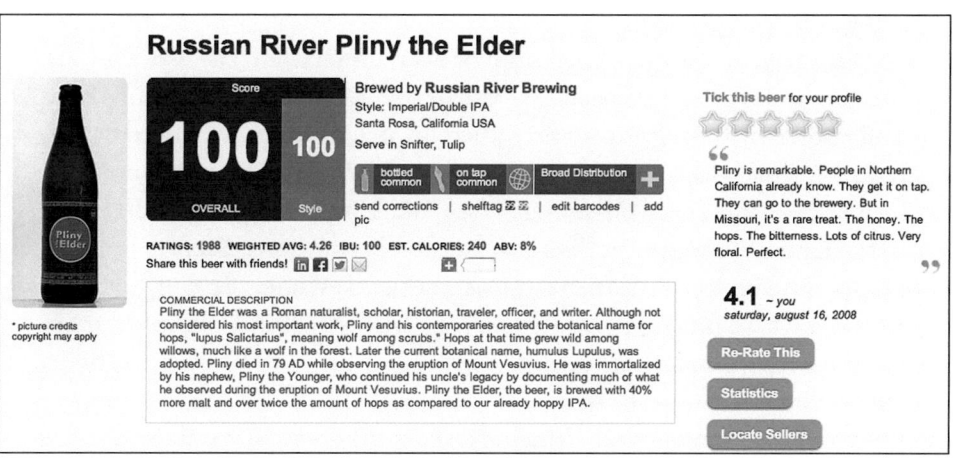

My rating for Pliny the Elder, August 16, 2008

claims that this interpretation of Pliny the Elder's identification of hops was an inspiration:

> We had several names, but nothing really inspired us. Finally, Natalie [Cilurzo's wife and Russian River co-owner] was looking through a brewing dictionary and looked up hops, which led us to Humulus Lupulus in the dictionary. This led us to Lupus salictarius, which [the book claimed] was the original botanical name for hops, which roughly translates to "wolf among scrubs," as hops growing wild among willows was likened to wolves roaming wild in the forest. This entry pointed us to Pliny the Elder, the Roman naturalist (among other things) who came up with that botanical name for hops. (qtd. in Steele 167)

Regarding the wolf, Pliny the Elder writes that

> each of these trees is in size as large as the fig; the blossoms are of an indescribable sweetness, and the fruit is similar in shape to a lupine, but so rough and prickly, that is never touched by any animal. (117)

Whether or not hops are what Pliny refers to in this passage, there exists an association (lupine/lupus) with the bittering agent. To arrive at a meaning that associates a Roman naturalist with contemporary craft beer, one must trace the network that juxtaposes or connects contemporary brewing (what is done with corn or the soaking of grain to extract sugars) with ancient practices (what is described by Pliny). In this network of connections are assumptions connecting a current object or practice (the contemporary hop) with a Roman knowledge of wild hops, often as if that knowledge is contemporary. Assumption, as later chapters will also show, is a craft gesture.

Hops have not always been used or even understood the way they are today. Stan Hieronymus's detailed research shows that although hops were well known by the eighth century, their aroma, flavor profiles, and usages have evolved within a ecology of consumer, brewer, legal system, and farmer ever since (*For the Love of Hops* 48). That ecology ties individuals to the land to products to laws to tastes to observations. *Ecology* is a geographic and biological term as well as a networked one: "Ecology includes all the ways we imagine how we live together" (Morton 4). Ecology, more than just a recognition of nature, is a way of understanding connectivity, connections to things or to ideas or to places that allow surroundings or environments to come into being regardless of historical accuracy (such as Roman knowledge of hops). "Place becomes a space of contacts, which are always changing and never discrete," Jenny Edbauer writes about ecologies and meaning (10). Such contacts can occur between a person who lived two thousand years ago and a beer bottled a month ago: "An ecological augmentation adopts a view toward the processes and events that extend beyond the limited boundaries of elements" (Edbauer 20). Pliny, as my brief overview shows, extends beyond boundaries (person, beer, taste, song, hop) that are often constructed in language or in habit in order to differentiate experiences. The experience, as in the case of Pliny, extends from one meaning to help shape one of the other possible meanings. This extension includes the boundaries, not only of a person or a tasting note, but of place. Pliny, as I show in this chapter and the next chapter, is a delicious double IPA. But it is also an ecology of place.

On August 16, 2008, when I rated Pliny the Elder, I lived in Missouri. I had moved to Missouri from Michigan, where a great deal of my beer knowledge had improved over the five years I lived there. When I left Gainesville, Florida, in 2002, my beer knowledge was mostly limited to Stone's Arrogant Bastard, Flying Dog's Gonzo Imperial Porter, and the— at the time—indulgent purchase of Verhaege's Duchesse de Bourgogne. This knowledge was limited by place and beer distribution (Florida, at that time, was not a major site of out-of-state distribution) and simple lack of knowing (my tastes continued to evolve). My ecology of beer place was a limited network of meaning. After leaving Gainesville, my craft knowledge expanded upon purchasing a six-pack of Bell's Kalamazoo Stout at a small convenience store on Woodward Avenue in Ferndale, Michigan. With Bell's, I discovered a regionalism and supposed limited boundary for beer production (at the time, Bell's was not distributed to Florida), which was Michigan beer. Florida beer, when I lived in Gainesville, barely existed (no Swamp Head, Saint Somewhere, or Cigar City yet, for instance). My ecology was based on prior assumptions (availability) replaced by new assumptions about place and beer. I extended my assumptions as I became more knowledgeable, but I was limited by the small ecology of meaning I relied on to understand what beer as taxonomy might mean; that is, Florida beer or Michigan beer.

My personal connection to these three places (Florida, Michigan, Missouri) was fleeting; as soon as I felt comfortable in a boundary of place, I moved. As an academic I have held four tenure-line jobs over a period of twelve years in three different states. I am not, in other words, tied to the land I live in beyond a job. My relationship with Missouri or with Michigan is, thus, temporary and fickle. I have no sense of residential terroir because the land or place does not seem to contribute to my identity the way being that from a country or, in Kentucky being from a county, does (*seem* being the key word). Pennsylvania is part of my sense of craft identity for its mythological relationship to place. That sense derives from the *seems* evoked in a series of connections traced and made visible by an anchor of experience (a Jewish/beer star).

I observe beers I drink in specific places (such as Missouri or Michigan) as they *seem* to relate to me. At some point while living in Missouri, one observation must have been that I wanted to try Pliny the Elder, a beer not distributed to Michigan or to Missouri and brewed far from either state. At that moment I made an effort to extend beyond a specific boundary or meaning. Pliny the Elder does not topologically equate Michigan or Missouri, the places where I would have had this observation. Pliny the Elder is not geographically bound to the region where my craft identity was being shaped.

Because of an ecology of networked material at my disposal online (references, reviews, discussion, hype), at some point I made an assumption about Pliny and its assumed quality (grapefruit, hops, resin) that circulated in the spaces of contact I experienced at the time. I assumed Pliny embodied these characteristics long before I tried the beer. This assumption—as the ecology of items was shared with me on message boards, videos, newspaper reports, and other spaces that extended beyond my physical location where Pliny was not sold—led to desire ("I want that!"). This assumption led me to purchase Pliny online (my trading does not begin until 2009) from South Bay Drugs and Pharmacy in San Diego, a region with a beer identity distinct from where I lived. I must have discovered South Bay on RateBeer in a trade forum on online purchases. In such a forum, participants make assumptions about the quality of online options available (good packaging, crazy packaging, expensive packaging, quick delivery, slow delivery, price, shipping costs). These assumptions, as well, enter in to my ecological perspective, as they do for other people who want Pliny the Elder shipped to them. Eventually, the assumption ties me to the retail moment (calling in my credit card number and ordering over e-mail) and then to a package shipped to my state. My ecologies, then, extend from a number of activities: where I live, the sites I frequent, the assumptions I make, the e-mails that arrive in my inbox, the comments I read online, and other items. These ecologies are place bound—but not only bound to physical space such as region or state. If I were to begin my interest in Pliny today, my assumptions would have to change direction. Most online retail stores do not ship beer to Kentucky. South Bay has become Bines and Vines, and it, too, does not ship to Kentucky. My ecologies need to shift. My sense of terroir, that is, needs to shift.

Terroir

These assumptions I make about ecologies and my first time trying Pliny the Elder tie a beer to a naturalist to the land. Pliny is named after a historian's supposed interested in an agricultural phenomenon, and even in that brief reference point, Pliny evokes a sense of terroir. Beer writer Martyn Cornell dismisses this land connection—as if Pliny has terroir—as being based on a series of misplaced assumptions repeated to the point of being accepted as is, without critical thought or questioning. Cornell questions the rhetorical ecology of Pliny, noting that Pliny the Elder never mentioned hops; instead, hops have been read into Pliny's usage of the Latin phrase *lupus salictarius*:

> I think it's somewhere between possible and probable that lupus salictarius WAS the wild hop plant: Pliny puts it among other wild plants from which the fresh shoots were harvested for cooking, like asparagus, and hop shoots are still cooked today, while "willow wolf" is a good description of what hops are capable of in the wild as they grow up trees for support. But that's a long way from "definite," and to write as if Pliny's lupus salictarius was unequivocally the hop plant is wrong. ("So What Did Pliny the Elder Say about Hops?")

Even if Cornell is correct in breaking down the historical usage of *lupus salictarius* (and I accept his breakdown), the term's ecology generates an assumption that exceeds accuracy or the questions of accuracy (i.e., did Pliny the Elder mean hops or not?). Assumptions and accuracy do not have to be equal for a given meaning to circulate. I can decode a problematic reading (as Cornell does) and understand that Pliny did not mean hops, and I can still be persuaded by the assumed association. Cornell's tension is a rhetorical one, and that tension plays out in assumptions about space and beer production formed over social media.

The assumption that land and certain types of artisanal products maintain a specific connection to each other (which I've already hinted at with this tension) is called *terroir*. Michigan, Missouri, and Kentucky are spaces generating terroir; that is, some type of food or beverage is associated with the state where it's produced. Terroir assumes that the land, soil, air, and temperature of a specific region affect the production of food or drink.

Kentucky, of all places, has a limited sense of terroir in beer history or beer's relationship to the land itself. Despite his extensive descriptions of nineteenth-century brewing, Stanley Baron offers only one mention of Kentucky in his historic overview: "In Kentucky there had been at least one brewery prior to 1800, but at the start of the nineteenth century this enterprise evidently lapsed" (130). For Kentucky to have a sense of beer terroir, one would assume it has a significant relationship to land-based ingredients, such as hops. If hops have been known to Kentucky brewers, they have only been known for a short time. And even though breweries such as Bavarian, Schaefer-Meyer, and Geisbauer operated in Kentucky in the nineteenth century, the notion of a Kentucky beer identity is a fairly new phenomenon. The terroir of Kentucky does not allow for any kind of extensive knowledge.

Such knowledge traditionally has been associated with land. One might think of Pliny the Elder's initial thoughts about hops (as the assumptions regarding his writings claim) as an early sense of terroir, an observation of the land and its effect on consumption. Terroir, as Elizabeth Barham notes, is in many situations a political concept used to protect regional food and beverage production by anchoring that production to specific parts of the world. Anchoring a product to the land produces economic assumptions as well: chiefly, that a product's success depends on its exclusive right to the land's name. Focusing on label-of-origin politics, Barham writes,

> Terroir also reflects a conscious and active social construction of the present by various groups concerned with rural areas in France (social and economic organizations, state agency personnel, academics) who jostle for position in their efforts to recover and revalorize elements of the rural past to be used in asserting a new vision of the rural future. (132)

A label of origin places a limited boundary on terroir's circulation. "Terroir and goût du terroir are *categories* that frame perceptions and practices—a world," Amy Trubek writes. "Terroir and goût du terroir are categories for framing and explaining people's relationship to the land, be it sensual, practical or habitual" (18). A Santa Rosa beer, such as Pliny the Elder, would, by this definition, be understood for its quality because it comes from Santa Rosa (Sonoma County) and all of the elements that compose the air, soil, and temperature of Santa Rosa, not because it was shipped to Missouri from a San Diego shop. If Santa Rosa or Sonoma County wanted to politicize this production, representatives of those places could, following Barham, lobby for a label that limits all very hoppy beers with the flavor of grapefruit and pine to their geographic location. Not following this logic or endorsing such acts, Trubek adds to her definition of terroir the memory of place (rather than place as a political designation):

> In France, terroir is often associated with *racines*, or roots, a person's history with a certain place. Local taste, or goût du terroir, is often evoked when an individual wants to remember an experience, explain a memory, or express a sense of identity. (51)

Those roots connect modern Pliny the Elder, an IPA, with the naturalist Pliny the Elder, who, one repeated narrative claims, identified hops. The category or name establishes roots via assumptions. Pliny the beer is rooted in Pliny the person. In this case, however, the roots are not in a place but in the idea of a historic person. Even when a historian such as Cornell challenges this idea, the idea of that person's acts prevails and creates roots in the concept.

While brewers do not always identify with historical figures, brewers often identify with the local environment when they incorporate the kinds of hops, yeast, or barley the area provides. This work allows for a feeling of connectivity to land and the assumption that one's work has roots in the land. The work is rhetorical for how it anchors meaning to land. These roots, many believe, affect consumption in a positive manner overall, and thus roots contribute to an ecology of drinking. Garrett Oliver notes this in his work at Brooklyn Brewery:

> As we connect ourselves more deeply to our farmers, we want to connect the people who are drinking the beer more closely to the farmers as well, so they know there are actual people behind what we're doing, which I think is what differentiates craft beer from something else. (qtd. in Brooklyn Magazine)

Dustin Brau of Minnesota's Brau Brothers comments on the six acres of hops and barley surrounding the brewery he runs: "[The farmland] keeps us homebrewers in a way because it lets us do new things and keep trying" (qtd. in Lewis, "Brau Brothers" 30). Connection to the land is also the logic behind Stone/Jolly Pumpkin/Nøgne-Ø's Special Holiday Ale collaboration:

> The resultant brew that came out of the summit at Stone was anything but pale. Intended to use indigenous ingredients from the three brewers' locales, the three got close. The white sage came from the California farmer that supplies the Stone café with produce. Most of the chestnuts came from Michigan, where Jolly Pumpkin's

based. And while they couldn't bring in juniper berries from Norway, they settled on bringing them in from Europe, and used Italian juniper. Then came the rye. And caraway. (Scheitrum 25)

The small New Hampshire brewer Throwback, too, bases its identity in the land surrounding its beer production. Co-owner Nicole Carrier notes, "Our vision is to try and get all of our ingredients within 200 miles of the brewery. Depending on the beer, we're about 65 to 90 percent there" (qtd. in Lewis, "Throwback Brewery"). National Public Radio covered Ava, Illinois' Scratch Brewing, whose co-owner "Aaron Kleidon went for a walk in the Illinois woods and returned with a bag of lotus seeds. The seeds were bound not for his dinner plate, but for his pint glass" (Bland, "Forget Barley and Hops"). Scratch, like these other examples, draws from the local environment to foster the idea of terroir: "The microbrewery specializes in beers with seeds, leaves, roots, fruits and fungi foraged from a nearby wooded property. The brewers have even made a saison from chanterelle mushrooms" (Bland). These practices suggest a terroir based on roots, or what Carrier's partner Annette Lee calls "beeroir." The land (preferably the surrounding local terrain) and the beer are networked. With Pliny the Elder, the roots are in a historic figure rather than solely in Sonoma County; with the local movement, the roots are in farmers, land, or products cultivated on the land.

This land connection reflects terroir's assumed association with wine, since wine comes from the terroir-affected grape specific to a locale. Despite exceptions like the ones I note, the narrative of land ecology dominates wine's discourse more than beer's. For many, terroir's taxonomy is fixed in place (much as its products are). "Establishing the links between terroir and wine character is an allusive and difficult task," Jonathan Swinchatt and David Howell write (4). "Never refer to soil dismissively as dirt," Brian Sommers warns. "It is literally the foundation of quality winemaking and the basis of terroir" (60). "Why not just use the more familiar word 'vineyard,'" James Wilson writes in his comprehensive text *Terroir*, arguing that "terroir" is a word synonymous with wine (56). This association of wine with terroir generates an appellation, a reference to the location of a wine's production, the anchoring of wine in a place. Burgundy means the place called Burgundy. Columbia Valley directs attention to the wine's connection to the Columbia Valley in Washington State. Appellation, like its theoretical counterpart interpellation, is the hailing or calling of identity into being; only in this case, identity is tied to land. The land calls the product into being. The taxonomy—the specific place that holds a specific meaning—gives identity to the product, often a wine. Such is the traditional network of terroir.

At some point beer, too, gained a spatial origin meaning and, in turn, a spatial identity. Some of the meaning is connected to farming and staying local, as I note, but some of this meaning conflates style and place, a conflation that, in turn, creates a spatial identity reflecting terroir. Tom Acitelli traces that point to the 1999 BrewGuide (later Beer Advocate) review of Sierra Nevada Porter, which tied this particular beer to the West Coast. In their historic review of the porter, the Alström brothers split identity from style and placed it in a network that included location:

> A porter was an "excellent" porter only if it looked, smelled, and tasted like an excellent porter. But the review also tells us that it was now understood that styles could be broken down further. It was like terroir with wine: it mattered where the beer came from, not because, as with wine, the geographic origin of the ingredients could define taste, but because the geographic origin of the brewer could. (qtd. in Acitelli 283)

West Coast style signifies a particular hoppy take on the IPA—big Cascade and Simcoe hops, floral, grassy, straw in appearance, often with a low, caramel malt body. Such is Tom Acitelli's definition of "bitterer beers made by more hops, especially the Cascade variety first used in craft brewing by Anchor in 1975 for its Liberty Ale" (174). According to these location assumptions, Pliny the Elder is a West Coast beer. Bell's Two Hearted Ale (Michigan) is not, while Alpine's Nelson (San Diego area) is West Coast, even though both are hoppy IPAs. Alpine represents the West Coast style. West Coast, of course, is not a style such as porter, kölsch, or stout. West Coast is a location transformed into an assumed terroir-based style. The style—regardless of style guidelines—becomes a taxonomy of terroir because of where the beer is brewed. That categorical expectation of location, however, can be disrupted. Heady Topper's Alchemist (Vermont), Toppling Goliath's pseudoSue (Iowa), Fat Head's Head Hunter (Ohio), or Three Floyds' Zombie Dust (Indiana) border that same taxonomy of West Coast style held by Alpine IPAs or Pliny the Elder. With these different meanings circulated by brewers influenced by a location-based style, terroir's categorical designation—or its taxonomy—limits a discussion of how the production of a specific product (food or drink) might be tied to a specific place. To be "hoppy" might mean to be tied to a particular place, like the West Coast. Yet, to reduce location to the political or to wine (or even to legacy with the Russian River example) is to deny the many ways terroir allows an individual's understanding of the product to occur and even overcome a taxonomic expectation. That is, appellation-based categories limit regional ties to beer. A taxonomy with West Coast as a style demands that all beer brewed in this style be from the West Coast even if the beers are located elsewhere.

When I wrote a rating about Pliny the Elder in 2008, I understood the beer as possessing a specific spatial meaning because I already imagined its place in Santa Rosa, Sonoma County, as special. That imagining was based on all kinds of factors. Sonoma County (or Northern California in general) occupies a place in my particular mental and emotional ordering of beer in America. In addition to Russian River's presence in downtown Santa Rosa or Bear Republic's presence in nearby Healdsburg or Lagunitas' presence in Petaluma—Sonoma County is the birthplace of Jack McAuliffe's New Albion Brewing Company. New Albion is the mythical origin point of contemporary craft beer (apart from Anchor's role in the craft beer origin narrative). Craft beer small stories make that point explicit. Almost all craft beer historical narratives begin with the story of McAuliffe returning to the United States after his navy service and reproducing the beers he had enjoyed while on duty in Scotland. "While others dreamed and schemed, he did it," Stephen Morris writes (181). "One of California's true microbrewing pioneers" is how Jack Erickson describes McAuliffe (*California Brewin'* 21). When Tom Acitelli retells McAuliffe's story, he titles one chapter of the tale "The West Coast Style" in order to highlight McAuliffe's role in creating this distinctive IPA, and possibly craft beer in general. West Coast is as much an association with a contemporary hop-forward brewery such as Alpine as it is with Jack McAuliffe. That association carries over into me as well. In my personal taxonomy, Northern California breweries (Russian River, New Albion) are arranged accordingly in my mind and cluster together in a sensibility of California beer that, at several points in my life, has had me yearning for a Pliny the Elder. I can stand in front of a wall of locally available six-packs of IPA (Founders Centennial, Bell's Two Hearted, West Sixth IPA, Sweetwater IPA) and, if my taxonomy shifts to the imagination of West Coast beer and what it stands for, I may think: I want a Pliny. That personal ordering, when allowed, can lead to online ordering, as I once did with Pliny when I lived in Missouri. Sensibility is distributed mentally (across my emotions and clustering) and physically (usually via FedEx).

Craft versus Crafty

With this personalized ordering, I generate, encourage, and even distort taxonomies and the rhetorical assumptions they support. When beer generates a sense of a political or professionally accepted craft appellation, it does so not from a personal ordering such as my own but from an industry-recognized taxonomy: craft. Craft is a specific taxonomy. Craft defines an industry and it defines a way of thinking. Often credited as being among the first to use the term "craft brewery," Vincent Cottone established a specific way of thinking about beer: "I use the term Craft Brewery to describe a small brewery using traditional methods and ingredients to produce a handcrafted, uncompromised beer that is marketed locally. I refer to this beer as True Beer" (9). Compromised beer, following Cottone's terminology, allows for *crafty* as an opposing taxonomy. Crafty isolates breweries associated with craft and declares them outside the taxonomy. These taxonomies have, like appellation, ideological implications. These taxonomies extend a generic understanding of terroir as a way to name a product and its various associations. Instead of basing terroir on land, the public debate of craft versus crafty has become a way for the industry to differentiate between beer that, in place of being land based, has an ideological terroir (genuine beer made by small, independent breweries that produce fewer than six million barrels per year and use traditional ingredients) and beer that appears to have this terroir but is, in fact, produced by a conglomerate (e.g., Blue Moon, Miller's Leinenkugel, or the InBev-owned Goose Island). The distinction is rhetorical (how we describe and identify with each label) and political (which, of course, is also rhetorical). A 2014 National Public Radio story introduces the craft versus crafty debate by framing it as one of taxonomic confusion:

> There was once a time when it was easy to throw around the term "craft beer" and know exactly what you were talking about. For decades, craft was the way to differentiate small, independently owned breweries—and the beer they make—from the brewing giants like Coors, Budweiser and Pabst Blue Ribbon. (Bland, "As Craft Beer")

And now, the taxonomic story relates, the distinction is not so easy to ascertain.

The Brewers Association takes credit for this gesture of differentiation—using rhetoric not unlike what Barham describes for European food politics—with its December 13, 2012, statement on craft versus crafty. The statement, amended in 2014, aims for a political distinction of craft as ideological terroir. The distinction, not unlike the revolution narrative I previously described, is based on an ideological binary of us versus them. In its press release, the Brewers Association wrote,

> The large, multinational brewers appear to be deliberately attempting to blur the lines between their crafty, craft-like beers and true craft beers from today's small and independent brewers. We call for transparency in brand ownership and for information to be clearly presented in a way that allows beer drinkers to make an informed choice about who brewed the beer they are drinking. ("Craft vs. Crafty")

Craft, in this case, resembles the wine labels Burgundy or Columbia Valley or any other designation that for ideological or economic reasons ties a product to land. Even if craft does not signify land (like West Coast IPA), it is used as terroir, a definition that is designed to pick up cultural legitimacy if a general public accepts its terms. Legal definitions are based in protection. The legal taxonomy associated with wine and specific foodstuffs attempts to protect the brand from being diluted by other places or producers. The legal taxonomy attempts to keep the classification outside a personal ordering, or what Geralyn and Jack Brostrom call "schemes":

> The identification of unique outstanding terroirs has engendered schemes to protect those place names from fraud and competition. Terroir therefore serves to underpin the market potential of wines and to add value. France's *Appellation d'Origine Contrôlée* (AOC), introduced in the 1930s, is the modern model for such legislation. (242)

The French model for appellation protection was based on champagne, blended wine sold in 750-milliliter cork and caged bottles. "Certain areas were judged to be in the 'Champagne region,'" Trubek writes, "and only wines produced in those areas could be sold with the 'Champagne' label. This was the beginning of a system that protected and promoted French wine and would ultimately be extended to cheese and other products" (26). Crafty, for some critics in the industry, is a scheme to redirect a taxonomic terroir from one type of production to another so that *craft* can be protected, much as *champagne* is protected from cheap imposters. Blue Moon, for instance, circulates as an example of a cheap craft imposter. In the French example, champagne sold without the "Champagne" label would be crafty.

Beer, in the contemporary craft example, sold without the explicit labeling of manufacturer origin (place, to some extent) would be deemed crafty. The taxonomy of crafty is meant to educate the consumer regarding production origin so that authentic choices can be made. Terrapin's John Cochran (whose brewery is partly owned by MillerCoor's Tenth and Blake subsidiary) reflects on this appellation of craft versus crafty as not a scheme or an attempt to undermine reputation but as a recognizable trade organization ordering the classification of a product within a larger field of similar products:

> Theoretically, these three criteria [Brewers Association criteria] are all OK. Especially when one considers them as what they really are. They are an attempt by a trade organization, the Brewer's Association, to define their clientele. Taken in that light, no big deal.

No big deal, following Cochran, if one recognizes that the appellation is not natural (it does not exist on its own) but rather is generated by a political moment (protecting a label called "craft" from being undermined by larger forces). August Schell Brewery's Jace Marti, reacting to his brewery's designation as crafty for using corn (and not barley) in its brewing, angrily rejects the crafty political taxonomy because it ignores historical context, such as Schell's 152-year-old rationale for this brewing choice:

> [August Schell] used a small portion of another locally grown ingredient he called "mais" as is hand written in our old brewing logs, better known as corn. He didn't use corn to cheapen or lighten his beer. He did it because it was the only way to brew a high quality lager beer in America at that point. By the time high quality two-row malting barley was finally cultivated and available to use, our consumers had already been drinking our high quality beers for many years. We continued to brew our beer using this small portion of corn because that was the way we traditionally brewed it. ("August Schell Brewing to BA")

Ingredients, as indicators of a taxonomy, do not exist only in a given moment, as when a trade organization issues a claim of authenticity, but they exist in a series of historical moments that must be traced and included in the current network we are experiencing. As Mitch Steele writes in part of an interview conducted by Maureen Ogle for her blog, historical context needs to be addressed when we subscribe to labels or taxonomies:

The use of "adjuncts," such as rice or corn began in the United States in the 1800s because American malt was of suspect quality and sometimes resulted in harsh, heavy beer. At the time, big brewers were located in the Midwest—St. Louis, Milwaukee, Cincinnati—where the summers are brutally hot. American consumers wanted a lighter, more refreshing beer. Brewers added adjuncts to compensate for the kinds of barley/malt they had access to. ("What Is in Your Beer")

This context should dilute some of the rigid crafty taxonomy, though it likely does not entirely dilute the distinction for an industry or a consumer base that remains fixated on issues such as ownership, place, or ingredients. Joseph Tucker, who runs RateBeer, tries to alter such a rigid definition with a declaration: "Craft Brewing is a genre. It is not a quality certification." Outlining a completely different taxonomy from that of the Brewers Association, Tucker offers other characteristics of craft such as "local" and as brewers having "relationships with consumers," as well as generating categories apart from craft that are not judgmental: industrial brewing, Belgian traditional, and American regional. Tucker's definition avoids the craft versus crafty controversy and allows for an evolving sense of terroir by introducing new anchors of experience into the definition. I, too, am working toward that sense (the *seems* of terroir) by expanding the network of actors in a given terroir moment.

Some of the ideological appellation present in the craft versus crafty debate is tied to size and not to ingredients. Size is also rhetorically constructed. Small, according to the debate's narrative, is legitimate; it represents grassroots, local, and independent. Big does not; it represents corporate, greedy, and committed to shareholders over the consumers' interest. The rhetoric of this exchange repeats confidence narratives and remains committed to stories styled as David versus Goliath (as the revolution narrative does). A *St. Louis Today* response to craft versus crafty declares,

> It makes a difference. By supporting small and independent craft brewers across the country, we are giving them a chance to thrive in business, create more jobs, boost the economy and compete against the massive corporations that have controlled the market for so long. (Papazian, Peace, and Kopman)

In this narrative, size equates authenticity. Authenticity marks terroir:

> Tired of watching mainstream beer sales fall while the craft beer craze soared, large international companies like MillerCoors and Anheuser-Busch InBev have hijacked the playbook of small, independent brewers. The results are faux "crafty" beers like Blue Moon and Shock Top, which appear to be created by smalltime operations, while actually being produced by the world's largest brewers. Naturally, the authentic little guys aren't pleased. (Tuttle)

Writing as "The Pour Fool," Steve Body expresses outright anger at conglomerates such as MillerCoors who pass off industrial beer as craft. Body's narrative repeats the size argument: big versus small; those that occupy corner offices in high-rises versus those that operate in industrial parks:

> As a viable and achievable alternative to the big corner office and the expense account and the millions in salary and bonuses, and the trophy wife and the mega-mansion in a gated enclave, how about . . . the thrill of discovery as the first batch of Amber comes out of the tank in that brand new brewery, tucked away in an industrial park . . . the first tasting and the smiles all around . . . the opening of the taproom and watching hundreds of beer lovers flock in to taste this new thrill. (The Pour Fool)

When Beer Advocate asks its members via an online poll, what does craft mean?, the first response to check on a provided list reads, "It relates to the size of the brewery and how much beer it sells" ("What Does 'Craft' Mean in Craft Beer Poll?"). One Burlington, Vermont, bar manager notes his "mission is to showcase rare, unique and traditional expressions of craft brewed beer, hand-made by the 'little guys'" (Jeff Baker). CNN Money's Denis Wilson writes, "Though you can't taste a beer company's size or ownership structure, some see these qualities as essential distinctions." Craft versus crafty is a terroir-based battle over telling the story of ingredients and size.

    I don't frame beer within a pseudolegal taxonomy (legal appellation) because in this framework there is no room for me and my personal ordering. There is only room for a debate over what is authentic or what is allowed per size or output. Taxonomies limit the boundaries of experience—in language, in place, in thought, and in taste—in a quest for assumed authenticity. If I succumb to land-based legal (or quasi-legal) associations of a product with region or style or brewery size, I cannot enter into that system of categorizing consumption. There will be no place for my personal ordering. There will be no place for me outside taxonomic gatekeeping. Craft obsession is not just about beer but about me as well. In the craft versus crafty binary, I can find no place for my obsession: I like Goose Island, but I don't drink Miller Lite; I like Terrapin, but I'm not interested in Budweiser. My personal ordering is a blended taxonomy of terroir—ideological, land based, and otherwise.

Clustering Terroir

My personal ordering of beer terroir is not limited to the West Coast, regardless of brewery size. In other personal orderings of beer terroir, I might also break the craft/crafty binary by placing Michigan, San Diego, Colorado, and Oregon as terroir-based sites because of my clustered association of beers with each region. These clusters, which in their connectivity reflect social media logics, may or may not pay attention to ingredients or brewery size. These clusters might be, for instance, based on my knowledge or consumption of specific regional beers. My knowledge serves as an ordering system regardless of logic or style. For instance, I might order these clustered areas as such:

> Michigan: Bell's, Founders, Arcadia, Dark Horse, New Holland, Jolly Pumpkin
>
> San Diego: Stone, Alesmith, Lost Abbey, Alpine, Green Flash
>
> Colorado: Great Divide, Odell, Funkwerks, Crooked Stave
>
> Oregon: Hair of the Dog, Cascade, Logsdon, Deschutes

In each cluster, the breweries may or may not brew similar styles. (Funkwerks, for instance, produces beers that are nothing like Great Divide.) These clusters are personal, based on my tastes as informed by culture, context, production, association, and consumption. They are based on my purchasing and trading habits. They are based on my own internal myths, stories I tell myself about beers, which I drink occasionally or hardly at all, but which I hold specific memories of (such as sitting at Great Divide when my daughter was two years old). They are, in a sense, personal geographies I carve out of networked affiliations of region. In this networking, I confuse state with city. I confuse cities with nearby towns and villages. I flatten regions to be homogenous when they are not (Jolly Pumpkin, for example, does not resemble Founders; Denver is not Fort Collins). It doesn't matter; in my ordering, these are all terroir beer regions. As Chicago, for example, expands in my ordering to include

Avery Brewing, 2009

Pipeworks, Revolution, Spiteful, and Piece, it still includes Goose Island, even if Goose Island is now supposedly "crafty" because it is located in the InBev network of beer ownership. With Chicago or other areas, I build and enter into an ecology. I am, of course, not the only one who understands terroir in this manner of classification.

"Terroir possesses multiple meanings, but they all refer back to a system of ordering and classifying a particular place," writes Trubek (54). I encounter in terroir a confusion of ordering and classifying practices. I understand that terroir means place; I understand that appellation refers to the specific naming of place for legal protection; I understand that beer produced in Sonoma County doesn't fit these previous ordering systems for terroir. Still, Sonoma County represents, for me, an ordering these other meanings don't. Terroir is a folksonomy. *Folksonomy* is the new media term for ordering and classifying systems in which any object or idea may be labeled with multiple meanings (such as wine and beer for terroir, or beer for Michigan instead of other regional categories such as automobiles or snow). A user of Flickr, for instance, might attribute the tag "house" to a picture of a house or might attribute "grandma," "Michigan," "nightmare," "celebration," or any other term that the user feels should be associated with the image; the associations often come from feelings or memories as much as they might be pulled from communal or definitional knowledge. Folksonomy, as David Weinberger has written, defies assumptions about organization. Regarding folksonomies, Weinberger writes that "we have to get rid of the idea that there's a best way of organizing a world" (10). Terroir, as a folksonomic system, is assumed to be a "best" way of organizing alcohol production and its labeling. Outside of this "best" definition's basis in dirt, terroir is a network of meanings and ideas. My understanding of this network begins with how I include my own perceptions within perceptions of place. Any other approach "assumes that [terroir] is a quantifiable, concretely *knowable* phenomenon" (Trubek 65). I don't know anything about my personal geographic clusters apart from a limited perception: beer. I can't quantify that knowledge by referring to soil samples or air quality. My knowledge is, admittedly, messy (unlike traditional appellations, which can be neat and orderly). My knowledge, in this messy arena of clustering, differs from many other knowledge sets regarding terroir. Despite that messiness, for me the terroir of these places is based on specific beers produced there.

Even those brewers who are interested in using local ingredients don't use the terms *appellation* or *terroir* to describe their beers. Writers interpellate (call into being) the status of a beer-based terroir in ways consumers and often producers don't. Michael Jackson, in particular, applied appellation to English beers in order to cluster (as I cluster) a specific drinking experience around locale:

> In the British Isles, we are hazy on designations of origin and do not regulate appellations of style, but we have hung on to regional differences among our beers. Even within the single-style bitter, very dry examples are most commonly found in the South-east (Shepherd Neame in Kent; Brakspear's in Henley; Gale's near Portsmouth; and Young's in London). This may be because the South-eastern breweries are nearest to the hop gardens of Kent and Sussex, and the traditional Kent hop variety, Goldings, gives quite a dry character. ("Appellations of a Different Nature")

Stan Hieronymus traces the concept of beer terroir from Belgian abbey monks ("Trappists understand the importance of place") to the role water quality plays in differentiating beers from one another to Sam Calagione's declaration that "'[b]reweries have terroir as well. But instead of revolving around a patch of land, ours are centered on a group of people'" ("The Dirt on Terroir"). Several craft breweries situate terroir as central to some of their production by centralizing their identification within the concept of regional appellation. Writing for *Draft Magazine*, Christopher Staten outlines a contemporary craft movement whose focus is to produce "native" beers in America. By native, Staten means beers whose terroir is strictly regional. This, we might assume, would follow the European thinking in which regions are associated with certain styles. (Cologne for kölsch, for instance). For the most part, though, Staten means yeast when he discusses native beers and terroir:

> Native beers have the potential to define the American craft beer industry's legacy. The array of yet-to-be-cultivated yeast strains floating past our windows could even mark new, distinct American brewing regions, not unlike Belgium's Senne River Valley, which became famous for its spontaneously fermented lambics.

Staten differs from my understanding of place. I don't cluster together regional beers by yeast (or water or air) in order to reflect on brand. I do so by personal taste—as it is informed by various experiences (what I read, what I hear, what I discuss, what I consume). As with any social media experience, I focus on me, in addition to the subject I engage with. Hieronymus, in response to Staten, asks, "Does it matter?" ("Native Ales"). "Does it matter?" suggests that having a native branding—based on yeast or some other material item—is not important. A brand does not necessarily situate terroir with a beer. Hieronymus points out No-Li Brewhouse's copyright of "Spokane Style" as an example of native branding having little categorical meaning beyond its assumed marketing value. As No-Li has it on its website, "'When you pride yourself on using only the finest ingredients and the greatest attention to detail,' said co-founder and Head Brewer Mark Irvin, 'you know what Spokane Style is. You can taste it'" ("No-Li Receives"). The phrases "finest ingredients" and "attention to detail" lack any sense of specificity demanded by terroir—whether the ordering is taxonomic or even personal. (When I tried No-Li's IPA in Asheville, North Carolina, far away from Washington State, I could not taste any "Spokane Style" in it.) Even if terroir is folksonomic (it may contain multiple meanings at once), these terms are too generic to be any type of category. Instead, some form of naming must occur if there is to be a *seems* sensibility of native beer that consumers attach themselves to. If I attach myself to Northern California, I do so for reasons beyond "finest ingredients." I taste something else in the attachment than generic labeling. Native means something else to me.

No-Li IPA, an example of "Spokane Style" native branding

Some beers, such as Urban Chestnut's Seitz Farm Terroir Lager and New Belgium's Le Terroir, incorporate terroir into their naming in order to get at the *seems* sense of the native. Some breweries showcase only native ingredients. Dogfish Head's D.N.A. (Delaware Native Ale) used only Delaware ingredients. Grand Teton brews Idaho Pale Ale, which they claim is the first beer brewed only with Idaho ingredients. And for Oregon's 150th anniversary, Deschutes brewed Oregon 150 Ale and Maiden Oregon Ale, made only with ingredients from Oregon. Some breweries go to lengths to develop the native concept as a distributed rather than single (state ingredients) concept. Odell Brewing's limited release Footprint showcases the concept of a regional and native beer, a beer whose ingredients come only from the imprint of the brewery's distribution network:

> Footprint includes hops and barley from Colorado and Idaho, wheat from Kansas and Wyoming, Arizona prickly pear, Minnesota wild rice, Nebraska corn, New Mexico green chilies, South Dakota honey, and oak barrels from Missouri. The final blend boasts a rich golden hue and an oaky stone-fruit nose, and a delicate sweetness from the wheat and honey that is balanced by a subtle spicy dry finish. ("Odell Footprint")

As a *Phoenix New Times* writer comments about this concept,

> People like to say it's not about where you're from, but rather where you're going. Weird thing about beer is, where you're going in a way becomes where you're from. Choices of where to distribute are not made lightly—the impression of a brewery can be just as impacted by the people who drink it and the places in which it's drunk outside the state of origin. A brewery's fans, regardless of where they live, become part of its persona. Sometimes it's good to pay homage to them, too. (Fowle)

These two definitions of terroir indicate the beer's footprint (the states its ingredients come from) and the consumer (who is part of the beer's persona). The beer leaves a digital footprint as well: online reviews.[1] These reviews extend the beer outside a specified geographic footprint (i.e., I learn about the beer even if I don't live where it is distributed).

Every beer leaves a digital footprint across Facebook, weblogs, YouTube, and elsewhere. By noting that a specific terroir-organized beer also leaves this additional footprint, I extend terroir from the physical space (dirt), from the current conceptual space (roots, consumption), and from the personal space (me) to the online space so that a network of all of these spaces is realized. If terroir is emotional (or people based) as Trubek claims, then the online interactions shaping a beer are as important as the ten-state footprint Odell draws on to brew its one-time release. I, no doubt, read about Footprint in an online space before I acquired it, possibly via an aggregated feed of blogs I read every day. My 2008 review of Pliny the Elder is part of these digital interactions once it, too, is read by someone else. In that reading, my persona (and others' personas as well) becomes part of the footprint. The consumer's persona is as important as a beer's ingredients; talking and writing about the beer help distribute it as well as suggest its taste. Terroir, we might say, is an aggregation. Aggregations are not static; they change over time and space. Aggregations are social media logics of organization and expression based on assumptions and anecdotes as much as they are based on taxonomies.

By saying that terroir is an aggregation, I note two levels of networks: the distribution network (the ten states Odell sells beer in) and the terroir network (ingredients, people, online interactions, reviews, assumptions, and so on). This aggregation assembles in one place (the beer) the sense or *seems* of a place-bound meaning. Apart from its bottle or can or label, beer assembles the terroir network into the object itself. The sense of place

Bottle of Odell Footprint RegionAle consumed in Kentucky

My rating for Odell Footprint RegionAle, an example of a beer's digital footprint

(San Diego, Michigan, Oregon) comes from how a consumer aggregates a variety of items. This aggregation is at the heart of social networks. Navigation of information demands aggregation; it is otherwise impossible to follow every friend's activities without Facebook's news feed or every news item without Google News. Terroir extends this kind of navigation of beer and place. Even the review I write to RateBeer contributes to terroir aggregation. I may write the review in Missouri (where I once could buy Odell off the shelves) or in Kentucky (where I wrote the review outside Odell's distribution network). Once that review is caught within the overall network of Odell (a network that includes the beer as well as the review), I contribute to the aggregation of terroir. I help construct a feeling of what Odell is, of what its identity is, of what kinds of meanings and memories it might produce. I am, as well, in the footprint. Even when I move outside the distribution footprint, my persona plays a role as the footprint becomes digital. I have been to Odell's brewery and taproom in Fort Collins, Colorado. I have moved from the digital to the physical. But even if I hadn't visited, I would still be within this terroir network because of my consumption and reviewing habits. In chapter 4, I extend this sense of aggregation further by exploring specific concepts related to aggregation and the example of a small Oklahoma brewery that defies terroir expectations.

CHAPTER 4
Craft Terroir

> They're enriching their beer.
> That's definitely enriched beer.
> That's an enriched beer, dude.
> —*It's Always Sunny in Philadelphia*, "The Gang Solves the North Korea Situation"

In the previous chapters, I've shown how craft beer moves through networks. Those networks are obvious (distribution channels) as well as less visible (terroir). With physical distribution, the networks function as trucks and pallets making their way from point (brewery) to point (warehouse) to point (retail or restaurant). Networks also function as advertising, the delivery of the message via media to the consumer. The networks are also affective, tapping into emotions or feelings we carry over from other activities and interests. Networking a naturalist, Pliny the Elder, and contemporary brewing results in the emotional naming of a West Coast hoppy IPA. "Every food practice directly depends on a network of impulses (likes and dislikes) with respect to smells, colors, and forms, as well as to consistency types," Luce Giard writes (185). As the network stretches from the pallet to the browser, that sense of impulse heightens.

In his 1932 book *Let There Be Beer*, Bill Brown described the process of receiving beer in the late nineteenth century as one framed by the network of impulses, anticipation, and media. As beer moved from one location to another, eager consumers knew when their anticipated products were released by reading notices posted on public boards:

> Arrival dates of beer liners were posted on black boards in the better bars. They were studied closely then as importing merchants study the lists of arriving mail and freight boats today. Man welcomers were on the docks awaiting all beer ships, striving to be the first up the gangplank and into the ship's bar for a preview of the latest brew to arrive at their shores. (282–83)

If there were a nineteenth-century terroir, it might be summed up as both the German brewing methods (based on *Reinheitsgebot* law) typical for the period and the emotional aspect of waiting for posted beer liners to arrive. Waiting for the delivery of a keg from Germany in the nineteenth century as advertised on a board indicates the affective response found in a folksonomic terroir.

This emotional response resembles contemporary beer drinkers waiting in line for a special release, posting anticipation for a release on Rate-Beer and Beer Advocate message boards, and asking about releases on Facebook, on Twitter, and over e-mail. A RateBeer ISO can be the twenty-first-century version of waiting for a public notice in the nineteenth century. For early twentieth-century American beer drinking, Tom Acitelli attributes this anticipation and waiting to the sense of place or locality:

> And the beer they drank was a local thing. Breweries and the beers they brewed were delineated by geography. What you got in Cleveland, you couldn't get in Brooklyn; the brands in Pittsburgh would seem unusual to someone from San Diego. (6)

Waiting for a beer to be released in Cleveland meant waiting for a Cleveland beer. Aggregation changes this sense of waiting. ISO means that a beer released in Cleveland does not disqualify my waiting for it in Kentucky. When I wait for a Founders' Backstage beer to be released, for instance, I don't wait in Grand Rapids, Michigan (though I could drive six hours to a release at the brewery). I wait in a parking lot at a Liquor Barn store in the Beaumont Center off Harrodsburg Road in Lexington, Kentucky. My sense of locality shifts from what beer drinkers in the nineteenth and early twentieth century experienced. No more kegs arriving by boat. My emotional connection and impulse, however, have not diminished. I get excited about a Backstage release the way a nineteenth-century beer drinker may have been excited about an incoming boat. I identify that release as part of the evolving Michigan aggregation my personal ordering fosters.

Emotion was a major component of my breakdown of terroir in the previous chapter. Emotion is what Don Feinberg, cofounder of Ommegang brewery and Vanberg and DeWulf importers, ties to specific brewers whose reputations are already familiar to him. "I want to have as real a relationship as I can with as real a culture. And I will continue to seek out and fight for the beers of Terroir [*sic*] that represent cultures I do know," he writes. Those beers might include the Belgian portfolio that Vanberg and DeWulf imports or the specific tastes Feinberg highlights as important to him, Russian River and Allagash. Emotion and beer, like craft versus crafty debates, highlight rhetorical tensions. While it is no Russian River or Allagash, Budweiser taps into similar terroir emotional connections or a sense of the local through one of its many commercials distributed over television and online networks. "Do you know where your beer is brewed?" one commercial asks ("Where Your Beer is Brewed"). Pointing out the twelve Budweiser breweries across America, the commercial adds, "Your next Budweiser is closer than you think. You might say we're America's largest local brewer." To solidify this sense of locality, Budweiser directs consumers to its website Trackyourbud.com, where drinkers can identify the footprint of a purchased Budweiser. Drinkers contribute to Budweiser's identity by networking drinking (interpellation) with the specific brewery that produced the can or bottle in their hand (appellation). While *terroir* is not a synonym for *local*, Budweiser conflates the two terms in order to produce an emotional connection for its consumer. Such a conflation, like crafty, would not be well received in a craft beer social network.

It's easy to be cynical about Budweiser's conflation of locality with advertising, or even to call this ecology connecting digital tracking to a brewery "crafty."[1] Despite having Budweiser brewed at a plant nearby or almost nearby (for me that would be St. Louis, a five-hour drive away), Budweiser is not a local beer. Its definition of terroir (tracking where the beer was made) does not fit into my aggregation of St. Louis (the place we normally associate Budweiser with), an aggregation that includes Schlafly, 4 Hands, Perennial, Six Row, Civic Life, and Urban Chestnut. Budweiser's definition of local would not fit with any local movement found across the country. Its definition is more akin to Greg Koch's critique of crass commercialism: "I promote local pride, not jingoism."[2] Budweiser's definition also resembles Feinberg's comment that "a beer without Terroir [sic] is a type of brand." Budweiser, of course, is a brand. The ad, however, believes that *someone will include* Budweiser in a personal or local terroir aggregation by visiting the website just as someone might label Blue Moon or Shock Top as craft beer. As soon as people decide to "track their Bud," terroir occurs. As soon as I aggregate or track my sense of Sonoma County, terroir occurs. Leaving aside issues of quality or taste, the logic is similar. Folksonomies were never meant to please all our concepts of place and beer. Folksonomies, for good or for bad, are associative.

Budweiser's all-inclusive nature of terroir would upset those who find terroir to be carefully defined in relationship to place. Jef Van den Steen, writing extensively about lambics, might find discomfort in a definition of terroir that includes Budweiser's superficial locality. Writing about Brussels, for instance, Van den Steen notes how important locality is to beer, particularly lambics:

> Until the late 19th century it was assumed that the wild yeasts required to get lambic to ferment occurred only in the valley of the River Zenne (in French: Senne) that flows through Brussels. Thus in 1839 the area in which lambic can be brewed was limited to Brussels and the immediately surrounding areas. (17)

In his 1996 *Scientific American* breakdown of lambic, Jacques De Keersmaecker positions the local even more specifically, drawing attention not just to place but to time as well:

> Not only does spontaneous fermentation of wort take place consistently only in a small area around Brussels, but it does so only from October until about April, when outside temperatures remain under 15 degrees C. Some seemingly minute conditions that could affect the balance of microbial flora and the growth rate of the microorganisms would also affect the fermentation sequence and, therefore, the final product. Just how minute some of these conditions may be is a matter of conjecture. (78)

From the nineteenth century to today, these definitions of lambic are believed by many *to be the definition.* That definition, or taxonomy, would exclude lambics produced by Allagash, Rivertown, Upstream, Upland, and others that do not have access to the Senne and its specific wild yeast strains. In that sense, *lambic,* such as terroir, would be a limited term for understanding a given experience. Its aggregation would be purely location based. Lambic or gueuze, the blends of lambics, would not be what the *Los Angeles Times* calls "a magic word that will make you sound like a craft beer expert" since it would be bound to a place far from Los Angeles, where the newspaper's readers are located (Verive). I would only be able to assume a beer is lambic, for instance, if I were drinking a Cantillon, not a Rivertown, as I will note in the final chapter.

Beervana blogger Jeff Alworth writes that because Cantillon's Jean Von Roy situates lambic within the tradition and place of Belgium and the specific Belgian valley of Payottenland (or Pajottenland), no other beer should be named a lambic if it does not share these features. Like the Brewers Association, Alworth makes a direct call for taxonomy, as opposed to a new-media-shaped folksonomy:

> It is the tradition of lambic-making, and now that the style is enjoying a bit of a renaissance, he'd [Von Roy] like you to remember this long tradition and what it means and has meant to his family (and the families of the other lambic-makers). When you think of lambic, think of the beers these brewers have kept alive in this little corner of the world for so long. It's not a huge request. (Alworth)

It is not a huge request to follow an anticipated taxonomy (whether a brewer or blogger makes that request) by acknowledging the vital role history plays in categorization schemes (lambic or otherwise). Traditions, as much as they preserve, also stifle meaning, and taxonomies display that problem. (Most brewers and drinkers, for example, no longer cling to the English distinctions between beer and ale or the German *Reinheitsgebot* because of how these taxonomies limit contemporary notions of craft). Settling on the anticipated taxonomy (what lambic is), Alworth assumes that his passionate connection to the taxonomy is strictly fact based, and not emotional. That is, Jean Von Roy may have an economic interest in the lambic label the way many food industries use the law to enforce appellation. But Alworth, a blogger who lives in Portland and far away from Cantillon, may also have interests beyond the legal or economic; he may be relying on persona as well. He may be relying on his love and appreciation of Belgian lambics, emotions that I, too, share. Persona, as I noted in the previous chapter, is an important actor in the network that generates terroir.

These emotional connections can be anticipated and presented as factual. When Stephen Beaumont writes on his blog that "Belgian beer is beer that is brewed and fermented in Belgium. Period," he is expressing an emotional taxonomy (no American craft brewer can brew a style called "Belgian") as a factual taxonomy (the label "Belgian" cannot define a type of beer or style because its land-based associations are too numerous to fit in one category) (Beaumont). "Belgian," for these writers, is already anticipated as a distinct category, and such categories must be defended. Instead of settling for that anticipated and expected response, I aggregate my lambic experiences in order to extend lambic from the yeast and air in Belgium (the common response) to an overall meaning that allows for my persona as well as other cultural or even economic meanings. Terroir, as a rhetorical process of social media, aggregates a number of meanings, even if we turn, in the end, to one definition.

Writing in the *Wall Street Journal*, William Bostwick situates his knowledge of lambic as such an aggregation, moving from the taxonomic status of Belgium—where he begins his lambic narrative noting its "centuries-old process"—to his first lambic experience in Maine, far away from Payottenland:

> I tasted my first American lambic in the woods north of Portland, Maine, in a rough-hewn shack behind the Allagash brewery, best known for its crisp, lemony White beer. There, members of an adventurous sect of American brewers are creating an astonishing and ancient beer anew.

An aggregated meaning is what most lambic consumers, such as I, possess. We are not able to experience lambic only in Belgium or via Belgian imports. Lambic as a sense of terroir has evolved and changed, moving physically and conceptually out of Payottenland and into homes and bars across the United States. My lambic aggregation (as terroir) is informed by Belgian lambics I've consumed but also by American breweries' lambics as well. One could say the same about Budweiser's sense of locality. Despite the promise of selling more beer by this advertising gimmick, Budweiser aggregates its production into the more generic term "local." Once Budweiser enters into a personal aggregation with its consumer base (if that ever does occur), it can be local for someone, even if not for me. Lambic works that way for me (and maybe not for a Belgian purist or someone who insists that lambic must come from the specific locale[3]). As Ron Jeffries of Jolly Pumpkin states, "How did I find out about lambics? Well, I like beer" (qtd. in Schroppfy). *Like* is the most ambiguous of all taxonomic systems. It is an assumption of taste. Like is the directive of social media taste, where a click or + sign assumes commonality or agreement. Like is what drives many relationships, between object and consumer, between object and industry, or between object and object. Like stretches the rhetorical and consumption tensions at stake in craft obsession. "I like beer" is an assumption, an assumption that, when combined with other assumptions and experiences, can define a given state, such as what is or is not lambic. Aggregation as an assumption or collection of assumptions reflects the social media assumptions we make about most of our experiences. I want to push this sense of like and assumption a bit further in my exploration of a networked terroir.

Aggregated Assumptions

For the most part, we associate locality with a place and not with what we like. Budweiser does. I do as well. Such is the traditional meaning of terroir.

"The traditional beers of Flanders and Payottenland are unlike any on the planet," Jeff Sparrow argues. "Each beer is more a product of the *terroir* of the brewery than simply the actual ingredients" (57). Terroir aggregates ingredients. When I map my mythic triangle of Pennsylvania, as I did in chapter 2, I identify my relationship to a specific place because of how I perceive a sense of locality relevant to Pennsylvania, one that connects me to a bad first beer review, the mob, family ties, and being Jewish. To that, I could add the birthplace of my daughter or the place of my wife's first academic job, if I felt that these items extend my associations of locality, or if I needed these "ingredients" to aggregate my identity within a place. In Kentucky my sense of "eating local" or "drinking local" is based on a notion of place that aggregates sentiment (support local business) with taste (fewer beer or food miles to the point of consumption equals freshness) with economics (keep dollars at home so that the local economy can prosper).

Roland Barthes understood this aggregation of ingredients into one sentiment or image or idea as "a message without a code" ("Rhetoric of the Image" 36). Reading an advertisement for a line of Italian Panzani products, Barthes calls such a message "Italianicity" for the way the ad's display of ingredients (a tomato, pasta, onions, and garlic in a string bag among yellow, red, and green colors) make up a sentiment of being Italian even if one does not know how to use the ingredients to make Italian food. Knowledge of *being Italian* already exists in the aggregated objects. Examining the assembled objects generates an association called "Italian." "The perceptual message and the cultural message" are assembled by the viewer of the ad so that a sense of what is Italian is understood ("Rhetoric of the Image" 36), even if that sense is not representational. Terroir functions similarly, whether it is identified in Sonoma or Payottenland, as locality is made the focal point of perceptual and cultural meaning. Knowledge already exists in a given cultural and perceptual meaning of place.

This focal point directs attention to one experience over another, often championing the local. During World War II, food writer M. F. K. Fisher wished for a more local beer drinking experience than the one she felt was dominating consumption:

> With trains full of soldiers and supplies rather than pale ale, perhaps factories can discover, as their fathers did thirty years ago, that a beer carried quietly three miles is better than one shot across three thousand on a fast freight. (333)

Even as I believe in such assumptions regarding locality, a place, as I've been describing so far, is an aggregation, not a pile of dirt or organisms in the air or even distance between brewery and glass. As a social rhetoric, place is not one single focal point of attention. "What is acting *at the same moment* in any place is coming from many other places, many distant materials, and many faraway actors," Bruno Latour writes (*Reassembling* 200, emphasis mine). Latour recognizes that materials, influence, people, advertisements, word of mouth, and various other items are always part of the current moment, whether one is drinking a Cantillon or a Budweiser or a beer from three miles away. An object or place may feel as if it is one thing (Lexington, Kentucky, or Cantillon), but it, in fact, consists of many physical and nonphysical items brought together, as Barthes demonstrated with an Italian food advertisement. What Latour calls *the same moment*, like the phrase *drink local*, is the place we associate with our beer. Whatever I may think about drinking local at Country Boy Brewing, Blue Stallion, Ethereal, or West Sixth Brewery in Lexington, Kentucky, materials (malt, hops), influence (other brewers), and faraway actors (employees' previous jobs or investor connections that led to the breweries' construction, consumers buying beer, the company that manufactures the cans, the origins of the equipment, the styles brewed or not brewed, former usage of the brewery, and even trademark lawsuits) are also part of the drinking local experience. (As an example of the last item listed, trademark lawsuits, in May 2013, brewing company Magic Hat sued West Sixth Brewery in Lexington for trademark violation. The response to this lawsuit in Kentucky, which was a show of support for West Sixth, reflected an allegiance to the local.)

"Drink local" as a statement of preference aggregates these parts into a specific local brewery that I invest my attention in. Drink local is a distributed campaign showcasing the network of individuals interested in local consumption. What is acting in my place when I drink local, as Latour might say, is part of what acts elsewhere when others opt to drink local. Even if we intend otherwise, the declaration for local—what we can also call "localicity"—always includes the other items aggregated into its specific sense of terroir. Even the call to engage the local is an aggregation, a movement from one place of discussion to the next. What is acting *in my place* when I announce my support for the local is what is acting on Beer Advocate's website when the Alström brothers advocate local exploration:

> Visit your local brewpub, pull up a seat at the bar and explore their beers. Visit a local brewery, take the tour and have some samples. Take home a growler of beer, too, because not only will the beer be extremely fresh, but you'll also be tempted to bring the empty back for a refill. (Beeradvocate)

The Alströms' statement regarding locality carries over into the moment that I or someone else in Lexington takes home a growler from a local brewery. Their statement regarding locality carries over into online moments such as a Google+ post I offered on May 30, 2012, of a West Sixth can and glass: "Drink local and make rolls for duck burgers."[4] For New Albanian's Roger Baylor, drinking local is an act of identity formation that allows for a unique investment outside of other influences: "Brewing locally is the pursuit that best unites the various stylistic, 'create and buy local,' consciousness-expanding, educational-broadening strands of beer endeavor into an expression that is unique to Kentuckiana. No other place can be exactly like we are" ("Wednesday Weekly: As They Say"). No other place can be exactly as we are because of the many Kentucky factors that create a Kentucky sense of local identity. Kentuckiana beer culture exists because of aggregation; Kentuckiana identity terroir is not a given on its own. Bluehorn Creative's Kentucky for Kentucky rebranding campaign—whose slogan is "Kentucky Kicks Ass"—showcases some of these aggregated items by drawing attention to Hunter S. Thompson, Johnny Depp, bourbon, the invention of the gas mask, the first place to sing "Happy Birthday," and other specificities (Kentucky for Kentucky). No other place is based on such items. Thus, we have Kentucky locality or a sense of Kentucky-icity (the state of being Kentucky). No other place, as well, can be like Indiana, Portland, California, or elsewhere, and that, as I began the previous chapter, is why I was already drawn to Pliny the Elder before tasting Pliny the Elder. My investment was aggregated for me into Sonoma County as a same moment consisting of other moments (historical, cultural, impressionistic). Budweiser, despite its nonlocal reach, wants that investment as well. It wants to be a part of the moment. *The moment*, though, is more than a glance at the brewery nearby or even the brewery found on a website by typing in an area code. The moment for craft beer, following Latour, is terroir. Terroir exceeds one moment or glance.

Terroir offers a common recognition of this point for wine—the earth, water, and minerals are always a part of the wine experience because they consolidate into a recognizable moment. Even this traditional taxonomy

My Google+ post about drinking locally

recognizes aggregation. Latour's moment, because of its complexity, must be traced; its actors must be identified through difficult descriptions and attention. Each connection, each item in the network, must be carefully described (Pliny the person, Pliny the beer, an e-mail update, an online purchase, Missouri, grapefruit, Sonoma County, another trade done in Kentucky years later, drinking at the Russian River brewpub with my daughter, etc.). Latour's moment does not assume that only earth, water, and minerals make up a place. Budweiser locality—for the average consumer—can be summed up in a website that tracks your Bud; there is no tracing in the network sense when one engages with Budweiser this way. The consumer makes a quick assumption without tracing or describing the other actors involved in brewing Budweiser (actors that might challenge the idea of locality because of mass production or the actual factory involved). Assumptions are moments of delivery. They establish an easy reception of a message (Budweiser is local, for instance, because the website shows me a nearby factory). In craft beer we can make a similar assumption regarding terroir as long as we acknowledge the humans and objects specifically coming together "in the same moment" that are not bound to the earth; that are, in fact, aggregated in their networked moments of delivery. Lambic is not bound to the earth anymore than Budweiser. Among these humans and emotions might be assumptions such as a lambic can only come from the valley of the River Senne. The size of a bottle is another assumption. The ecology of appellation and Champagne that I noted earlier returns with bottle size because of how assumption generates aggregations in various networks of meaning.

Object Aggregation

A 750-millimeter cork-and-caged bottle is part of one assumption network. Even, as Garrett Oliver writes, the 750-millimeter cork-and-caged bottle is not bound to wine (or even to champagne) and has long been associated with beer culture; a typical assumption when encountering the bottle in a grocery or liquor store might be "wine" ("'Wine-ification'"). That assumption might trigger positive audience response (wine is good; this must be good) or negative audience assumptions (beer is acting too much like wine; it's pretentious). The assumption associates the bottle with a place or habit. For instance, 375-millimeter bottles might trigger *my* California assumptions. Russian River and the Lost Abbey use the same 375-millimeter bottle for Consecration, Supplication, Angel's Share, Cuvee de Tomme, and other beers. When I receive Almanac's Barrel Noir in a trade (the same trade that delivered the May 2013 Pliny the Elders), my California assumption is triggered again. Almanac uses the same size of bottle as Russian River and Lost Abbey do, and it is from San Francisco. All of these breweries are further aggregated for me by bottle type, size, and location.

Bottle assumptions, Clay Risen writes in the *New York Times*, confuse aggregation: "Many beer drinkers are uncomfortable with the notion of drinking beer like wine, to be split among several people and pondered. And the idea of drinking a 750-milliliter bottle alone can be daunting." Gina Pace, of the *New York Daily News*, repeats this assumption. "Stick a cork in it," she mockingly writes. "Wine is done." Pace's reporting highlights bottle size as the basis of this assumption. Bigger bottles, Pace assumes, are novel, and in this novelty beer drinkers share wine drinkers' habits:

The so-called large-format bottles range in size, shape and style, from metal-capped offerings that look like normal beer bottles on steroids to cork- and cage-topped carafes fit for Champagne. Like bottles of wine, these drinks are meant for sharing—especially the massive 1.5-liter "magnum" bottles.

Assumptions, as they are repeated by Pace and in other popular news coverage, stem from the aggregation of culture (how a beverage is thought to be consumed), habit (the kinds of bottled beverages one buys), memory (thoughts of packaging), and taste (what comes out of a bottle that shares the same size). Based on these aggregations (aggregations encountered in news media, experience, and elsewhere), the consumer makes a positive or negative assumption when viewing the 750-millimeter bottle on a shelf. Jay Brooks identifies the negative aspects of assumptions regarding bottle shape or size:

> The other assumption is that everything else is trying to be like wine, that anything trying to be a well made, good product on its own has to be aspiring to be like wine, it can't just want to be good for its own reasons. ("Big Bottles Equals Wine?")

Brooks, whose blog documents visual histories of beer advertising trends and attitudes, points to a number of large-sized bottles that predate current interest in the 750-millimeter cork-and-caged size. In that sense, he traces the "in the same moment" aspect of the bottle by pointing to Budweiser's and Anchor's earlier usages of the bottle size. Van den Steen notes that cork-and-caged bottles were used for lambics in the late nineteenth century: "The bottles were sealed with a self-cut (almost square) and tied tight with cord. The first bottles were placed in a hayloft between the warm hay bales and . . . exploded" (22). In Édouard Manet's 1882 painting *A Bar at the Folies-Bergère*, on the counter in front of the barmaid are 750-millimeter bottles of Bass beer. Will Anderson's *The Beer Book*, a 1972 guide to collecting beer memorabilia, offers numerous photographs of late nineteenth-century 750-millimeter bottles from breweries such as City Brewery of Elizabethtown, New Jersey; Dawson and Son from New Bedford, Massachusetts; Buffalo Brewing from Sacramento, California; and Park Brewing from Winona, Minnesota, among others. Advertisements from Evans's India pale ale from Hudson, New York, and Imperial Beer from Beadleston and Worerz in New York City also depict 750-millimeter bottles (Anderson 40). I add to these observations the scene in Quentin Tarantino's *Django Unchained* in which one of the lead characters is handed a flip-top 750-millimeter bottle of beer. The year is 1863.

These usages, once traced, show us that what is acting in this moment—the 750-millimeter bottle—happens in other moments (early usages). *In the same moment* indicates that objects have histories that extend assumptions regarding terroir. Even a 1977 Lowenbrau commercial, without the 750-millimeter bottle present, taps into this emotional history. A group of men are at a steakhouse. One of the men orders "the biggest steak you've got and a bottle of Lowenbrau." A friend at the table responds, "You're a genius" ("1977 Lowenbrau Commercial"). In this *same moment*, beer is conflated with wine, when an expensive meal is accompanied by a supposedly expensive beer. The assumption is that Lowenbrau is as good as an expensive wine (even if it is brewed by Miller, the brewery with cheap connotations). Assumptions don't need proof because they are emotional networks of meaning. Assumptions can be culturally or historically forgotten, as Oliver argues. A 750-millimeter bottle, assumed to be beer acting like wine, can also limit opportunities to rethink terroir. If I or anyone else stops in a grocery aisle possessing a wine assumption and notices a 750-millimeter bottle, terroir aggregation stalls or becomes something else entirely. I, as much as the bottle, play a role in aggregation. Not every consumer has access to these aggregations I identify; not every craft consumer is caught within the obsessive nature of networked terroir as I am. Without access to this network of moments I briefly trace here, I may assume that beer has no connection to the 750-millimeter size (Oliver's critique of Risen), and I may assume that "beer is acting like wine," as many newspaper accounts attest. The network facilitates assumptions—from what is lambic to what is it to be Italian to what is local to what one drinks out of a 750-millimeter bottle—into knowledge. That knowledge, though, comes from one's desire to trace the network and enter into these aggregations.

Oklahoma Assumptions

Assumption generates the terroir network, acting as another element aggregated among the physical and historical items collected within a sense of terroir so that it becomes an "object" affecting other objects within various networks of meaning. Despite my initial reservations regarding anecdotes, I will interrupt this chapter with my own assumption anecdote about purchasing a 750-millimeter bottle of beer. Recently, my assumptions about terroir were disrupted by Prairie Artisan Ales, a small brewery out of Krebs, Oklahoma. I discovered Prairie's beers at The Beer

Trappe, a local beer shop I frequent in the Lexington neighborhood Chevy Chase. In 750-millimeter bottles, Prairie Artisan Ales stood out on the shelves as another local (American as opposed to their Belgian inventory) Shelton Brothers–distributed beer. By producing saisons and sour beers in a small town in Oklahoma, Prairie Artisan challenges beer assumptions regarding these styles, assumptions typically associated with locales such as Belgium, where the saison reigns as indicative of the region's beer production. Belgium is often identified with the tradition of brewing saisons, just as it is for lambics:

> *Saisons* were brewed at the beginning of winter in a farmhouse brewery in order to quench the thirst of the farmhands who worked in the fields in the summer. The saisons that were brewed in the winter had to survive the spring without becoming too infected. Sometimes these beers were called *saisons d'été* or summer *saisons*. (De Baets 98)

"A true farmhouse ale," Phil Markowski adds, "conveys a sense of origin; a great one, transcendence. You feel the rusticity, imagine the field and sense the unpredictability of the season—the liquid summation of 'terroir'" (24). The wild and funky characteristics of Prairie Artisan beers can be placed within the larger network of beers called saison, Belgian, sour, or more specifically lambic—even though these are not identical taxonomies; they are *assumed* taxonomies where meaning conflation occurs. Prairie Artisan beers assume these characteristics even though they are not brewed on a farm or for farmhands' thirst. With Prairie Artisan I may sense the rusticity Markowski describes, but rusticity is not often associated with Krebs, Oklahoma, a city that one social media website claims is famous for "its many Italian restaurants" ("Krebs, Oklahoma"). We can point to the specific conditions that give rise to Cantillon's lambics, as Van den Steen suggests—the wild yeast living in the Belgian air that settles in the wort and creates off flavors. Can we point to the conditions that produce a saison in Krebs, Oklahoma?

Even more than the wild yeast, as I've noted in this chapter, emotional connections to lambic and Belgium make Cantillon's take on the dry and somewhat funky saison more special than what other breweries do. When I rush to a local store to buy Cantillon (after my waiting and waiting, delivery is marked by my receiving a tweet that a few bottles have arrived and my waiting may have ended), I do so because of taste (the beer tastes good) as much as I do so for the emotional connection (produced by any number of forces I've engaged with: taste, hype, scarcity, Belgium). As I noted with my previous Cantillon anecdote, the beer's star-like status already situates its terroir in the drinker's mind long before the first sip. Even beer writer Ben McFarland warns beer drinkers that drinking Cantillon Vigneronne requires such knowledge first: "This marvelously musty and mildewed three year old sherry-like ale is not really for learners, but rather for learned lambic lovers" (*World's Best* 99). According to this narrative, Cantillon needs to be in one's mind before consuming. It needs to be learned as a terroir experience.

The same emotional connections that extend from a Belgian valley to the beers it spawns apply to American beers as well. The sour that makes a beer like Russian River's Consecration or Lost Abbey's Cuvee de Tomme amazing is not bound to San Diego or Santa Rosa (the yeast is not native to California; the barrels are not native to California), but the emotional connection is. We create emotional categories—instead of taxonomic distinctions—and treat the beers and breweries as having like-minded terroir conditions. With place, we can group Bell's, Jolly Pumpkin, New Holland, and Founders together as much as we can group Great Divide, Odell, Crooked Stave, Funkwerks, and New Belgium. Emotional terroir allows us to do so. Emotional terroir is an aggregation. That terroir can be place bound (California or, more specifically, San Diego) or style bound (Funkworks and Crooked Stave in Colorado aggregate with Russian River and Lost Abbey).

All this causes me to ask, what is my emotional connection to Krebs, Oklahoma? I was born in Oklahoma on an army base, returned once in the early 1970s, and I have no idea where Krebs is located. I Googled the city, and I discovered that thirteen years ago its population was 2,051. This population number might have been calculated before the brothers Chase and Colin Healey, who run Prairie Artisan Ales, showed up in Krebs and began brewing beer. There may now be 2,053 people in Krebs. All the information I have to go on is what Google shows me. Google won't show me my emotional aggregation, and it won't tell me that Prairie Artisan Ales defies terroir. I tell myself that.

Prairie Artisan Ales upsets everything about the emotional expectations that connect land and beer. Budweiser's declaration of locality upsets strict definitions of terroir as well, but it does so because of its marketing ploy. A Budweiser does not defy terroir at the moment it is consumed. Based on taste and emotional response, it remains Budweiser. One does not confuse Budweiser with any other beer whose connections to a specific locale exist in our minds. Prairie Artisan Ales defies terroir. I initially experienced the idea of terroir defiance when tasting the lambic beers that Upstream—in Omaha, Nebraska—was producing via a rooftop coolship. Nothing about Omaha said lambic to me. Omaha, on the other hand, meant in-laws, who live in nearby Lincoln, and big snowstorms and boredom (for me). Upstream's gueuze lambic yielded notes of apple and tartness that reminded me of many Belgian gueuzes. I experienced that feeling of "being reminded" again when I drink a Prairie Gold from Prairie Artisan Ales. This is not a lambic, I said to myself while reading the bottle's label. Nothing on the label indicates lambic. Prairie does not use a coolship. It doesn't blend beers to make Gold. It can't make lambics. But Gold tasted like a lambic: tart, lambic aroma, lemon, semidry. When I rated the beer on RateBeer, I included these terms. Whether or not anyone else makes this association does not matter. My own system of aggregation or network terroir prompts these thoughts for me (it works off of persona). With these senses conjuring images of familiar taste and associated location, Prairie Gold defies terroir. Oklahoma does not say lambic to our emotions the way Belgium or the valley along the River Senne might. Gold does. Gold changes my emotional connection to the aggregation known as lambic.

Bottle of Prairie Gold

Gold defies terroir because of aggregation. I have tried other Prairie beers since the moment that established this introductory anecdote, and I have found each one to embody everything I love in saisons and semidry slightly funky beers—for those of us who love such things because of how we aggregate taste. We can place Prairie Artisan Ales among some of the best breweries in the craft beer business for the production of saisons and semidry slightly funky beers—along with Upright, Jolly Pumpkin, Southampton, and Hill Farmstead. We can place Krebs, Oklahoma, within the networked aggregation that brings to the foreground an idea such as saison, lambic, funky, or even Belgian. We can do so even if we recognize that Jolly Pumpkin (or whatever) is not Prairie Artisan Ales but rather part of one's networked terroir or cluster of experience. When I asked my wife to spend our honeymoon in Belgium, I recognized that sense of aggregation as the space of beer consumption. As long as we are getting married, I seemed to say, let's celebrate in a place that aggregates everything I then enjoyed about beer: Orval, Cantillon, Westmalle, Chimay, Delirium, Achouffe. Belgium served as an aggregation point where disparate meanings come together to generate one meaning, and our celebration would participate in that meaning system. When I sat in my Kentucky home drinking Prairie Gold, I recognized that special aggregation again. Couch. TV. Glass. Lexington. The Beer Trappe. These are not the points of aggregation. They are not focal points of attention. My emotional response is the point of aggregation; it forms the assumption I make. Defiance does not need to be a violent act, a rebellious act, or an act of resistance (like a revolution). Defiance is also an emotional and rhetorical reorganization of the aggregation we have come to accept as commonplace.

Distribution also contributes to how we defy terroir. If Prairie Artisan did not establish a distribution agreement with Shelton Brothers the way some similar saison-oriented American breweries have done (Jolly Pumpkin, Jester King, St. Somewhere), could I, in a place like Lexington, Kentucky, have the opportunity to confuse and defy a fairly common sense of terroir? Shelton Brothers takes Oklahoma to Kentucky in this case—much like the way it has brought Belgium to America. Terroir is a distributed and delivered experience (and I will discuss delivery more completely in the next chapters). Terroir is not a place-based experience in the ways we have come to understand it. If I—and everyone else who loves saisons and semidry slightly funky beers—continue drinking these fine beers from Krebs, Oklahoma, our sense of terroir will be completely fucked up. To be fucked up is to be completely confused about any given taxonomic distinction. To be fucked up is to be caught in the social network of folksonomic distinctions. When we are fucked up, we have to allow our senses, tastes, and intellectual framework to open up to Krebs, Oklahoma, the way we have opened up to Portland, Maine, or Portland, Oregon, or Belgium or any other aggregated sense of place. Because of one brewery? Yes. That's all it takes. One brewery in some kind of obscure farmhouse situation in the middle of nowhere where a little over 2,000 people live can fuck up a common sense of terroir. (For the record, Prairie Artisan Ales did announce the construction of a new brewery in Tulsa after I first wrote this chapter. Still, my introduction to Prairie began with Krebs.) Hill Farmstead did for Greensboro, Vermont, Oklahoma now does with Belgium; it distributes terroir and fucks up whatever we may think is the natural order of beer and location. Distribution fucks up assumptions, particularly when that distribution is not only physical (moving beer on trucks) but emotional.

Aggregated Taste

For those who are dedicated to the taxonomic status of terroir, my gesture to transfer it from a sense of place to one of aggregation may sound like amateurism, an amateurism that wants "fucked up" to become a classification for beers that defy terroir expectation. The expert understands the delicate and important connections that place generates for the consumption of wine or beer and would never suggest "fucked up" as a category. The amateur—who calls for "fucked up"—undermines expertise. Social media stress the amateur as the basis for user-generated experiences (like folksonomic definitions). I was an amateur when I misrated Weyerbacher. I am an amateur when I redefine a traditional sense of terroir.

Andrew Keen critiques Internet and social media culture because of the amateur's rise, calling those (i.e., the amateurs) who write or share content online "monkeys," who "can use their networked computers to publish everything from uninformed political commentary to unseemly home videos, to embarrassingly amateurish music, to unreadable poems, reviews, essays, and novels" (3). Keen laments the loss of old media giving way to "search engines, social media, sites, and video portals" (9). New media replace the expert, Keen argues, with the unimportant and problematic amateur whose fascination with the banal and the everyday works against the official and the institutional. With the amateur, we experience "the decline of the quality and reliability of the information we receive, thereby distorting, if not outrightly corrupting, our national civic conversation" (Keen 18). With craft beer, the expert, some similarly claim, conveys a nuanced and reliable comprehension of the delicate relationships among air, water, yeast, and dirt so that terroir remains a static definition bound to location or legal definition and is not caught up in personal networks of aggregation as I outline here. Aggregation marks a sense of the amateur, not the professional, and, by accounts such as Keen's, is disrupting the national conversation regarding beer by making such a conversation one to which *anybody can contribute*.

Andy Crouch proclaims aggregation to be an amateur experience regarding beer. Crouch remembers the initial appeal of aggregated beer writing spaces such as RSS that, via RSS readers (such as Google Reader), allow writers to distribute ideas to readers without their having to go to individual websites. Via RSS, writings arrive within one RSS reader (Google Reader, Feedly, the Old Reader, Netnewswire, etc.). Reading experiences extend from one or a few sources and eventually include multiple sources (from the armchair beer reviewer videotaping himself in his bedroom to the "professional" beer writer whose work is edited and published in a recognized magazine with a Universal Product Code prominently displayed). The appeal of RSS, Crouch feels, does not expose multiple writings (and multiple viewpoints); instead it yields to repetition by amateur writers (bloggers). Originality is victim to the "anyone can publish and distribute" model that RSS promotes and supports:

> I remember being genuinely excited when I first experienced the RSS beer heaven that was Real Simple Beer Syndication. Confronted with hundreds of beer blog entries every day, I thought for sure that some distinctive voices would result. Over the years, I find myself coming back to the professional beer writing set (not that its members are all top-notch either) for readable content. Perhaps the retread nature of so much beer writing was initially necessary as beer writing established itself. ("Another Lament")

Retread indicates the amateur, of a topic or subject returned to multiple times, often without knowledge of previous mentions. Pete Brown echoes Crouch when he comments on the "rut" of online beer writing, a rut that sounds like amateurism:

> Our online beer conversation does seem to have settled into a complacent rut. It's not any one person, but taken as a whole we all seem to be writing about what awesome beers we've had recently, how extreme they are, how rare they are, how hoppy or how aged they are. Beer blogs have become an online beer geek diary, a hi-tec [*sic*] glorified form of ticking. ("Wikio Rankings")

One writer's retread or repetitive rut is another's contagion. The retreaded narrative or critique annoys when it adds little to a circulated conversation. On the other hand, such retreads, or contagions, indicate a widely circulated conversation: that is, a common focus on a particular idea whose repetition speaks to broad interests, or following Tony Sampson, where "imitative rays relate one person to a world of things" (41). An anecdote about one's first time drinking a beer is not a retread when the tracing of its repetition reveals a common experience whose meaning extends beyond the repetitive moment and into a larger conversation of "things." The same holds true for terroir discussions.

When Crouch laments "retread" writing, he might imagine writing that does not extend or advance a conversation, writing trapped in basic approaches to terroir or aggregation because of how it stays *in a moment* (and doesn't connect moments). Crouch might have in mind writing typically associated with social media, "the kind of quick, unfocused thought that results in a scarcity of coherent sentences and a limited vocabulary," which Marc Bauerlein has been cited as claiming that social media platforms encourage (Keller). Crouch might have in mind something akin to Bauerlein's critique that "a more circumspect glance finds that bad grammar, teen colloquialisms, and shallow ironies litter the blogs, comment threads, and social networking sites" (132). Crouch might have in mind writing he feels does not involve grand narrative ideas. He might have in mind the video amateur, whose understanding of expression, Jean Burgess writes, is "buried deep in the DNA of the brand" (54).

That DNA, however, distributes craft terroir by allowing assumptions and fucked up moments to circulate and be shared (enriching overall understandings of beers and the places they come from). Deep in the DNA of YouTube's amateurs, Crouch might have in mind reviewers like the Michigan couple who videotape themselves drinking beer for a series they call Sunday Morning Beers (Life with Beer). Uploaded to the LifewithBeer YouTube channel, the videos celebrate the couple—sometimes in their pajamas—sitting side by side, in matching recliners, sharing thoughts on a beer or two. Or Crouch might have in mind the Georgia-based VideoBeerReviews YouTube channel, where on June 1, 2009, the members reviewed Pliny the Elder (reading the Pliny the Elder hops story off the bottle's label) (VideoBeerReviews). In a retread or contagion moment, VideoBeerReviews identified pine in Pliny, too, but not citrus or grapefruit. Fellow online "amateur" Greg's Beer Reviews five hundredth review notes the "piney hops" and "citrusy" aroma of Pliny the Elder before also reading the label's recognition of its historical namesake ("Beer Review #500"). Rob of the blog *The Daily Beer Review*, whose reviews are not on YouTube, might not be distinctive enough for Crouch as well. In his March 3, 2011, review of Pliny the Elder, Rob also notes the label's story of the historical Pliny and remarks on the pine and citrus flavors (Beer Drinker Rob). If retread is merely repetition, Crouch would reject such observations, whether performed from a recliner or a laptop, a video or a blog. RSS aggregation of online reading, in this case, provides the recirculation of common ideas (such as a beer's taste or the aroma of pine, observations, as I noted, that Crouch also has made) and wouldn't actually aggregate experience. Retread also offers a rhetorical gesture associated with contagion acts, the ways anecdotes are as well. When I put these Pliny moments into relationship with the previous Pliny moments I've noted, I see the larger conversation regarding this beer. In that sense, retread also shapes a sense of terroir. Retread offers an important part of an overall craft obsession.

When I first began reading about beer online, I, like Crouch, relied on Real Simple Beer Syndication.[5] When the RSS beer feed was disabled, I switched to a long list of 241 beer blogs aggregated on Google Reader. When Google Reader was shut down, I switched my RSS to the Old Reader. My reliance on so-called amateur writing has not waned. "Who the hell reads this stuff," Alan McLeod, of *A Good Beer Blog*, asks about online beer writing ("Do Writers"). It appears that I do. I read this "stuff" every day. My reading aggregation continues because the process of understanding or assembling terroir does not end. As a beer outsider (I am an academic writing about rhetoric and digital media; I am not a beer historian or an expert at tasting), I don't share Crouch's objections to amateurism. In fact, the so-called amateur writings, posts, images, and reviews that I encounter online inform my terroir-based thinking as much as other parts of the aggregation network do, parts that also include Crouch's writings and other professional publications. My own beer weblog, *Make Mine Potato*,[6] can be read from RSS and once was available from Real Simple Beer Syndication. I don't review beers, but I do try to write about experiences, ideas, rants, travels, my kids, daily consumption, and other matters that may seem amateurish. If I am not an amateur academic writer, I am likely an amateur beer writer.

My beer writings are aggregated in other ways as well. Whenever I rate a beer on RateBeer, for some reason I don't understand, I allow RateBeer to send my rating to Twitter. This may be a moment of simple information sharing (look at what I am drinking today), or it may be my role in extending digital footprints (my terroir reaches farther via the tweet), or it may be a moment of the humble brag (look at what I'm drinking!). A great deal of information on Twitter is shared in such ways: photographs, links, retweets. The minute my tweet is sent out from RateBeer it is aggregated in my followers' feeds. Those feeds are further extended and shared, or even retreaded. Every now and then on Twitter, for example, someone named Natedawg27 (Nathaniel Southwood) identifies me in a tweet by my Twitter name and informs the Twitterverse that I have a "top story" in the Nate Dawg Bugle.[7] Like any writer—academic or otherwise—I love having a top story, and I'm honored to have a top story, or, at least, the assumption of a top story. Only, I don't know Natedawg or his Bugle. And what is being billed as a "top story" is neither top nor a story. It's a tweet I have sent out via the RateBeer option to tweet your ratings. If my tweet is a top story, critics such as Crouch or Keen would likely condemn it as quintessential amateurism and surely a sign of the decline of online writing. One such tweet billed as a top story was, in fact, a rating for Troegs Scratch 71. The tweet was probably two or three sentences long. Whatever minimal importance it had for me, the Nate Dawg Bugle was "impressed."

My tweet is not a top story for a Bugle newspaper or even retread writing but a moment of Internet aggregation regarding sense of place. This Dawg site, run by the Paper.li "start your own newspaper" social media site, aggregates content the way Google News does or Real Simple Beer Syndication once did or the way my understanding of terroir does. Users aggregate a selection of sources that they find valuable. Such aggregation marks a great deal of contemporary reading habits, including my own. New media apps sort information for us based on what we tell such apps we like or don't like (as Amazon does for our consuming habits) and organize these tastes or interests around various associations and metadata. Our tastes dictate aggregation in most cases; in this way, I subscribed to Real Simple Beer Syndication, or I organize my current RSS by the

Screenshot of NateDawg27 aggregating drfabulous

Screenshot of Nate Dawg Bugle aggregating a RateBeer rating

category "Beer." Beer is a generic taxonomy for my online reading. In the case of my top story, the person running Nate Dawg Bugle seems to find random RateBeer rating tweets as worth aggregating. Did his readership tell him that my two-sentence ratings are worth aggregation? Or did he merely fall into Crouch's rhetorical trap of retreading content? Or did a computer bot simply tap into keywords I shared as being indicative of the terroir (the sense of beer related to experience or place), which Natedawg27 finds important and at some point may have scheduled his aggregator to locate? These keywords take the place of content. They become the "amateur" writing Crouch finds so problematic.

Keywords shape discourse. Soil, water, and yeast shape discourse regarding terroir. Keywords anchor meaning in sentences, essays, movements, and larger conversations and create what Raymond Williams called "a shared body of words and meanings in our most general discussions" (15). All discussions share terms and ideas, whether tasting notes (citrus, pine), experience (first time), or ideology (revolution). One area of content—expressed via shared words—I find myself returning to or retreading in this discussion of aggregation and terroir is Pliny the Elder, which is my exigence for this chapter and the previous one and is a keyword, for me, regarding terroir. On August 17, 2008, on *Make Mine Potato*, I wrote about my first experience drinking Pliny.[8] "The honey. The hops. The bitterness. Lots of citrus. Total floral aroma. This is the beer obsession revolves around." I don't find my writing particularly professional or informational. It is a bit of retread as well. It is, however, just as much a part of the terroir of Pliny as any other mention I've shared in these two chapters. My discussion of Pliny the Elder is preempted in the same blog entry by a photograph of a bottle of Vered IPA (Vered is my daughter's name), a homebrewed IPA made by my brother-in-law with my daughter's picture on the bottle. Daughter and Russian River juxtapose in what is still part of my parental beer tale from the introduction, for that parental story aggregates the way terroir aggregates moments to bottles to blog posts. My daughter has entered my sense of Russian River/Pliny the Elder terroir. Terroir might convey a professional taxonomy; the blog writer might convey amateurism. Neither meaning, though, is stable in a world of aggregation. Aggregation—RSS or the terroir sense of aggregation I demonstrate in this chapter—allows for a networked experience that the expertise of terroir, as its taxonomic status defines it, does not accommodate.

Even if I am an amateur in my shift of terroir from dirt to aggregation, I frame terroir within the context of social media. When I read the network of aggregations I receive in my reader on a given day, I encounter reviews, news releases, historical work, reports of industry fighting, a comic, videos, rants, excitement, critiques, tweets, and so on. Real Simple Beer Syndication is defunct, but the professional side of aggregation is still captured by websites such as Beer Pulse and Beer Journal, and the amateur aggregation is captured by sites such as Paper.il, all of which aggregate for readers

Vered IPA brewed by Wes Detweiler

press releases, personal writing, and news items. My reading experiences via aggregation involve a great deal of waiting (like Bill Brown's drinkers waiting in the nineteenth century for beer). I obviously wait for someone to write. Reports of beer releases start my feeling of waiting (when it will come out, will we get it in Kentucky, which stores will get it, how many cases will local stores get). If terroir, then, is as much emotional as it is physical, the feeling of waiting, in the nineteenth century like today, must be incorporated into this network of meaning.

With this waiting, I interrupt these aggregations so that I consider a particular space that began much of this conversation I have been tracing, the Russian River brewpub in Santa Rosa. Russian River's Pliny the Elder, as I alluded to already, was a beer I had waited a long time to try, largely because of place assumptions. My blog post that juxtaposes my first Pliny with my daughter's picture on a beer bottle captures the emotional connection I have with Russian River on the level of being a parent. One parental beer tale I take with me into all of this aggregation, and noted in the introduction, is my visit to Russian River with my daughter during my fortieth-birthday beer trip to Northern California.

Waiting for Terroir

Bill Brown documented the waiting involved in nineteenth-century beer drinking. Acknowledging "beers worth waiting for," Eric Asimov lists what he considers to be vintage ales served at a dinner at Gramercy Tavern: a 2002 Victory Golden Monkey, 2001 and 2004 Brooklyn Monster Ales, and a 1998 J. W. Lees Harvest Ale ("Beers Worth"). Blogger Jay Brooks has discovered a 1941 Schlitz advertisement that portrays individuals waiting in line to vote ("Beer in Ads #730"). And HeBrew's Messiah Bold (its maker, Jeremy Cowan, was featured in an anecdote in chapter 2) is credited in its tagline as being "the beer you've been waiting for." Each day I wait for feeds to produce for me ideas and information relevant to craft beer. Social media, more generally, might be described as information waiting. At some point, we expect and anticipate, someone will post an idea, news item, photograph, or other piece of information. According to one study, the typically tolerated wait time for a Web page to load is two seconds (Nah). Waiting is temporal, but it is emotional as much as it is knowledge based.

Some people wait for a beer's significance to be explained. Pete Brown describes how craft drinkers wait to taste their beers, and in that waiting, the significance of what they are drinking can settle in via taste:

Being beer writers, there's no chink of glasses and quick, deep pull. In this company the correct procedure is to contemplate the beer a little more carefully, looking first at its appearance, then swirling it to get the aroma, before holding on your tongue to appreciate its fullness of flavour and texture. (*Three Sheets to the Wind* 63)

The unnamed beer's meanings arrive with patience. Even if Cilurzo drew upon the naturalism of Pliny to name his double IPA after the noted historian, is Pliny the product of terroir and of waiting? Pliny's emotional significance depends on waiting. I am not the only one to recall waiting prior to trying Pliny for the first time; in fact, I am part of a larger network of contagion waiting moments, moments that might resemble Brown's tasting scenario or simply waiting in line patiently. One beer reviewer begins a YouTube video review of Pliny the Elder by stating, "I've wanted to try it for quite a long time" (Moeckel). A reviewer on Beer Advocate writes, "I have waited a long time for this to be available and it was worth the wait" (Rkuhnel). Another Beer Advocate rater proclaims, "I'd been waiting to try this beer and I had a lot of expectations and it met and exceeded every one" (Willijschmidt). Waiting is part of the overall terroir aggregation experience that repeats and retreads.

I, too, experienced the sense of waiting for Pliny and Russian River beyond that first online order. In the fall of 2010, we landed in San Francisco for my fortieth-birthday trip, a trip my wife offered so that I could celebrate getting old by drinking beer in a part of the country whose terroir greatly affected me. In a rented Pontiac whose gearshift was set below the steering wheel like a 1970s muscle car, we followed our Garmin's directions to Santa Rosa to make our first stop of the trip at Russian River. Unfortunately, the Garmin took us through downtown San Francisco on our way to the brewpub. As we moved slowly through the city and stopped at every traffic light on the way, I lost my cool. The emotional buildup of waiting overcame me as I sat in traffic. I freaked out. I began yelling in the car. My target, Russian River, felt hours away. I also had misjudged the time it would take to drive to Santa Rosa and grew increasingly frustrated along the way about the time we were losing driving (and not drinking). My wife, likely, was watching my meltdown and quickly regretting the idea of spending my fortieth in Northern California.

Without the freak out, my experience was not unlike Trubek's own travels to Sonoma County (contagion). As she writes,

> As part of my research on terroir and the taste of place, I spent time in Northern California, especially in Sonoma County. My family accompanied me for the first part of the trip. We arrived in San Francisco and did all the usual airport activities—luggage, car rental car seat—and then packed ourselves into a shiny red car and our way north. (108)

In the back of our not-so-shiny car was my daughter strapped into a rented car seat. To my left was my exasperated wife. In the driver's seat was a fanatical beer drinker. I was driving to Russian River because of terroir. Besides Pliny, there are other beers with strong hop profiles. Besides Consecration and Supplication, there are other beers aged in barrels. Besides Temptation and Beatification, there are other sour beers. My associations with Russian River are taste based, of course (I like their beer; I pause before Pliny reaches my lips; I take in the aroma first), but also emotional since, when planning the trip, I gravitated toward Russian River first and not toward other breweries offering similar options. What I've read (listed here), what I've consumed, what I've thought. These, too, are characteristics of terroir. They accumulated in an overall sense of waiting for a moment to appear. I had been aggregating this trip for a long time.

Aggregation is not an immediate experience. It involves waiting. My experience with waiting, waiting to visit Russian River, waiting through San Francisco traffic, waiting through a longer than expected drive, is part of the terroir network that encompasses information distribution as well as a beer's taxonomic status. This experience, too, is felt when craft beer lovers search out the rare and once-a-year-released Pliny the Younger, described thus by Russian River: "Pliny the Younger was Pliny the Elder's nephew, in the case of this beer, the 'Younger' is a triple IPA. Pliny the Younger is hopped three times more than our standard IPA, and is dry hopped four different times." Every February, Russian River releases a limited amount of Younger at its brewpub and distributes a few kegs to selected accounts in its network of distribution. The waiting for Pliny the Younger begins prior to and during the release week as patrons wait in line for the chance to experience a small four- to eight-ounce pour. "Pliny the Elder Released," a *Huffington Post* headline reads, "Fans line up" (Robertson). "This is what the line for Pliny the Younger Looks Like" a Serious Eats story states, with accompanying photograph (Hoffman). By 10:00 A.M., February 2013, three hundred people were waiting in line outside Russian River's Santa Rosa brewpub, the blog *Beer Nuts* reports

(Strader). "The moment you have all been waiting for!!!" Seattle's Brouwer's Café declares on its blog to announce the 4:00 P.M. 2012 tapping of Pliny the Younger ("The Moment"). To this day, I am still waiting for Pliny the Younger. Since I live in Kentucky, which is not part of Russian River's distribution network, and since my meltdown may have convinced my wife never to return with me to Santa Rosa in a not-so-distant February, I may wait for some time.

Pliny the Younger offers up an aggregation made of reputation, hype, desire, and waiting. All of these items aggregate into the taxonomy of triple or double IPA that Pliny the Younger holds (and it has almost a quarter of the ratings as Elder has on RateBeer). Waiting is investment (time, emotion, money). Waiting connects to what Marshall McLuhan and Quentin Fiore called engagement. "Because of electric speed," they write about technological engagement, "we can no longer wait" (*Medium* 63). The speed of digital delivery—like waiting a lengthy two seconds for a Web page to appear—makes involvement instantaneous. The website One Second shows how many Tumblr posts, Instagram photos, and tweets appear every second, a time span—no matter how quickly passed—we can assume people are learning about each other. McLuhan described such involvement as the product of cool media, media that engage or cause involvement. In an age of involvement, waiting shifts from mere standing around to a type of media engagement.

Hayagreeva Rao associates McLuhan's notion of cool media with the rise of the craft beer movement. Rao calls those who built craft beer "market rebels," thus drawing on the "revolution" trope I identified with craft confidence narratives, a trope that engages readers with the sense of independence and individuality:

> The challenge for market rebels becomes how to forge a collective identify and mobilize support by articulating a *hot cause* that arouses emotion and creates a community of members, and relying on *cool mobilization* that signals the identity of community members and sustains their commitment. (7)

Cool media, McLuhan taught, enact participation (users fill in details of images or sound in order to make sense of the message delivered). Hot media, he countered, do not enact participation (the message needs no further work; no waiting is required). Terroir—such as what kinds of beer deserve the label "lambic"—is a hot message that evokes intense feelings because recipients of the message may feel no need to alter it.

These feelings indicate a sense of commitment or belief different from the aggregated (cool) terroir I am promoting, one that allows for recipient engagement; I fill in the message with other items based on my specific engagement (persona, assumption, taste, waiting, etc.). That Pliny the Elder or Younger enacts a hot cause (we respond directly to the message of rare release with no further interpretation or consideration) or cool mobilization (we become engaged by lining up and waiting) need not be directly caused by Russian River or any particular actor in the overall aggregated terroir network. For Rao, though, this network has ties to actual distribution networks: "Beer enthusiasts were rebels who constructed a hot cause (the atrocious taste of mass-produced beer) and relied on a cool mobilization (small brewpubs using traditional methods and authentic artisanal techniques that offered distinctive beers and, therefore, added to cultural diversity)" (45).

One aspect of this cool mobilization, as Rao understands craft beer, is the enthusiasm that beer evangelists engage with when promoting the products they love to consume. One aspect of this cool mobilization is terroir, whose sense of place is tied to promotion and its delivery via aggregation. These individuals who promote, whom Malcolm Gladwell calls "Connectors," will be an important part of the next two chapters' focus on distribution and networks. In particular, Connectors, and I am one as well, play a significant role in mobilizing distribution from its physical form—delivering beer from brewery to market—to its rhetorical form—delivering messages over time, participants, spaces, and, of course, beer itself. Like other aspects of craft obsession, delivery is not without its tensions and contradictions. Chapters 5 and 6 elaborate networked terroir as networked delivery in order to better understand the cool mobilization of distribution as a communicative act.

CHAPTER 5
Craft Delivery

SOCRATES: So you affirm that pleasure is felt in the act of drinking?
CALLICLES: Certainly. —Plato, *Gorgias*

In the 1935 short film *Three Little Beers*, the Three Stooges are employed in the delivery department of the fictional Panther Brewing. In order to drink some of the beer they deliver to others, the Stooges enter a golf tournament where fourth prize is a keg of Panther. Most of the beer narrative toward acquiring the keg is interrupted by the golf story, complete with traditional jokes about noise on the golf course bothering golfers and jokes about not knowing how to play the game. The beer narrative returns to the film only in a final slapstick scene of wayward barrels rolling down

Scene from Three Little Beers. Columbia Pictures

the street, delivered to the wrong destination. Delivery, in this case, is out of control, and one would expect as much from the Three Stooges and their antics.

Beer Barrel Polecats, the Three Stooges' other beer movie, from 1946, takes up the theme of wayward delivery, too. Its narrative begins with the Stooges reading a pamphlet—"How to Make Panther Pilsner Beer." But the pamphlet's delivery of instructional information is countered by Moe's bad reading:

> MOE: Now let me see, in order to make ten gallons of beer, pour one can of hopes.
> LARRY: Hops!
> MOE: Hops.

Eventually Moe, Larry, and Curly each add three cakes of yeast to the wort, not knowing that the others have added the ingredient as well. The result is a predictable mess of overfermented beer and, eventually, exploding bottles. The message (beer-making instructions) fails to reach its destination (collaborators who cannot successfully collaborate) despite the ease of media used (pamphlet). In both of these Stooges' moments, delivery, the simple arrival of message or product, is unsuccessful.

Delivery is important for beer. Unlike the Stooges' antics, *Smokey and the Bandit*'s canonical 1977 narrative about a twenty-eight-hour Coors beer run from Atlanta to Texarkana and back to Atlanta involves success. While Bandit and Snowman deliver the beer on time, a question remains. How did all these cases of Coors beer end up in Texarkana, a dry county, in the first place? By law, one would not have been able to buy Coors in Texarkana, Texas, in 1977. The film's narrative has delivered an incorrect message. The joke is on us, the audience, who in 1977 may have thought that Coors could be purchased in Texarkana (or even that Coors was rare and worthy of a twenty-eight-hour smuggling escapade).

The joke of misunderstood messages (not reading instructions properly, not knowing others have added ingredients, not portraying geographic facts correctly) is a familiar contagion in popular culture's relationship with beer. In the 1933 film *What! No Beer?* Jimmy Durante's character, Jimmy Potts, standing at the fermenter, asks Buster Keaton's character, Elmer J. Butts, "Do you think we put in enough yeast?" When they open the fermenter to check, a flood of foaming wort comes pouring out. Beer evokes misunderstanding. In *Day at the Races*, Groucho Marx's character, Otis B. Driftwood, calls out, "Two beers, bartender!" His companion Fiorello

(Chico Marx) adds, "I'll take two beers, too." This, too, is an unsuccessful moment of delivery (they will end up with four beers!). In a Buffalo Wild Wings commercial, a homebrewer treats his friends to "homebrew," complete with the imagery of overfermenting carboys in a mad scientist living room. ("Buffalo Wild Wings"). "So you brew your own beer?" one friend asks. "For you, bratwurst beer," the homebrewer notes to his friends' disgust.

Bratwurst beer sounds like an unsuccessful delivery of the craft beer message (different types of so-called extreme ingredients that make craft unique and exciting) masked as parody. A similar parody occurs in a *Three's Company* episode in which Mr. Roper is making beer in his living room (not in his kitchen, the expected place of homebrewing). "This is pure stuff," he tells his wife. "Everything that touches this beer has been sterilized." Mrs. Roper responds, "So, that's your problem" ("Days of Beer and Weeds"). Mr. Roper fails to deliver his message (try my beer). Mrs. Roper treats his failed explanation as a chance to mock his sexual prowess. In place of acceptance, the beer message is met with scorn and ridicule.

Delivery is important for beer, but unlike these examples of failed beer delivery, the overall message that craft delivers is success. There are more breweries currently in operation, we are repeatedly told in newspaper accounts or craft brewer interviews, than any time since Prohibition. Craft has overcome the stranglehold of conglomerate beer production by capturing approximately 7 to 11 percent of the overall market. As Brewers Association's director Paul Gatza argues in one of the trade group's press releases, craft owes its success to the delivery of a specific message—flavor over blandness: "Increasingly, beer lovers are turning to craft brewed beer from small and independent producers to satisfy their thirst for bold, innovative and flavor-forward beers." ("Brewers Association Releases"). Flavor, that is, without bratwurst.

Nestled within these successful narratives are small stories of failure—not grand economic failure, but instead stories of popular culture failure as the characters and narratives associated with popular culture treat craft and beer overall as a miscue or misunderstood message. In these exchanges, actors engage in a beer communicative act, and the message fails. We hear this lack of success repeated in not only the examples I begin with but also in contemporary texts mentioning beer, moments when something has gone amiss. In hip hop artist MF Doom's "One Beer," for instance, a lament for single beer purchases, when only six-packs are available, occurs: "Powers only one left, the pack comes in six / Whatever happened to two and three." Or we hear lack of success in MF Doom's

"All Out of Ale," where he contemplates, like the Three Stooges or Mr. Roper, making beer when there is no beer to purchase, particularly when Sunday blue laws prevent beer shopping: "Sunday in the A-T-L and I'm all out of ale. . . . / Got all the ingredients and a recipe, might as well." He "might as well" as long as he doesn't overferment, as popular culture repeats in its messages of beer brewing out of control. Nestled within *Breaking Bad*'s early story line was a scene of Hank's homebrewed—and possibly overfermented—Schraderbräu bottles exploding (he and his wife misunderstand the breakage message when they hear the explosions; they think they are hearing gunshots). In these examples, delivery fails. Too much yeast. Barrels gone astray. Out of beer. Explosions. These are odd moments of beer delivery. These moments are nowhere near as odd as Frank Zappa using beer to irritate the devil in "Titties and Beer." Zappa chants the song's title so many times—he overdelivers the message—that the devil regrets buying Zappa's soul in the first place. "A tinge of doubt," the devil eventually concedes, "crosses my mind when you say that you want to make a deal with me" (Zappa). In addition to making a mess on the floor, beer can save one's soul as well, it seems, when overdone.

Terroir, in the earlier chapters, suggested a controlled delivery, different from these examples I offer; one that I framed as aggregation, a social media strategy for networking a variety of forces that may or may not belong together. I aggregate the Three Stooges, the Marx Brothers, *Three's Company*, a chain restaurant commercial, MF Doom, and Frank Zappa in this chapter's opening paragraphs to create an initial craft identity of delivery. Delivery is an important aspect of craft obsession: from delivery of the beer itself to delivery of the idea of beer. Beer must arrive physically and conceptually to the consumer. "The world is full of people who say . . . you can't do that," a New Belgium ad for Fat Tire declares, suggesting that idea delivery (support, potential, market share) is not a given for craft beer (New Belgium). Idea delivery must be cultivated for an audience, not taken for granted. Or else, "you can't do that," as Mrs. Roper might say about her husband's homebrewing, will be the response. Audience cultivation, at times, involves an aggregation of different factors, moments, or ideas. Thus, messages must be built up over time and not accepted at their initial reception.

Such is Greg Koch's contention when he recalls initial responses to his message of what a pale ale should taste like, as opposed to what a beer audience expected a pale ale to taste like prior to Stone's inception. Audiences—bars and restaurants interested in purchasing kegs—expected something akin to a light and fizzy mass-produced beer, not what Stone was offering in 1997. The first response to Stone Pale Ale, too, was a put down: "All too often, I got a quasi-quizzical look, as if they were still trying to figure out if I was serious, coupled with a polite-ish declination/explanation: 'It's just . . . so . . . bitter'" (Koch, Wagner, and Clemens 40). Stone, circumventing expected taste, should have failed, like these initial examples. Delivery, like contagions, requires familiarity. Exploding beer bottles and overfermenting wort are familiar ways of telling beer delivery stories comically; they are anticipated responses (contagions) to brewing that frame the experience as failure. Reading these initial examples of failed delivery, I, too, might have initially come to an assessment of Stone's potential for failure if I were a "beer expert" in 1997. But Stone did not fail, and its success is tied to the larger aggregation of taste and flavor associated with artisanal food movements of the 1990s, not overall familiarity (i.e., fizzy yellow lager). Anticipated assumption (as it was aggregated by retail and consumers) directed an understanding of delivery that eventually proved inaccurate. Delivery, because of aggregation, involves how ideas cross various spaces, moments, people, and times to create a message that often does not address familiarity or anticipated responses.

As I engage with delivery as a component of craft, I aggregate material online, moving over videos, ads, songs, movie scenes: what I read, what I write, and what I understand are the result of this aggregation. I develop a writerly terroir of delivery. I experience, as Bruno Latour writes, "the breath of technology pass [me] over" (*An Inquiry* 217). As Latour argues, the trajectories of technology "are not easy to grasp" and "they do not go straight." My aggregation is anything but straight. As I begin this chapter, I've followed a number of nonlinear trajectories to this point. "Everything in the practice of artisans, engineers, technicians, and even weekend putterers," says Latour, "brings to light the multiplicity of transformations, the heterogeneity of combinations, the proliferations of clever artifices, the delicate setups of fragile skills" (*An Inquiry* 216). From wayward beer barrel to taunting the devil, delivery is transformed via aggregations that do not travel in straight directions. There is no linear ordering to my aggregation of delivery-related moments. If I swap out one item for another in this aggregation, my delicate setup shifts to alternative understanding. Understanding, arriving at some semblance of meaning, need not move from point A to point B, and it does not need to be under my control (items can aggregate apart from any role I play). There exists a heterogeneity of possible aggregated moves before understanding may occur. Counter to some notions of delivery, such as the one expressed by Keith Grant-Davis, delivery is not necessarily the moment when meaning becomes controlled. As Grant-Davis claims, the person who can "define the fundamental issues represented by a superficial subject matter—and persuade audiences to engage those issues—is in a position to maintain decisive control over the field of debate" (267). A keg of beer. Homebrewing. Buying a single instead of a six-pack. These, too, might be superficial moments where delivery is out of control. With craft aggregation, as I'll show in this chapter, control may not, in fact, exist. Audiences may be persuaded by a delivered message for reasons beyond one or more speaker/writer's control of the message or its formation.

Aggregation

Aggregation, as I previously noted, is a Web phenomenon realized in many social and cultural trends including craft beer. In issue 27 of *Beer Advocate* magazine, editors Jason and Todd Alström coin the term "Beer 3.0" to describe the Web's influence on the craft beer community as an aggregation. "Let's face it," they write, "without the Internet, craft beer wouldn't be what it is today—more specifically, not as popular as it is today" (1). Beer 3.0, they claim, is the state where "access to beer-related data has never been easier." Information flows easily from beer producers to those who consume the products, and vice versa. This state of communication, in essence, is beer delivery placed within a technological framing as aggregation:

> Consumers and the industry have been brought together in mutual dialogue about beer. Feedback is instant. Everyone has an opinion, and everyone can be heard, by thousands. Brewers and their beers are followed online like rockstars [sic]. A beer or brewer can be hyped to stardom or trashed overnight. (Alström and Alström 1)

The Three Stooges' delivery is all over the place. MF Doom can't get a beer. In the Alströms' scenario, on the other hand, social networking facilitates consumer-producer relations throughout craft beer culture and its representation in mass media so that delivery is not all over the place and beer is accessible. Specifically, craft beer provides an example of delivery in social networking's communicative practices; it brings together (aggregates) craft beer agents. Like many social media applications, the mythical Beer 3.0 is celebrated as mutual, dialogue based, feedback centered, and user generated. My initial Weyerbacher rating, a Beer 3.0

moment, failed on all of these celebrated accounts. I rated outside any aggregated message regarding ratings and beer in general.

"Celebrate," a 2008 AT&T commercial, exemplifies the Alströms' point by highlighting the mutual interactions I lacked when I became involved in Beer 3.0. In the commercial, a brewer and a distributor join forces to sell craft beer.

> "You sure can brew it," the salesman tells the brewer.
> "Question is, can you sell it?" the brewer responds. ("AT&T Brewery Celebrate")

The answer is affirmative; through AT&T wireless communication, the salesman maintains continuous contact with the brewer, potential clients, and established accounts. The seller keeps both the brewer and the customer engaged in a consumption experience. The network facilitates connectivity and, thus, delivery. At one point in the commercial, the salesman, securing account after account, asks the brewer, "Am I going too fast for you?" The speed and delivery of wireless communication provides immediate financial payoff, we are told. Beer cannot keep up with networked sales. "More bars in more places," the commercial's statement puns. With wireless, there will be more (beer) bars in more places. There will be more cellular phone bars as well. Phone bars deliver content. Message received. Sales occur.

These examples demonstrate a shift in how delivery works in the age of networked communication. Barrels roll away. Bars are filled in more places. In particular, these examples focus this shift within the specific area of craft beer and its overall relationship to rhetorical delivery. The rhetorical concept of delivery has long played a role in communicative technologies (even as rhetorical criticism places less emphasis on delivery than it does on the other rhetorical canons). A message, we assume, must be delivered to an audience, and speakers and writers navigate various options when delivering that message. One aspect of beer delivery aggregated across a number of media and writerly voices, as I have noted, is revolution. The revolution message, as repeated by various brewers and writers, convinces beer drinkers that what they are experiencing is novel, innovative, and a response to the boring and monotonous product of major conglomerates who have kept great taste—despite the promise of a canonical 1970s Miller Lite commercial—out of the recipe for brewing. The Web page for *Beer Pioneers*, a film, describes its project as part of this revolutionary message delivered to a sympathetic and enthusiastic craft audience:

THE REVOLUTION: Today, craft beer and microbreweries have been fully integrated within North American culture, even if at only ten percent of the market share! More breweries have opened (and stayed open) since the last peak in the late 1800s—and all of these newcomers today are producing traditional or experimental beers! (*Beer Pioneers*)

Phrased in the right way, revolution acts not as a retread term delivered to an audience, as some critics of memes and contagions might attest, but as a convincing term attached to the craft beer narrative and accepted by its audience as authentic. Fizzy yellow beer is on its way out. Flavorful beer is on its way in. The revolution has prevailed. I, among many others, am swayed by this message's appeal. Delivery, in this case, is persuasive. As revolutionary declarations are repeated, they are aggregated into convincing statements. In the larger network of interactions, however, these declarations are convincing because of the many spaces where they occur, the amount of times they are spread across these spaces, and how they are repeated in these spreadable moments. If one person or one film claims revolution for craft beer, the message is less persuasive than if revolution is aggregated. The revolution must be networked.

Aristotle's concept of lexis (style) claims that "it is not enough to have a supply of things to say, but it is also necessary to say it in the right way" (bk. 3, sec. 1). *Revolution* has been one such term, often said in the right way for craft beer enthusiast audiences. Aristotle, though, frowns upon delivery, adding that "delivery seems a vulgar matter when rightly understood" (218; bk. 3, sec. 5). As William Fortenbaugh writes, Aristotle recognizes "the fact that style actually determines delivery" and thus diminishes the ethics of delivery (because style can deceive) (252). This association of style with delivery is also found in Plato's *Phaedrus*, a dialogue in which Socrates prefers the stylistics that oration delivers over the artificiality of writing. "You can lead me all over Attica," Socrates tells Phaedrus, "or anywhere else you like simply by waving in front of me the leaves of a book containing a speech" (7; 230E). Speech, for Plato, is the ultimate form of delivery because of its aesthetic appeal (a better version of style). "Delivery," Cicero claims, "is the dominant factor in oratory; without delivery the best speaker cannot be any account at all, and a moderate speaker with a trained delivery can often outdo the best of them" (qtd. in Johnstone 124). *Revolution*, for instance, is a stylistic term; its aesthetic appeals to our desire to overturn a given status quo in favor of something more personal, better crafted, or less mass produced. It outdoes "the best of them," so to speak. Its message reaches us in powerful and persuasive ways. Even Mr. Roper, brewing in his living room, taps into that stylistic gesture. He engages in a revolt against the status quo of packaged macro beers.

Delivery, in the classical sense, is oral communication, the way one expresses an idea effectively, and for Plato, the way one expresses an idea beautifully. Fortenbaugh writes, "Delivery helps make discourse not only clear and enjoyable, but also persuasive" (246). Delivery is aesthetically based; its ability to persuade is located in how the message sounds or looks. While persuasive, delivery also pleases. Moving away from this particular emphasis, Malcolm Gladwell updates the classical meaning of oral delivery with the notion of "Connectors," people who "know lots of people. They are the kinds of people who know everyone" (38). Connectors don't need aesthetics or to please as much as they need knowledge. Connecters are bodily delivery systems (people who communicate ideas to others they know). Their linkages are often conveyed orally in conversation, and style plays a minimal role, if any. Aesthetics, for Gladwell, seems unimportant. A Connector says (literally or metaphorically), "I know you. Let me tell you how." Or, "I know about X. Let me tell you what it's like." A Connector engages. I discovered this engagement in chapters 1 and 2 as I traced my anecdotal interruptions. Each interruption served as a virtual Connector allowing me to follow a stylistic set of patterns across people and ideas. Each interruption told me something about the other connection. Each interruption allowed for a rhetorical engagement with unlike items and material. In the next chapter, I will perform a similar set of interruptions for craft beer release days.

Delivery suggests style (word choice, tone, diction), body gesture (rigid posture or energetic gesturing), the importance of media (the space where ideas are placed), Connectors (the items or people who allow messages to be conveyed), and aesthetics (the appearance and presentation of the message, idea, or product). Connectors are also part of bodily gesture. As James Fredal writes about bodily presentation, "Nonverbal or presentational media function to serve thought, deliberation, expression, and judgment as well as verbal, only they do so in different ways" (255). In digital media, delivery becomes emphasized as the prime, nonverbal force for conveying meaning where nonhumans (the links or platforms or images engaged) become delivery mechanisms. Regarding digital presentational media, Marshall McLuhan famously noted that "the medium is the message" because "it is the medium that shapes and controls the scale and form of human association and action" (*Understanding Media* 20). In particular, McLuhan found that electronic media alter specific aspects of delivery, particularly those media that engage with the everyday. Many of the media McLuhan highlighted also have aesthetic appeal. Books. Games. Ads. Comics. Television. These are, for McLuhan, forms of delivery that allow everyday encounters with meaning and ideas: "The electric puts the mythic or collective dimension of human experience fully into the conscious wake-a-day world" (*Gutenberg* 319). Connectors—people or media—participate in these mythic experiences. If only McLuhan had experienced Anchor in the late 1960s (one of the few craft beers of his time period), he might have included beer in his list and traced its various Connectors.

Connectors engage. The label "craft" stems from the communal sentiment for artisanal works (as in William Morris's nineteenth-century Arts and Crafts movement) or what Richard Sennett calls in his book *The Craftsmen*, "the special human condition of being *engaged*" (20). The craftsman (in beer or in art) is engaged with the object being produced in a way the noncraftsman supposedly isn't (i.e., mass production of the noncraft item removes the ability to be engaged because all of the product reception experiences are the same). The craftsman supposedly engages with the delivery of aesthetic value over mass production; the medium (or craft object) delivers the message. In that engagement, a specific meaning and value system is understood. The nineteenth-century Shakers movement in America emphasized this point as well. Known for their handcrafted furniture, brooms, and quilts, the Shakers, like their nineteenth-century counterparts in the Arts and Crafts movement, denigrated the industrial in favor of the handmade and, in doing so, preached a specific type of engagement (and even, revolution). Of their eighteen communities, one of the largest was the village at Pleasant Hill, a twenty-minute drive from my house in Lexington. Visiting the village, one can experience "the authentic" craft lifestyle delivered as reenactment; village employees recreate the anti-industrial message begun in the nineteenth century. The legacy of that authenticity exists in contemporary craft as well. "I like to brew the way they brewed 115, 120 years ago," Bob Sylvester of St. Somewhere declares. "I want to brew an authentic product, authentic meaning true to the style, true to what it is" ("Conversation with Bob Sylvester"). Authenticity, in this case, signifies the long-standing tradition of craft as handmade (as I noted regarding brewery size or authenticity in the craft versus crafty debate). Authenticity, then, is engagement with the delivery of previous time periods or claims of authenticity. Engagement enacts human experience in the wake-a-day world.

Aesthetic Delivery

Craft, from William Morris to craft beer to Shakers, engages the delivery of aesthetics. Flavor. Color. Aroma. Labels. Bottles. Design. Handmade. These are keywords we can associate with the general taxonomy of aesthetics. The new aesthetic, Ian Bogost suggests in his *Atlantic* essay of the same name, refers to a computer-driven movement, but it is also relevant to craft and the production of things. Objects or things, as Bogost summarizes James Bridle's new aesthetic movement (and from Bridle borrows the term *new aesthetic*), are experienced, not just observed. Objects are engagements. And by being an experience, objects take on meanings and relationships beyond being owned or used. In this vision of craft, where the object is central, things have agency. Things engage. A beer, we can add, has agency; it can function as a Connector. Thus, beer can activate a moment of delivery (such as a pamphlet instruction or barrel rolling away). Bogost's position—which is not specifically about beer—differs slightly from Bridle's project on the weblog of the same name. As Bridle describes the new aesthetic, "It is a series of artefacts of the heterogeneous network, which recognises differences, the gaps in our overlapping but distant realities" (Bridle). Bridle's aesthetic includes phones, fake shops, global positioning systems, digital art—items that supposedly showcase this gap between felt experience and an assumed reality. Beer, too, is a part of this aesthetic. As the blogger Craft Beer Girl writes,

> A well-designed package can get me to buy almost anything, and this phenomenon definitely holds true when it comes to beer. While it's no secret that the beer industry and product marketing go hand in hand, the craft beer market is introducing a new aesthetic, playing to a . . . dare I say it? More sophisticated beer drinker. (Ellsworth)

Design closes the gap between experience (drinking beer) and reality (whatever ideas the beer's label stands for so that persuasion causes one to purchase the beer).

Bogost, less concerned with gaps, argues that this aesthetic raises questions regarding how we explain agency. Bogost is not interested in consumerism—such as how a label or ad *causes us* to purchase a beer because of its delivered and persuasive message. Instead, Bogost's response to the question of aesthetics and objects is carpentry, a theory of explaining by making. Carpentry replaces the practice of explanation. Carpentry is a craft practice. Making, Bogost claims, explains on its own:

> The things we make in and beyond the bounds of the New Aesthetic might have different goals: not art that helps us couple machines to one another, but philosophical lab equipment that helps us grasp, as best we can, the experience of objects themselves. I've called this practice *carpentry*, making things that speculate how things understand their world. Carpentered objects need not be fashioned from wood, but they bear the same mark of hand-manufacture, care, and craft—not just the craft of the artist, but the way that craftwork helps reveal how things fashion one another, and the world at large. ("New Aesthetic")

Craft, the nineteenth-century Arts and Crafts movement argued, fashions a world outside industrialization, favoring the handmade and the artist over the impersonal mass-produced object. Craft highlights an initial concept of carpentry—ideas as objects (chairs, tables, and lamps all exemplify a specific ideology of the handmade). Relationships, Arts and Crafts claimed, come from the artist, not the machine and objects associated with the machine or the machine's by-product of consumption. To understand the ideology, this version of craft argued, one need only look at the object and how it was made. William Morris begins *Art and Socialism* by asking his readership to "consider what remedies should be applied for curing the evils that exist in the relationship between Art and Commerce" (4). Technology has not brought pleasure, Morris contends, but destroyed it. "The wonderful machines," Morris sarcastically states, "have instead of lightening the labour of the workmen, intensified it, and thereby added more weariness yet to the burden which the poor have to carry" (5). If craft had agency for Arts and Crafts, that agency redirected attention from the industrial and technological to the artisanal and, in turn, rejected consumption in favor of aesthetic reflection. Craft revealed a specific type of fashioning of the world that the individual could appreciate and ponder. The object, in its making, explained an ideology. The aesthetic of the thing delivered the message.

Adam Gopnik, writing about the Shakers, argues that a completely different aesthetic existed among the craftsman of the celibate religious group. The Shakers responded to industrialization via their objects, but as they did so, they were not completely outside the industrial circulation of meaning. "Shaker chairs and other wooden objects were made in semi-industrial conditions for a growing middle-class market," Gopnik points out. He adds,

The urge to make consumer goods is, after all, one of the keenest spiritual disciplines that an ascetic can face: it forces spirit to take form. An ascetic drinking tea from a cup decides not to care what kind of cup he's drinking from; an ascetic forced to make a cup has to ask what kind of cup he ought to drink from. By the mid-nineteenth century, "Shaker" had become a brand name.

Craftsmanship, even with its suggestion of the handmade, was not divorced from brand identity. This contradiction is not just one of definition, or even of practice, but of delivered message. Arts and Crafts' redirection failed throughout most of the twentieth century, where the delivery of consumption—handmade and industrial—was not only rampant but enjoyable, as even Shaker craftsmanship in the village near where I live attests. Engaging with such objects, one does not necessarily respond with vitriol for the industrial, but instead one understands the object as explaining pleasure: this looks or feels nice. This rhetoric is relevant for craft beer as well.

Latour writes that "the technologies and consumer objects that the philosophers and moralists of earlier generations advise us to abhor" are the ones whose aesthetics we love (*We Have Never Been Modern* 136). A beer bottle is mass produced, often filled in an assembly line. Its aesthetic, however, explains something other than mass production. With craft delivery, attention has not been redirected away from consumption, particularly in the narrative of a beer revolution that, since 1980, has redefined a love of fermented wort from something to drink (or get drunk on) to something to savor and experience pleasure from (this tastes good!) to something that explains a concept (revolution). Even as a consumer may abhor mass production, the mass-produced beer may elicit a message of pleasure. This version of craft—as Bogost's sense of carpentry argues—functions as a logic and ideology. It is alive as a technological process of networked production. It is alive as the spirit of the handmade. It is alive as an aesthetic message. Craft is repetition of small stories. Craft is the terroir I have highlighted. Craft as a form of making explains handmade and industrial/technological logics. Craft is also, then, delivery.

Craft exists as aesthetic and as practice and involves an emerging culture of artisanal and handmade work framed within a new media environment and often exemplified in, among other items, beer. With aesthetics, craft, as in craft beer, reveals how "things fashion one another" in ways that Arts and Crafts may not have anticipated, for craft, today, is also technology that has things fashion one another. As Malcolm McCullough writes in *Abstracting Craft*, "Now there is reason to explore the possibility of craft in the emerging realm of information technology—with the computer as a medium" (21). Some of this material regarding craft and technology I explored via the ideas of contagions and aggregation. The logics of both are prompted by the very technological framing of social media where the computer is the obvious medium. Bogost does not differentiate between the handmade and that produced by technology; objects, Bogost writes, are objects regardless of how they are manufactured or where they appear: "What if we asked how computers and bonobos and toaster pastries and Boeing 787 Dreamliners develop their *own* aesthetics" ("New Aesthetic"). For Bogost, craft is an overall aesthetic that does not differentiate between the handmade or the machine made. A bottle coming off a massive assembly line at Boulevard or a bottle capped by hand at the local brewery—both are craft. Craft is an aesthetic with agency; it is an aesthetic of objects affecting objects, with and without computers. Or to reconsider Roland Barthes's question in *The Pleasure of the Text*, what might be the aesthetic of the consumer? (59). We could also ask the same of the consumed object. What is its aesthetic and what does it do? What does it make? What is its relationship to new media and to me, the consumer of such an aesthetic? What is it telling us?

Aesthetics do something. They form connections, deliver messages, or deliver some other kind of engagement (attention, disappointment, pleasure, excitement). In the world of consumerism (as Arts and Crafts critiqued), they enact purchases and supposedly support a problematic capitalist enterprise. Mass production takes such a claim seriously regarding the end effect of making a purchase, conflating various forms of artisanal and craft aesthetics so that neither appears to differ from mass production, but both create a purchase. As consumers, we experience both messages of the artisanal (craft fairs, pottery, art, textiles) and simultaneously the commercialized mass-produced visions of craft.

Even as Bogost argues that "craftwork helps reveal how things fashion one another," not all representations of craft or artisanal production are positive even as they fashion one another. William Morris lamented how contemporary "craft" canceled out the humanization essential for producing a meaningful life:

> I have been considering the loss of the thing itself, the loss of the humanizing influence which the daily sight of beautiful handiwork brings to bear upon people; but now, when we are considering the

way in which that handiwork was done, and the way in which it is done, the matter becomes more serious still. ("Lectures on Socialism" 150)

The supposedly handmade Shaker object did not cancel out the message of mass production (each handmade object is made to look like the other). Budweiser can use the word "batch" in its Project Twelve collection—twelve Budweiser brewers using the same yeast to create a unique beer—in order to generate the image of small (small batch) and artisanal or handmade. Or Blue Moon can declare that its beer is "Artfully crafted" in print and TV campaigns. These usages offer up the rhetoric of Morris's "beautiful handiwork" and play into Plato's notion of rhetoric as craft. Plato has Gorgias say that one can persuade by "no means of no other craft than oratory" (*Gorgias* 15; sec. 456b). Craft, in the rhetorical tradition of crafted oration, is generated by a "craftsman" or, in contemporary language, a Connector or even a Beer 3.0 delivery system of drinkers and enthusiasts who exchange the handmade as idea. Socrates and Gorgias debate how pleasure connects to craft, with Gorgias siding with the craftsman:

> SOCRATES: Now it is for every man to pick out which kinds of pleasures are good ones and which are bad ones, or does this require a craftsman in each case?
> GORGIAS: It requires a craftsman.   (*Gorgias* 77)

Craft can be pleasure, message, fake, or even dangerous. The craftsman, or the person or object(s) delivering the message, determines which via rhetorical choices and gestures. As I begin to trace out a craft delivery in this and the next two chapters, I don't want to cling to narratives of craft or crafty, good or bad, success or failure, or to even allow Morris's rhetoric to drive this discussion of delivery. Craft, as a folksonomic delivery, is both good and bad. We shouldn't forget that Tyler Durden, the protagonist of *Fight Club*'s mindless revolution, is an artisanal soap maker whose craftsman-like gestures shape a narrative with soap. Soap, as Durden states in the film's diegesis, is a con (an overpriced $20 bar of recycled body fat) and a potential weapon (it can be turned into an explosive). It is a form of carpentry (it stands for Durden's philosophy). It is a message (revolution). In the network of events traced and crafted throughout the film, soap has agency; it is social for the way it generates relationships in a larger network of meaning and for the way it aggregates meaning. Soap maintains a specific position within a larger network of activities it affects (consumer disgust, split personalities, leadership, mob rule, a romantic relationship). Whatever the aesthetic of craft might be in the situation *Fight Club* portrays, this aesthetic is not reduced to artistry, or to claims of value, or to a productive method of explanation, as Bogost's carpentry suggests. Instead of reducing craft to one of these items, following Bogost, such aesthetics can be turned into tracings of objects' relationships with other objects, or following the work of Bruno Latour, with other human and nonhuman agents. In other words, an account of a network (in a film or otherwise) can be traced (as Latour calls for) where nonhumans (soap, revolution) engage with humans (split personalities, soap makers, revolutionaries) to generate an aesthetic or, following Barthes, a pleasure, "braided, woven, in the most personal way" (*Pleasure* 59). Latour's tracing involves identifications of all the actors who construct a thing, object, movement, success, failure, and so on. Tracing reveals as many actors as one can identify in a networked delivery (it is impossible to trace all of a network's participants). Tracing is a type of storytelling, a way of narrating how something comes to be or what it might mean. The *Fight Club* revolution is personified in Durden as mindless, but objects' interactions trace a network in the diegesis that mixes the personal (Durden) with other moments (items in the film's plot). If we follow all of this tracing, we get a narrative. If we do this tracing, we enact delivery.

To understand craft delivery as part of this networked process, personal weaving can be appended to network theories proposed by Latour and Bogost since both authors seem to exclude the personal. Bogost, for instance, asks,

> Why couldn't a group of pastry chefs found their own New Aesthetic, grounded in the slippage between wet and dry ingredients? Computers are interesting, influential, and important, but they are just one thing among many. Just one tiny corner of a very large universe. ("New Aesthetic")

Since Bogost is not a pastry chef, I assume he is talking about others, not himself. I extend Bogost's question regarding pastry chefs with another culinary question, one not directed toward baking or even soap but toward a new aesthetic of object relationships, which, like terroir, captures *my* interest for the way it networks other objects in new media spaces I encounter. In turn, this aesthetic generates *my* obsession: craft beer.

Craft beer is my personal intervention in the object narrative I've briefly traced here. Why can't there be a new aesthetic of craft beer? I ask. To respond, I pose craft beer within this overall discussion of delivery in order to focus my attention because, like these examples I pull from Bogost and *Fight Club*, it, too, is an object capable of founding its own aesthetic (new or otherwise). It, too, is an object in a relationship with technology (social media). It, too, is a network of object-oriented relationships. It, too, exemplifies a type of carpentry that Bogost mentions in "The New Aesthetic." And in the network that craft beer exists within and creates, I find, among the many objects I encounter, a human object obsessed with pleasure who participates in the delivery of craft's overall meaning. As I've been showing throughout this book, I find myself in the networked aesthetic. Personal weaving occurs. I, too, become one of the many encountered craftsmen shaping pleasure.

Networked Pleasures

In 2009 the "I Am a Craft Brewer" video went viral; it showcased numerous brewers making the title's proclamation and—as if echoing William Morris—professing anticorporate beliefs in order to promote the artisanal production typically associated with craft beer. In place of promoting dominant corporate beliefs, the brewers proposed craft beer as a force networking their interests, in which all the objects and ideas associated with craft connect them to this product and its aesthetics. "I Am a Craft Brewer" is personal (each brewer presents his or her position) and collective (the overall force and body of craft). "Craft brewing," the brewers tell us in the video—each saying one word of the following—"is innovation, independence, curiosity, collaboration, character, and family."

Screenshot from "I Am a Craft Brewer," with Vinnie Cilurzo of Russian River

Craft beer is an object. As an object, it enacts values prompted by brewers. Craft beer, as an aggregation of forces, has agency. While he is not fond of the word *object*, Bogost describes the object as an operation, a process of transformation (*Alien Phenomenology* 25). "An object," Bogost writes, "is thus a weird structure that might refer to a 'normal,' middle-sized object such as a toaster as much as it might describe an enormous, amorphous object like global transport logistics" (*Alien Phenomenology* 23). For the brewer, the object (beer) is artisanal. A toaster oven may not appear to be artisanal (even, as I'll see in the final chapter, as it appears in my beer photographs' aesthetic framing). But a beer, such as Pliny the Elder, is artisanal. As an artisanal thing, the beer object transforms; that is, it delivers a message that reshapes or affects what or who receives the message. The video, in this case, attempts to transform its audience; "I Am a Craft Brewer" redefines my, the beer drinker, relationship with beer (i.e., I am buying an artisanal product; I am participating in an aesthetic, I am connected to this message). "We must spread the message," Sam Calagione declares in the "I Am a Craft Brewer" video. If these featured individuals in the video are craft brewers, then I must be a craft beer drinker. This message is delivered. I, in turn, continue to spread the message within the networks I enter. I share the video. I like the video. I comment on the video. I enter into a spreadable, networked relationship with the video's overall idea.

The message is spread by me and by the object. Bruno Latour advises that in any network study, "the first solution is to study *innovations* in the artisan's workshop" because "in these sites, objects live a clearly multiple and complex life through meetings, plans, sketches, regulations, and trials. Here, they appear fully mixed with other more traditional social agencies" (*Reassembling* 80). The object is not just a thing but those events, moments, people, processes, and so on that create or surround the thing as well; the thing is the result of all of this activity, and it becomes itself an activity. Within any object exist many actions and transactions. In a given craft beer (artisanal) moment, we might encounter the packaging, production, contents, hype, advertisement, and consumption, to name but a few of the actions occurring within the object itself. In the "I Am a Craft Brewer" video, for instance, the object is obvious (beyond the video itself): a glass, bottle, can, barrel, or keg of beer. The overall object projected throughout the video—the one we might call craft beer—includes such items, but it also includes more items not visible in the video's overall message: the places of consumption, distribution, drinkers, online discussion, ingredients, shipping issues, beer tastings, consumption itself, retail, hype, relationships among craft brewers, marketing, and so on. The overall circulated object is a network of all of these activities and more. The video is one space where this network engages with these ideas. Others exist as well.

    Craft beer represents one type of network. Latour argues that networks are not made; they already exist: "A network is not what is represented in the text, but that readies the text to take the relay of actors as mediators" (*Reassembling* 131). Networks, for Latour, are not physical or material items. A network, Latour writes, "is not made of nylon thread, words or any durable substance but is the trace left behind by some moving agent" (*Reassembling* 132). When I call craft beer a network, I am not pointing to a physical object and representing it (as a graph or infographic might accomplish), nor am I pointing to the object itself (the beer), but I am instead acknowledging the tracing left behind by its various agents whose interactions construct the network in question, one called craft beer, whose focus is delivery, for this and the next chapter. Latour adds, "The very poverty of graphical representation allows the inquirer not to confuse his or her infra-language with the rich objects that are being depicted" (*Reassembling* 133). In addition to all of the agents I list above, I, too, am leaving behind a trace of this network (as I noted earlier regarding footprints and terroir). I do so because I, too, am a craft beer drinker. I am confusing my language with the object, and that—despite Latour's concerns—is not a problem.

    Within this tracing, I can consider the personal's role in the networked delivery of beer. Thus, my purpose is to trace a specific type of network, a craft network, in order to understand not only how objects affect one another within a series of relationships, as Bogost or Latour or even *Fight Club* might ask, but how I, too, am part of these affected relationships, as Plato's declaration of the craftsman evokes. My digital footprint is more than just a footprint like Odell's footprint or my rating of Odell's beer; it is an active member of a specific network delivering meaning to audiences. There exist all kinds of metaphors for this tracing, as Latour notes, and while graphic visualizations may be popular for how they simplify or explain a phenomenon, Latour faults them for "believing the world is made of points and lines" (*Reassembling* 133). Instead of a visual representation of craft beer or a chart mapping how objects respond to objects (as many online infographics of beer show) in some type of delivery system, I return to Bogost's interests regarding craft and the activity he calls *carpentry*. Carpentry, we are told, is a response to writing and any popular representation of networks; academics (like me) *write* about networks or relationships. They don't, as Bogost points out, construct either (much as Durden makes soap or Shakers make furniture or Cilurzo makes a delicious double IPA). Some of us academics—not unlike *Three's Company*'s Mr. Roper—make beer, of course. I tried to make beer in graduate school; the result, like the delivery failures I began the chapter with, was two batches of malt-extract-based beer and a huge mess on my kitchen floor from not knowing how to siphon properly. Most of the batches sat in a Gainesville closet until I moved to Detroit. Then they were thrown out. Now, and quite wisely, I write.

"Writing is only one form of being," Bogost proclaims (*Alien Phenomenology* 90). Carpentry, on the other hand, involves "constructing artifacts as a philosophical practice" (*Alien Phenomenology* 92). Carpentry is a response to writing, a way to explain what writing supposedly cannot. Bogost writes that "carpentry entails making things that explain how things make the world" (*Alien Phenomenology* 93). Greg Ulmer, citing Hannah Arendt, associates the ability to reason (or, we might say, be philosophical in making the world) with craft and, thus, with making: "Aristotle and the Greeks invented their new higher reason from an analogy with the know-how of craftsmen. Craftsmen started with a prototype, an idea, and created an artifact by means of the choices or options that Aristotle called *proairesis*" (*Avatar Emergency* 151). The artifact explains. Proairesis, choice based on ethos, extends to the object one chooses to make (Bogost's sense of carpentry or Durden's soap or Russian River's Pliny the Elder). Craft brewers, evident in their well-circulated promotional video, maintain a type of artisanal ethos based on what they make. This ethos, dependent on claims of authenticity, often determines the craft versus crafty label. "I don't put rice in my beer," Adam Avery claims in the "I Am a Craft Brewer" video. Rice equates homogenized production (big brewers who use cheap ingredients). The artist makes something regardless of ingredient cost. Or as Burkhard Bilger profiles Sam Calagione in the *New Yorker*: "Calagione makes more beer with at least ten per cent alcohol than any other brewer, and his odd ingredients are often drawn from ancient or obscure beer traditions." Not using rice projects ethos. Ancient or obscure traditions project ethos as well: willing to take chances, being unique, appearing exotic, presenting one's self as radical. "Real radicals, we might conclude, make things," Bogost declares (*Alien Phenomenology* 110), and we can easily imagine Durden being radical and making soap bombs or Avery being radical and brewing with grain, or Calagione being radical and brewing with juniper berries. Unfortunately, I do not share this artisanal ethos of making—not because I am unsympathetic to the craft cause. The opposite. I am a craft beer drinker (which includes drinking Avery and Dogfish Head beers). I am very sympathetic. I like so-called exotic ingredients in craft beer. Put simply, I am not good with my hands. I can't make things, including beer, as I've noted (malt extract or all grain). I am not radical. I do, however, write.

This discrepancy regarding carpentry, craft, and aesthetic delivery does not mean that I have no character, nor does it mean that—despite the tendency to cite revolutions in craft beer—craft brewers need to be radicals in order to engage in some semblance of carpentry. Even without a so-called radical edge, craft brewers maintain an ethos when producing objects that have meaning. They produce objects that share ideas, that help fashion small stories. I am interested in extending the notion of carpentry and its associated proairesis to the craft network I am tracing because I, too, am part of this network. My presence and participation (not my handiwork) contribute to the making of a craft network (proairesis) that explains how craft beer generates the social. I engage with carpentry while showing a specific carpenter act. I am not "making" the network to show relationships, as Latour claims we do not do, but I am already in the network as an object with other networked objects that interest me and interact with me, something akin to Latour's "quasi-objects": "They attach us to one another, because they circulate in our hands and define our social bond by their very circulation. They are discursive, however; they are narrated, historical, passionate" (*We Have Never Been Modern* 89). I am one of those agents that leave a trace as I narrate, or as Bogost might say, I am one of those agents making things that explain the world. I saw this process when I discovered that my anecdote about tasting beer for the first time resembled and repeated other anecdotes of first times. The previous anecdotes affect my own stories; the tale circulates through hands (the bottles or cans we hold) and ends up in writing (it is read). By telling such an anecdote, I will eventually affect others. I am in the network but only because I am building the traces within the network with others as well. Without my anecdote, another network exists, but not the one I helped trace. My traces reveal my object-based interactions.

Latour does not include himself as a part of the given network he explores: in his network studies, Latour wasn't involved in Aramis's creation; he is not an engineer; he is not a lawyer. But *I am* a craft beer drinker.[1]

Whatever craft network I discover, I am a part of it because my beliefs, interests, tastes, purchases, writings, etc., are part of the craft network. Carpentry occurs, only I am not the only carpenter present. I am not the only one engaged in this type of delivery. I shift Bogost's concerns with carpentry away from the individual building to explain the network in ways writing won't support. The network is not the result of an individual entity making a thing like a table or a beer. Instead, the network consists of a number of actors making the thing together—even if they don't realize they are doing so or know the others involved—and delivering it in a complicated manner. I am one of those actors. All things or objects are carpentered networks.

I also recognize the participant culture that theorists such as Clay Shirky, Axel Bruns, and Henry Jenkins frame as a foundation of social media, and that, as I noted earlier regarding my first rating, does not always work smoothly. Such theorists, though, maintain the individual as central to participatory media. When Axel Bruns, for instance, writes about the prosumer, he means an individual whose identity as consumer and producer is mixed: "The role of 'consumer' and even that of 'end user' have long disappeared, and the distinctions between producers and users of content have faded into comparative insignificance" (Bruns 2). Bruns's version of the prosumer is one who disrupts the traditional model of producer, distributor, and consumer. When I consider the many agents at work in a given network, I am not concerned with whether or not they are disrupting one model of production or another. Instead, I am concerned with how I and others interact with such agents so that we, too, are part of the network we are both fascinated by and that we are building. "One obvious lesson is that new technology enables new kinds of group-forming," Shirky argues (*Here Comes Everybody* 17). Groups form and enable movements, moments, activities, beliefs, consumption, and other patterns of activity. I will trace a specific group formation as carpentry to better understand how a craft meaning may be developed and shared. This formation I will call *craft delivery*.

Connected Delivery

Leading into this chapter, I've juxtaposed craft beer, technology, and delivery in order to explore *engagement*. My obsession, in turn, is networked within these areas (and so, too, are others' obsessions as well). This craft obsession is not solely controlled by the juxtaposition of beer, technology, and delivery as Beer 3.0 suggests, but instead it engages connectivity. The audience (me, other beer drinkers, beer writers, people in the industry, etc.) enacts connectivity and engagement. When advising how to engage an audience, Quintilian drew a connection between delivery and the consumption of alcohol, of which beer may have played a role during his time. The speaker, Quintilian argues, must maintain a sense of control when speaking to an audience:

> Neither let him imitate the vices of the drunkard nor adapt himself to the baseness of the slave; nor let him learn to display the feelings of love, or avarice, or fear: acquirements which are not at all necessary to the orator and which corrupt the mind, especially while it is yet tender and uninformed in early youth, for frequent imitation settles into habit. (1.11.2)

Since the mid-1980s, the craft beer movement has not imitated the vices of the drunkard; instead it has positioned itself as an artisanal alternative to large-scale brewing (the imitated anecdote of revolution). Craft beer does so through bypassing large-scale delivery methods typically not associated with craftsmanship, opting instead for a networked delivery practice and the usage of Connectors. When we retell the story of our first time drinking a beer with our dad on a hot day, we act as Connectors. When we aggregate styles or locations into a network of terroir, we act as Connectors. When I take a photograph of a beer I am drinking and upload it to a social media site, I am acting as a Connector.

Connectors are a form of delivery. When it comes to successfully reaching an audience, conglomerates such as InBev and MillerCoors pose a challenge for craft beer, which does not use large-scale advertising for the delivery of its message, image, and content. A contagion allows identity to form; that is, my repeated anecdote allows for an identification with others sharing the same anecdote. Or, in the case of advertising as delivery, a contagion overpowers the meager budgets of craft brewers. Miller Lite, for instance, claims its beer has "triple hops," suggesting a special hop process where hopping occurs three times. Miller Lite allows the statement to be repeated, picked up by consumers, and realized as an increase in sales because of this repetition. Never mind that most beer engages with three distinct processes of hopping: bittering, flavor, and aroma. Connectors repeat the advertisement's message as is or they retread the message. Whereas a single ad or an advertising campaign serves the major beer producers, craft beer depends on a network of information systems and Connectors working together in a type of engagement more complex than advertisement to Connector to other Connector. In other words, the process differs from basic advertising retreads. In the age of new media, craft beer realizes its message delivered in a manner similar to Carolyn Rude's description of contemporary new media delivery, "in which multiple documents and other rhetorical acts may work together to change values and policies" (273). Carpentry, as I began to explain, is part of this overall process.

Economic scale offers one reason why craft brewers don't advertise (lack of budget), but methodology also determines a communal, networked engagement. Fritz Maytag, founder of the modern Anchor Brewing and one of the pioneers of the craft brewing movement, once bragged that he never spent a dime on advertising. "I have always believed," Maytag writes, "that 'If we brew it, they will come,' but from my earliest days as a brewer I have known in my bones that 'they' will only come and drink our beer if someone tells them that we have brewed it" (2). As Maytag notes, brewers benefit from contemporary networked communication technology that allows each member of the network to "tell" the other when a beer has been brewed and by whom (as Gladwell's Connectors tell each other of their personal knowledge). Such is Henry Jenkins's claim that oral connection plays a vital role in online information delivery: "Word-of-mouth recommendations and the sharing of media content are impulses that have long driven how people interact with each other" (*Spreadable Media* 2). This telling-as-interaction generates databases of information that, in turn, are delivered to audiences who generate new forms of communal knowledge and who redeliver this knowledge back to its source. Telling builds. Telling is a form of interaction. Tony Magee states,

> In beer culture, people talk. Distributors talk to retailers, who talk to consumers about who owns what. What will help us in the long run is that essentially we are not in the same business as the multinational brewers. We are selling community, and they are selling liquid. (qtd. in Voight)

Telling is community. Telling is building a network. When I first ordered Magee's Lagunitas online from Archer Liquors in Chicago (Lagunitas was not yet distributed to Missouri), I did so because somewhere, someone—online or in person—told me about Lagunitas and its Frank Zappa tribute beers. A RateBeer database of reviews supports this telling, where my engagement across multiple actors in the network informs me. Untappd, a mobile database recording of beers one has consumed at specific locations, is another form of this type of telling. So is the Bluegrass Beer Geeks Facebook group I am a member of, a space where craft drinkers from Kentucky and Southern Indiana tell each other about releases, purchases, and local events. So are other applications and sites. In contemporary terms, we call this activity Web 2.0.

Tim O'Reilly defines Web 2.0 as "the power of the web to harness collective intelligence" (O'Reilly). In the network of information platforms we call Web 2.0—Facebook, Twitter, weblogs, RSS feeds—collective thinking (and the creation of communal knowledge) allows members of these social media sites to share knowledge via posts, links, embedded video, updates, and other means. Web 2.0 often is called *social networking*: a collective networking of various online experiences and communicative acts. James Surowiecki calls this activity "the wisdom of crowds." Surowiecki argues that a large number of smart people function together better than one smart person does alone. Collectively, the crowd delivers a message better than a lone individual. Such a position runs counter to classical notions of delivery that emphasize the individual as the deliverer. In Web 2.0 the group is emphasized. Surowiecki, however, counters the power of harnessing collective intelligence with the damaging role influence might play in any collective experience:

> The more influence a group's members exert on each other, and the more personal contact they have with each other, the less likely it is that the group's decisions will be wise ones. The more influence we exert on each other, the more likely it is that we will believe the same things and make the same mistakes. That means it's possible that we could become individually smarter, but collectively dumber. The question we have to ask in thinking about collective wisdom, then, is: Can people make collectively intelligent decisions even when they are in constant, if erratic, interaction with each other? (42–43)

I told the RateBeer database that I disliked a Weyerbacher beer that everyone else, mostly, liked. I was outside a network of influence and ignorant of the overall Weyerbacher message since I was new to the practice of rating. No one yet had *told* me how to rate; I had no Connectors, no spheres of influence. Telling another Connector, as Maytag or Magee write, is a principal feature of any kind of crowd behavior when an idea is delivered to an audience. Telling is a form of delivery. Telling influences, as Maytag also notes, future behaviors (in this case, consumption). Advertising is one form of telling; word of mouth is another. Maytag's assumption is that telling will lead to positive influence. To overcome influence that leads to a populace being collectively dumber, as Surowiecki argues, individuals need "a wide array of options and information; and second, the willingness of at least some people to put their own judgment ahead of the group's, even when it's not sensible to do so" (61). When a pre–Web 2.0 audience told someone about Anchor beer, they did so by comparing options (Anchor versus a major producer like Budweiser, Schlitz, or Miller) and by putting their own judgment ahead of the group's (most consumers choose the major producer first since it is what they already know). Maytag depended on a growing collective intelligence willing to do this type of work and to deliver the information orally. Oral delivery is obviously no longer the only means of sending such information to an audience. Within Web 2.0 culture, social networking allows for a networked delivery of information via a metaphoric telling.

Walter Ong called the influence of orality on new media "secondary orality," a more "deliberate and self-conscious orality" dependent on writing and print in order to be electronic:

> Secondary orality is both remarkably like and remarkably unlike primary orality. Like primary orality, secondary orality has generated a strong group sense, for listening to spoken words forms hearers into a group, a true audience, just as reading written or printed texts turns individuals in on themselves. But secondary orality generates a sense of groups immeasurably larger than those of primary oral culture—McLuhan's "global village." (134)

Telling is a part of the electronic group sense that Ong highlights. "Encoding," Kathleen Welch writes, "is required to understand adequately how texts operate in secondary orality" (28). Encoding, for craft beer communication, might involve understanding how networked texts shape communicative acts in ways that include telling as much as they include other acts. In a social networked space, a writer "tells" the other. This telling generates group sense among participants in networked spaces motivated by the online trait of reviewing (expressing like or dislike for a product) as well as trading (the shipping of beers from one user to another that are not available where one lives), and daily communication (impromptu discussions on various topics). In the case of RateBeer and Beer Advocate, users feel loyalty to one site more than the other, though many users participate in both sites regularly. I use RateBeer for rating and trading; I use Beer Advocate to have discussions in the local Kentucky (actually, South) forum. I am told information, and I tell information. The sites, as well, act as Connectors for me; they engage me in this telling so that I am part of the group.

What might drive this group feeling or connectivity? In *The Time of the Tribes*, Michel Maffesoli traces the group-sense mentality of the tribe to the notion of vitalism. Vitalism, Maffesoli argues, is a nonrepresentational life force driving an affective participation in group settings. Vitalism is not a known entity but a secretive, emotional bonding that can be expressed via telling but also by other behaviors. Groups do not organize for purposes of morality but are mobilized by "collective emotions" (18). Such groups, Maffesoli notes, are called *tribes*. Tribes are marked by "the smallest details of everyday life which are lived for their own sake and not as a function of any sort of finality" (32). Tribes are not dependent on like-minded thinking in order to exist; relationships that lead to tribes, however, are based on proxemics. Proxemics can lead to friendly or antagonistic behavior. "Whatever it may be called," Maffesoli writes of this state, "neighborhoods, varied interest groups, networks—we are witnessing the return of an affective, passional investment whose structurally ambiguous and ambivalent aspects are well known" (127). Social networking spaces place individuals and information into proximity-based relationships where telling creates emotional bonding. Topic threads, updates, and back-channel e-mail conversations all generate a sense of proximity that, like McLuhan's global village engagement, can be as tense as it can be cordial. "That which we think of as a personal opinion belongs in fact to the group of which we are a member," writes Maffesoli (76). Influence is group directed and not entirely, as Surowiecki fears, individually created.

The reason to congregate online in a given space, share information, and rate or discuss craft beer in these proxemics spaces, following Maffesoli's understanding of membership, cannot be known: "One of the characteristics, and by no means the least, of the modern mass is surely the law of secrecy" (90). The secrecy includes why one becomes enmeshed in a tribe, why one contributes information to it, and how one delivers that information. The payoff for users is not financial and may not be persuasive, but it is typically affective. The reason to participate in these types of information exchanges, then, should not be framed within the understanding of a rhetorical purpose or goal of delivering an idea or message to an audience since such gestures require a degree of deliberation that group sense does not require. "Understanding the popularity of many Web 2.0 platforms," Jenkins observes, means considering what motivates people to contribute their time and energy without expectation of immediate financial compensation—whether these motives are attention, recognition, and identity building; the development of community and social ties; the creation of a useful tool; or myriad other considerations. (*Spreadable Media* 74)

What motivates is not an easy question to answer.

Such a position counters classical delivery's stress that a composition "must be suited to the nature of the subjects on which we speak. The care required in it is great, but that devoted to thought and delivery should be greater" (Quintilian 9.4.147). Participation in these types of affective exchanges works against this topos of purpose, an identified feature of delivery (know whom you are speaking with and proceed accordingly, as Quintilian argues) that we might position as "the" foundation of what delivery encompasses. To understand affective delivery, we engage with what Maffesoli calls "another culture, that of collective sentiments" (152). The collective intelligence of this supposed other culture is sentiment, what I cite Ong as calling "group sense." Telling taps into that sentiment.

If online delivery faces the danger of influence (per Surowiecki), then what do we make of a collective intelligence whose focus is sentiment, particularly when it comes to understanding meaning and ideas (per Maffesoli)? Such a logic suggests that groups come together, not necessarily to influence and shape each other's opinion via calm or emotionally delivered pleas, but to share affective moments, to tap into a type of vitalism that energizes and shapes their need to distribute information to one another, even when that need is not obvious or known to the participants. The sharing occurs not in one moment but in "related rhetorical acts over time" (Rude 273) or what Manuel Castells calls the new media trait "not made of content but of process" (38). As Jim Porter argues, in this type of digital delivery, "the choice of distribution matters to the success of communication" (214). The distribution, the secretive, shared telling occurring in a variety of places among a variety of chosen objects (beer, message boards, bottles, trades, events) and people (me, others interested in beer), is where the carpentry—the building of ideas—occurs, often for reasons that are difficult to pin down or clarify. One particular place where such activity occurs, and which is largely shaped by the ways information is delivered over social networking spaces, is the craft beer release day. That particular delivery moment will be the focus of the next chapter.

CHAPTER 6
Craft Tracings

You like hanging on Twitter, and we like beer.
—People Under the Stairs, "Beer"

The previous chapter's discussion of delivery, secrecy, proximity, actors, and carpentry prepares me for a tracing of one specific type of craft beer moment, the release day, so that I may better understand craft delivery. Release days come in various forms. Some craft breweries enhance their reputation by releasing limited quantities of special-release beers at their breweries one time per year; these beers will not be available via retail distribution. The reasons for doing so vary: limited space to produce high-quality beers and thus not enough output to distribute widely, the need to generate attention and hype so that reputation may be enhanced nationally, the ability to make a considerable amount of money on one day of operation, the desire to produce small quantities of high-gravity, barrel-aged, or sour beer for a specialized audience. Some release days are not brewery based but rather occur when a brewery releases into its distribution network a limited beer that will only be available for one time or for one time during the year. These releases (Bourbon County Stout, Kentucky Breakfast Stout, Black Note) may lead to allowances of single-bottle or single four-pack purchases at various retail establishments in the network.[1]

Over the last half a dozen years, brewery-based special-release events have grown from a few hundred people attending specific events or festivals to over six thousand people attending in the case of one specific release. Portsmouth Brewery's Kate the Great imperial stout release (in March), Russian River's Pliny the Younger double IPA release (in February), Surly's Darkness Day imperial stout release (in October), the Bruery's Black Tuesday imperial stout release (in October), and Three Floyds' Dark Lord Day (in April) are five well-known release days. Release days were once local draws; they now attract beer consumers from thousands of miles away or even from other countries. For the 2012 release of Cigar City's Hunahpu Imperial Stout, Beer Advocate members debated the value of camping out at the brewery the night before.[2] The debate soon became moot. Four thousand people showed up to buy three-bottle allocations in 2013.[3] In 2014 the same event drew angry crowds and almost caused a riot when Cigar City ran out of beer before distributing all of its ticket holders' allotments. For the 2012 Jackie O's December release party, one attendee complained that showing up the night before was no longer enough to secure some bottles.[4] On July 12, 2013, three hundred people lined up for Westbrook Brewing's special release of barrel-aged versions of Mexican Cake Imperial Stout, a stout brewed for the first time only two years earlier.[5]

A release day may be similar to other one-day events in which consumers line up to purchase products: Black Friday sales, concert tickets, or a new iPhone release. Delivery in these events, as well, might function in a socially networked manner, although this chapter focuses on two specific experiences that, like the last chapter, engaged me personally. My first example, a brewery-based craft beer release day, helps in understanding how social networks create a networked version of delivery. The building of the network—the concept of carpentry I borrow from Bogost's interest in how objects affect other objects—includes me as much as it includes other actors in the network.

Dark Lord Day

Out of the release events I listed above, I have been twice to Dark Lord Day. Dark Lord Day is hosted at the Three Floyds brewery in Munster, Indiana. In a small industrial park, thousands gather to purchase a specified allotment of the special release Dark Lord imperial stout, to drink guest taps from various craft brewers, and to share beers that they have brought to the event. In 2005 only two hundred people showed up; in 2012 over six thousand crowded the brewery, its parking lot, and the streets in the vicinity. By 2013 the event had spread to a nearby field to accommodate all the people and the live music. In 2014 eight thousand people attended. The only way to participate in the event—aside from setting up tents and chairs in the surrounding area—is to wait in line for the beer purchase, for entry to the brewpub, or for purchasing guest beers. Dark Lord Day, like the other release day I will discuss, is not a single event. It is an event carpentered over many events and by many individuals and objects.

Communication about the event called Dark Lord Day occurs in a number of social networking spaces prior to, during, and after the event. The website Beernews.org; the membership sites the Beerspot.com, RateBeer, and Beer Advocate; Beerpulse, Twitter; Facebook; Flickr; and various blogs network a series of announcements and follow-up information regarding the release date. Three Floyds, struggling to find an equitable system for selling its release beer, used Twitter in 2010 to announce the sale of Golden Tickets to the event (as opposed to previous years when attendees showed up without guarantee of purchase). The Twitter sale announcement was made on RateBeer, Beer Advocate, and Beernews.org. The March 17, 2010, Twitter announcement for the April sale came in two tweets, the first at 9:36 A.M.: "After work we'll put the pot of golden tickets at the end of your rainbow"; the second came at 7:05 P.M. the same day: "Darklord 'Golden Tickets' are available at: http://bit.ly/bjMWaW Have a great St. Patrick's day!" The tickets sold out in an hour and crashed the brewery's website. In 2012 the tickets sold out in four minutes.

To purchase a ticket, the buyer must have navigated a variety of sources of information since the time of sale was ambiguous or not clearly announced. While repeatedly hitting reload on Twitter was one option for discovering the right time to make a purchase, buyers likely were following threads in the various weblogs for days, if not weeks, up until the unannounced purchase date. That is what I did in 2010 when tickets went on sale during the time I was at an academic conference, and I spent hours in my hotel room hitting reload on the browser. In the case of the Dark Lord release, delivery does not occur at one moment or via one

2009 Dark Lord tickets

speaker, but instead it is distributed over a variety of spaces over a period of time. Delivery is also the publication of content by a collective intelligence participating together via modes of sentiment. Those who share information regarding the sale do not merely give an actual time or date (which is published by the brewery), but often they share other essential knowledge based on their general emotional responses to Dark Lord Day. The members of these sites share speculation, information, anticipation, disappointment, and ideas for the ticket announcement as well as for the event itself. This sharing is not homogenous and not necessarily in agreement with one another, as some areas of social media theory claim for generic sharing. Because of this network of moments and sharing, Dark Lord Day has the same kind of craft identity that I have attributed to myself in previous chapters, an identity based on the networking of disparate moments and ideas.

The arguments regarding Dark Lord and its release are based on a collective *sentiment* of craft, not logic or rationality. Cost, a need to actually buy this beer, and logistics seldom play a dominant role in one's decision to attend Dark Lord Day, and when they do, sentiment dominates. This type of delivery juxtaposes what Sennett calls "engagement" and what Malcolm McCullough calls the craft characteristic of "participation." Within the enhanced network of delivery that Dark Lord enjoys, participation becomes a major feature of its craft status. As McCullough writes, "There is reason to explore the possibility of craft in the emerging realm of information technology" (19). McCullough highlights how craft is a type of technological participation that conveys meaning:

> How to operate technology is not enough; it might be better to ask how to be when using technology. If it were possible to summarize this psychology in a single word, that world would be "participation." As is increasingly acknowledged by managers and technologists alike, effective satisfactory work depends on conscious involvement. This very sense is perhaps all that is meant by the new usage of the word "craft." (139)

Participation, in the network-styled delivery I frame as responsible for the release day, is the sentiment-based telling that informs various audiences (or Connectors) across multiple platforms in multiple moments so that physical and emotional involvement occurs. This telling (not unlike the sharing of repeated anecdotes) engages participation. That participation, as it networks a variety of forces, is craft.

Fragmented Tracings

The multiple exchanges delivering Dark Lord's release to a given audience (or more than one audience) are too numerous to duplicate, but we can explore some online interactions in order to understand, or encode, their functionality. Doing so lets me tell one Dark Lord story as a series of exchanges occurring across an obsessive social network. These networked exchanges do not lead to, as Carolyn Rude writes, a finite act of meaning, nor do they repeat the grand narrative gestures I have identified in this book as fundamental to certain types of beer narratives (revolution, for instance). "Delivery understood as a finite act, ending with the performance or publication, neglects (or at least does not emphasize) the impact of the publication on the rhetorical situation, the exigence that called the publication into being," Rude argues (274). Whatever the exigence that calls the release day into being (reasons such as I noted above), its impact is not defined by one moment or one message. The release day delivery includes the impact (what happens on the day) as well as the various networked texts that create the day for its audience. Those network texts, too, function as impacts. They also create a reason, or exigence, for participation. One rhetorical exigence would be "to buy beer not otherwise available." Another exigence might be aesthetic: "this beer tastes good" or "the bottle's artwork looks metal." Yet various exchanges regarding the release discount such points as the sole reason to engage with Dark Lord Day. Buying beer is one type of exigence but not the only one as sentiment demonstrates.

One approach to telling a Dark Lord story would be to trace the release day texts found on various online social networking sites in order to arrive at a primary moment of origin so that we understand the event's inception and impact. Just as an anecdote is often assumed to be the initiator of a linear story, so, too, could a tracing show a linear causality. But like the anecdote, the release day story does not progress accordingly, but rather it is interrupted by other media moments (transmedia). Release days, in what sounds like a contradiction, have no single point of origin or direct trajectory. Instead of performing a linear tracing, I follow a version of Bruno Latour's methodology regarding networked tracing; I isolate a few networked moments that represent how delivery is called into being. These moments are treated as fragmented events—snapshots—that, when put in relationship with one another, reveal some understanding of an activity occurring. *Some* understanding, I want to emphasize, not a total understanding. These moments will allow, following Latour's notion of the tracing, for an interaction "to *frame*, to *structure*, to *localize* another" (Latour, *Reassembling the Social* 194, emphasis in original). The isolation of these events (rather than a complete analysis of the day or the texts that create this day) is done with the understanding, as Latour notes, that "there is nothing more difficult to grasp than social ties" (159). Social networking is a continuous movement; we can never fully trace all connections, relations, or engagements as individuals and objects participate together in a network and build (or carpenter) some variation of the new aesthetic. Whatever I trace, then, is not a totality or full grasp of social ties. The representations I isolate demonstrate "fragmentation rather than convergence" as a key feature of social networking delivery (Castells 37).

These fragments isolate two dates, 2008 and 2010 (the first and last time I physically engaged with the event called Dark Lord Day), as nodes in this larger network of meaning. I include myself because I, too, am a member of the group sentiment I explore. I am part of this overall collective intelligence. I am part of the weaving. My craft identity is personified (for me) in Dark Lord (and as I will also explain, in other releases as well). Since these are linkable online moments, in the chapter notes I indicate their location by URLs rather than conventional citations, which I feel would fail to allow an accurate tracing to be followed. Readers can access the links in the notes for more complete threads and conversations that, in turn, link to other moments of "telling" as well. The note and its link act as a Connector and provide a more complete tracing of delivery. Overall, I present these isolated moments as the tracing itself with minimal commentary and in narrative form so that an impression or small-story view of the process of networked delivery can be read.

Networked Delivery

Every narrative, even if nonlinear, has some semblance of a beginning. Discussion on Beerspot.org for the 2008 Dark Lord release occurs on October 2007, months in advance of the release day. Because of Dark Lord Day's growing popularity, the message board thread begins with speculation that the event will be moved to the Hammond Civic Center and concludes with the eventual posting of an official Three Floyds poster countering that speculation by showing the release to be held at the brewery again (with promised "shorter lines").[6] Beernews.org begins its coverage of the release on April 3, 2008, with the entry "Three Floyds Dark Lord Day 2008 Countdown Begins."[7] The entry's purpose is informational:

The most celebrated beer release in the US takes place on Saturday, April 26, in Munster, Indiana. Nick Floyd, founder of the brewery, aka Floydicus, revealed just *some* of the details of Dark Lord Day 2008 on both Beer Advocate and RateBeer recently. The event will take place all day from 11AM–10PM with several bands playing music, and food and merchandise also being sold.

The RateBeer calendar for April 2008 lists several hundred members attending the event.[8] The Beer Advocate calendar lists exactly 365 members attending.[9] Founder and owner Nick Floyd updates Beer Advocate members with details of the release (including the promise of "faster lines").[10] The Brew Dudes post a video of their road trip, including the Three Floyds growlers of beer they are drinking in their hotel room the day before the event. At the event they declare, "After waiting in line for two hours, they finally opened the doors and started letting people buy the Dark Lord."[11] A synopsis of the 2008 event is recorded at the popular Indiana weblog *Hoosier Beer Geek*. "Let's talk about that line," one paragraph begins.[12] Because of the long lines, the *Chicagoist* coverage claims "never again."[13] A Flickr photo set by Fejnation shows people waiting in line around the Three Floyds brewery.[14] Another Flickr set by Bgramer shows more lines.[15] One Beer Advocate thread title, angry at the release selling out before all those in attendance could purchase the beer, reads, "I Came to DLD and Leave Empty Handed."[16] In addition, more reports of shortages appear at Beernews.org.[17] On TheBeerSpot.org, Farmhouswench describes a positive experience:

> We had a great time! Got there around 10, maybe 10:30. Walked right past the endless line to the tasting area in front and were greeted by many friendly and familiar faces. Picnic tables were as full as ever, but with nearly everyone waiting in line, it was far less crowded.[18]

One video posted on Flickr contains the caption "In line for probably 4 hours at this point. Yeah, four hours."[19] Almost simultaneously, my first tasting of the beer was recorded on RateBeer on July 5, 2008. I did not attend the release that year. I avoided the lines, though a friend from Indiana cut to front and purchased beer for us. By 2012, the 2008 concern over lines continues as Doug of the blog *The Brew Bros* notes that, while he has tried every Dark Lord since 2008, he has never been to the event because "I also really can't stand waiting in line and that specifically is another huge deterrent for me wanting to go to this event."[20]

These 2008 moments anchored by lines and shortages eventually are engaged by those attending in 2010. The earlier threads and moments join the 2010 moments to create one portion of a network of exchange. On RateBeer, discussions regarding attendance begin around January with threads such as "Dark Lord Day 2010" and end with expected thread titles such as "Dark Lord Day, how was it?"[21] On a January 4, 2010, RateBeer thread, member VandenBossche writes,

> For those of you that poo-poo the idea of DLD without ever attending . . . you're missing the point. The acquisition of the DL is incidental. The main attraction is the camaraderie amongst fellow beer lovers and the opportunity to try a host of new beers whether they be on tap or provided by other RB/BA folk.[22]

A 2010 Three Floyds website screenshot shows Dark Lord Day and Golden Tickets as two of the top ten Chicago trending topics on Twitter.[23] A Beer Advocate thread titled "Dark Lord Day 2010 . . . Details, Prior Indications from Previous Years" serves as a source for information, general griping, what to expect based on past experiences, where to shop in the area, and what kinds of bottles to bring for trades. "I had read a ton about DLD prior to making the 76 mile trip from South Bend IN, and my expectations were high," one blogger writes.[24] Beer Advocate member KarlHungus tells other members to remember 2008:

> My experience at Dark Lord Day 2008 was that it was the most unorganized event I have ever been too [sic]. Note that I said most unorganized event, and not most unorganized beer event. The part that really made me think, "wow, these people have absolutely no idea what they are doing" is when they came out with a jackhammer to put up tents a couple hours after the event had started. Why the hell didn't they have those tents set up prior?[25]

Overall, users contextualize past experiences by knowing ahead of time to set up trades that will take place on the day of the event.[26] Beer Advocate sets up a general information page as a resource for attendees.[27] On RateBeer, plans to meet up are established.[28] After the event, RateBeer member BBB63 writes about the sharing experience:

> The vertical of 2006–2010 DL seemed to be a hit. Glad to be able to share with everyone. The 2007 has really improved but still among my least favorite, the 2006 is at peak and possibly going downhill. The 2008 still has some ageing left and the 2009 is still pretty green. Time will still tell on the 2008 through 2010.[29]

Beer Advocate member Skeksi dismisses complaints regarding bottle allotment:

> Most of the complaints I read are from people who could have avoided their own headaches by planning better and reading the threads on this very forum, which have been up for weeks. You gonna tell me the other threads on here weren't full of people advising to get there early as hell? Yea, but fuck FFF right?[30]

On YouTube, a video pans over the guest tap trailer. At forty-two seconds, as the camera shows people waiting for the sale to begin, I can see the back of my balding head.[31] Even though we had tickets in 2010, we showed up at 7:00 A.M. to stand outside the gates to the brewery and wait in a sprawling line for the 10:00 A.M. opening. On the website Chicago Now, Nohit Naimpally writes of the 2010 crowd, "I know of a fair number of beer enthusiasts that were unable to get Golden Tickets, or even Dark Lord, but still had a great time at the event."[32] On Beernews.org a hosted video shows Three Floyds minister of propaganda Lincoln Anderson declaring that the release brings together "people of like mind."[33] Reflecting on the event's attendance, RateBeer member DrinkMcDermott links to an Examiner.com article he has written about Dark Lord Day 2005, the release's first year.[34] That link contains an embedded video shot at the 2005 event, at which only two hundred people attended.[35] He writes,

Me striking a pose after waiting in line at Dark Lord Day, 2010

Back then, only about 200 people came to the brewery, and they all fit inside the building. No bands, not a lot of beer trading. And since Floyds's brewpub hadn't been built yet, just a tasting booth with a couple of taps of other Floyds available.

The blog *SixPackTech* (which is not a beer blog) reposts the 2005 video, expressing recognition of people featured.[36] When Mark Dredge lists Dark Lord as a "Blockbuster Beer," he notes in his description that upon arriving at the event, he "joined a three-hour line. The standing in line sucks" (*Craft Beer World* 205). In April 2010 I record my second Dark Lord Day visit on my weblog *Make Mine Potato*.[37] I complain about the lines.

Imagined Delivery

These are fragmented participatory moments conveying an event. They are engagements created by various agents delivering this event in multiple pieces of networked information. In this first example, I mostly focus on the craft beer enthusiast tribe, the human agents delivering the event over various online spaces (with more space, I might also explore the nonhuman agents as well—the websites, the threads, the tickets, the guest taps, the lines). In this sense, engagement or participation doesn't mean actual physical involvement but something more akin to what McLuhan and Fiore call "total involvement," a communicative process where "information brushes against other information" so that a sense of knowing occurs even when it is difficult to grasp how that knowing takes place (*Medium* 76). They call this delivery "participation mystique" (114), and Maffesoli calls it the secret. "The mass audience," McLuhan and Fiore write, "can be used as a creative, participating force" (22). Why these individuals participate in delivering Dark Lord Day (including me), though, remains unknown. It's a mystery. Long lines. Cost. Lack of organization. Such logical factors do not override emotional interest in being with the group or sharing with the group. Sharing is a component of networked delivery. One could simple attend (or not) and not help create the growing network of information that leads to some virtual or emotional sense of Dark Lord participation. In this networked release day space, the contagion, as I have explored it, functions via the complex motives for sharing. As Michael Kriser reflects upon his 2013 experience at Dark Lord,

> Everyone that goes to Dark Lord Day can choose to be an entitled critic and write a Yelp-like review of the experience from a "customer" point of view (many of which come from people who have

never been there), or you can take a stake in the day yourself, bring a couple bottles to share, try some beers that are well "off the menu" and if you are so inclined, wait in line for one of the great craft beers that catalyzed an unstoppable craft beer culture we may never see the likes of again.

The expected delivery moment might be "consumption," but as Kriser notes, consumption does not explain the feeling or impact of a shared communicative event such as Dark Lord Day. Delivery's focus need not be reception (where value plays a role in how messages are received), as classical rhetoric teaches, but the network. The network—or the social network—assumes audiences are multiple and varied since multiple agents participate in the creation and dissemination of information.

The fragmented moments I've highlighted regarding Dark Lord Day do not reveal a specific agent or position in that communicative moment. Nor do they reveal, as Surowiecki argues, that influence can be detrimental to collective intelligence. Influence occurs as individuals tell each other about Dark Lord Day. That influence, though, is not persuasive as we might believe influence should be (people do not try to stop or encourage attendance). Nor is it deliberative since members of the tribe do not make an argument about buying or attending Dark Lord Day. Some people put their interests ahead of the group; some break with sensibility to tell about Dark Lord Day problems (bashing the event will not lead to its continued success, after all). Some send video; some send text; some send images. Some are ecstatic; some are disappointed; some are reflective; some are nostalgic. Regardless, collective intelligence or sentiment generates delivery. The group is both homogenous (united by interest in Dark Lord Day) and diverse (disjointed in the message it conveys about the release day). Surowiecki's question is "Can people make collectively intelligent decisions even when they are in constant, if erratic, interaction with each other?" (43). With a release day, the answer appears to be that erratic interaction or participation does not prevent a collective decision to attend and promote the event.

Even with all of this tracing, I cannot be sure that reception occurred anywhere in particular among Dark Lord Day participants (how many people actually have seen these videos or read these threads?) or was intended (when a posted video has 330 views, is viewer reception intended, or is this just a simple act of sharing among craft enthusiasts?) nor be sure that it was thoughtful or planned (as Quintilian proposes). Instead, a process unfolds, what Rude describes as the nonunified characteristic of new media delivery: "The message is delivered in multiple media by multiple voices over time" (283). For a moment like Dark Lord Day, we have to *imagine* delivery since no one moment stands for the act or for its overall effects. Craft, in networked delivery, evokes this sentiment of imagination. We imagine that all of these networked events perform together. The consequences of a networked delivery are not the gestures or intonations that a speaker or writer makes but rather the imagination of reception we create and receive over a series of moments and exchanges. Delivery is imaginary.

Delivery and imagination are not unknown to each other in rhetorical theory. Fredal summarizes Demosthenes's *Against Meidias* by questioning whether it was ever delivered. Rather than provide evidence, Fredal settles on the imaginary:

> The interesting question arises out of evidence of the speech's imaginability, seeing rhetorical action as a constitutional feature of the speech throughout the composing process. The question is not whether or not the speech was delivered by the historical Demosthenes but whether it is *imaginable* as the performance of a Demosthenes character. (256)

Whether or not a product or taste is delivered may not always equate the imaginable: griping, standing in line, sharing, interacting, being engaged, participating. These are the nodes of social media obsession over the network. And, as Maffesoli argues, vitalism (imagined energy) is not representational or definable but is, as he notes, mythical, the space where "experience and imagination reinforce one another" (59):

> The contemporary media, by presenting images of everyday life rather than visualizing the great works of culture, would be playing the role that used to fall to the various forms of public discourse: to ensure by means of myth the cohesion of a given social entity. (26)

"In the popular imagination," Surowiecki writes, "groups tend to make people either dumb or crazy, or both" (xv). That is not the case in the first example I provide. *I can imagine* the Dark Lord Day network, or I can point to the mythic performance it engages across a variety of actors without believing that the actors shaping these spaces are dumb or crazy. The online media space I draw mostly from to trace the release conveys a sense of social myth since its members' discursive exchanges are not necessarily bound by intimacy or community but by an imagined cohesion across various spaces. Social moments can feel representational (I was there) or mythical (I imagine what occurred). Thus Cicero, too, understands Demosthenes's delivery also as mythic:

> As the tale goes—it was his habit to slip pebbles into his mouth, and then declaim a number of verses at the top of his voice and without drawing breath, and this not only as he stood still, but while walking about, or going up a steep slope. (261; bk. 1, sec. 61)

Myth, in this case, is exaggeration. Exaggeration—putting pebbles in one's mouth while delivering verse—offers cohesion regarding what is or isn't possible for a given audience. When I trace a star across the state of Pennsylvania to note the mythic nature of my identity (as it is delivered to me via patterns), I, too, exaggerate in order to offer a cohesive narrative. I exaggerate as much as a brewer or writer declaring beer to be a revolution. Dark Lord is another form of exaggeration—the once-a-year release—that bonds a community of drinkers' narratives regarding lines, scarcity, taste, and trades. As I cited McLuhan earlier, new media delivery embodies "the mythic or collective dimension of human experience" because basic representation (what something means) is not as pleasurable as the exaggerated myth (what we imagine). Release days, as well, deliver myths. The myths are emotional (desire to obtain hard to find beer) as well as actual. The lines at Dark Lord Day are, in fact, long, as some of the fragmented tracings I enact reveal (they are not myths, in the sense of being "made up" or hyperbolic retellings). The delivery of such a message, however, occurs within a larger imagined or mythical event that one may or may not experience as it belongs to a larger sentiment that a metaphoric Dark Lord tribe evokes.

Delivery, in the social networked space, is imagined. This imagined state, as Maffesoli argues, is secretive (what happened?) and affective (sentiment) and an extended form of orality (Ong). The brief tracing of the Dark Lord Day release that I perform here is not meant to offer a conclusive understanding of networked delivery as craft technology but instead is meant to frame our understandings of such acts as what the classical tradition frames as oral, what Ong calls secondary orality, and what Maytag called "telling," as these notions are updated for the new media environment we live within. As Latour writes, the task is not to explain what a given moment is but rather to trace out its relationships, to describe those relationships as much as possible, and to maintain the desire for "details, I want more details" so that we might imagine an overall body of information in its collective, mythic state (*Reassembling* 137). Dark Lord Day is not the only event we can turn to for such purposes, but it does offer initial insight into the complexity of social networking as delivery. This delivery not only allows someone like me to attend or purchase Dark Lord, but it builds a series of ideas (scarcity, waiting, pleasure, thrill, sharing) that other moments of delivery may or may not construct. If a release is part of the new aesthetic, as the previous chapter explores, its value is not in one item (bottle) or event (sale) but in the craft sense of networked delivery. The other moment I want to offer as example of this process is the release of Founders' Canadian Breakfast Stout. Like Dark Lord Day, Canadian Breakfast Stout is also mythical. Its release, however, happens in a slightly different way.

Craft Tracing

In addition to Dark Lord Day, I share another specific networked delivery where carpentry occurs so that I can continue to understand how objects (including me) affect objects (including me) within craft. I contribute to the carpentry of not one or two releases but of the overall network called release. Unlike the one day at the brewery release day I've focused on, I shift attention to the release day in which a beer is distributed to the public for sale, but in a limited way. The one release I will focus on is Founders Brewing's Canadian Breakfast Stout, released in September 2011 for the first time in bottle form as part of the brewery's Backstage series of 750-milliliter bottles. I choose this event to focus another social media obsession as carpentry and to trace a supposedly simplistic moment (the selling of a one-time beer) complicated by the agents who construct the network. To do this tracing, I again include numerous pointers to where these agents appear in the network, where they might be read, where they might engage with other agents. Details provide the tracing. I interrupt my Dark Lord discussion in order to begin again.

Founders' Canadian Breakfast Stout (CBS) is a barrel-aged version of the brewery's regular breakfast stout (a coffee stout released during the winter months) with maple syrup added. Initially, the beer only existed as draught, and its reputation as exotic and rare centered on such limited access. One had to go to the brewery, sample it at a festival, or participate in a rare tapping at a specific bar within Founders' distribution network in order to try the beer in four- to ten-ounce samples. If I had been more alert to the guest taps while I was at Dark Lord Day in 2009, I could have sampled CBS, but I didn't. Many of the 2009 reviews on RateBeer express such an experience.[38] The bottle, in 750-milliliter size (the contagion of my previous discussion of bottle size), focused attention on the beer, as object, in unique ways as news of its release attracted more attention than draught availability had previously raised. CBS, like Dark Lord Day, eventually became a networked conversation across numerous spaces rather than a one-time event. These conversations occurred, for the most part, in new media spaces: blog posts, videos, shared images, news aggregation sites, and social media sites. CBS was listed—via aggregated ratings—as the fourteenth best beer of 2011 by RateBeer.[39] CBS, though, is not listed among Dredge's 350 of the finest beers known to man.

The hype over the release of CBS in a 750-milliliter bottle for the first time gained traction on September 16, 2011, when Founders blogged that CBS is on the bottling line.[40] The popular Beerpulse website reblogged the rarity and shock of that moment so that a wider audience might learn the news.[41] As interruptions challenge beginnings, discussion preceded the bottling and official announcement. On August 11, 2011, Evan Benn, beer writer for the *St. Louis Post*, tweeted a quote from Founders' president Mike Stevens that fifteen states would be allocated one thousand cases of the beer packaged in 750-milliliter bottles.[42] At the point of the Founders announcement, Beerpulse writer Adam Nason reminded readers that even earlier than Benn's tweet, the blog *The Beer Is Good* leaked the news that a new beer would be released from Founders, a beer that turned out (unknown to the blogger at the time) to be CBS.[43] Responding to *The Beer Is Good*, Nason commented, "The CBS release may not necessarily follow suit but it gives us some indication as to what we might expect."[44] In September RateBeer administrator Joet posted the Founders press release for the CBS October release and further expanded the audience to include others who might not have been aware of any of the earlier blog posts or tweets.[45] In the Midwest, in a September 23, 2011, post the *Chicago Foodies* blog expressed excitement over the pending release. "There will not be a lot available," the post warned.[46] Initial discussion of perceived rarity and mythical status (never before bottled) allowed for the network's growth.

With these details, one might expect a conclusion to the beer's network. The beer was anticipated, eventually released, and some consumers purchased it. In this case, the release is not a festival or a moment for bottle sharing, so community cohesion is not necessarily realized in a physical space beyond that of waiting in a line at a local retail store for the delivery truck to arrive with its allotment of CBS. The release, beyond its actual

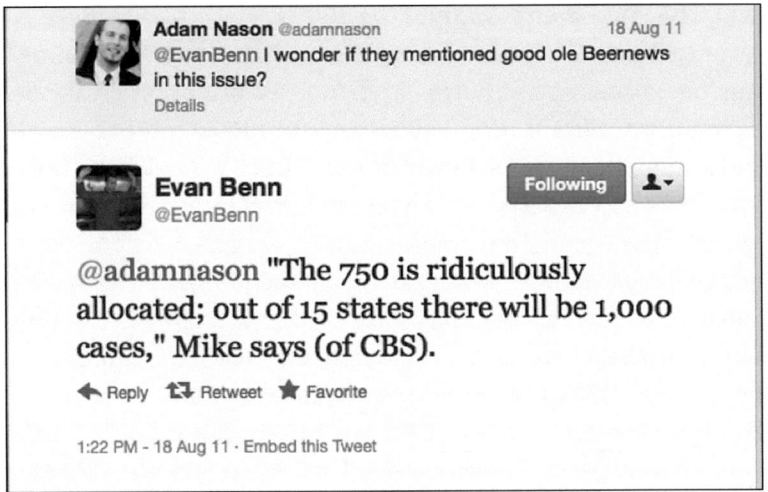

Screenshot of Evan Benn's tweet and Adam Nason's response, showing carpentry in action

appearance on store shelves, generated further discussion and interest regarding issues of distribution, taste, hype, and other matters, and thus extended the release beyond one day to a distributed series of moments built by those who consumed or did not consume the product.

The conversation focuses, at first, on availability. Even if it's in the network members' interest not to share availability or scarcity stories (and thus have better access to the release if it remains somewhat under the radar), they often do. As a major Connector of craft beer information, Nason provided on his blog what he termed "an incomplete run down" of the distribution states for the beer.[47] Many links in the rundown showed exact bottle distribution as well as which stores had sold out. The lack of access to distribution, even in states where Founders is normally distributed, led some consumers to proclaim a "CBS Fail."[48] Aleheads blogged the beer's local tapping (to coincide with the bottle release): "The CBS began pouring at 4:15PM . . . it was gone by 4:50PM."[49] Websites crashed under duress from online orders (where available) or from those looking for availability news.[50] A New Jersey drinker noted how the Coverleaf bar's tapping of the beer "kicked in under 10 minutes."[51] A Cleveland beer drinker posted that "Whole Foods sold out in about 40 minutes."[52] Mark and Shaun's *Beer Blog* described their frustrations with getting a bottle:

> I called my local wine store 10 times during release week, tried multiple locations, veritably begged them for it, and they ended

up releasing it mid-day via tweet (and the dreaded Facebook post) when I was at work, miles away. It disappeared in 10 minutes. My other angle was through a raffle. . . . Suffice it to say, I did not win. Some guy allegedly celebrating his birthday won the last of the six. I momentarily imagined him opening it up and finding it filled with Bud Select. I must say that such a thought was not unpleasant.[53]

The blogger of *Hop Bunnies* drove five hours to Grand Rapids to wait in line at the brewery for a bottle.[54] On the night of the release, Beyond the Pour filmed a review of CBS.[55] Shoreline Beverage in New York was accused of selling its allotment too early.[56] Beer Avatar described some price gouging.[57] It's Just the Booze Dancing brought up the issue of price gouging as well.[58] Founders commented on the release snafus and dispelled rumors of state, store, or specific market favoritism:

> On another note, there seems to be some concern or confusion on how are beers are allocated per state. We are proud to be a Michigan-based brewery and all specialty releases take this into consideration. We at Founders will never forget our home state market. In terms of CBS, the state of Michigan received an allocation of 21% of the entire batch of CBS. No other state saw more than 12% of the total availability. That being said, no state is treated more fairly than another (including MI). Distributor allocations are simply based on a representation of total number of accounts they represent for Founders. Should rumors of this exist to the contrary, know that they are just that: rumors.[59]

In response to the distributed rhetoric of complaints and access concerns, Big Red Liquors in Indiana released a video promoting the release and announced the 5:00 P.M. sale of their "miniscule" allotment at the downtown Bloomington store.[60] The writer of *Beermonger*, who works in retail, appealed to craft beer drinkers to tone down the hype regarding distribution and sales.[61] Flickr user Mainbr86 posted an October 6 picture of his beer fridge that featured two bottles of CBS in the side door.[62]

At another point in the release's delivery, the rhetoric switches from complaining about access and distribution to consumption. An October 15, 2011, picture uploaded to Flickr shows Cicerone Annette May holding a bottle of CBS proudly.[63] The blogger behind *The Beer Is Good*, who initially scooped the CBS release story, eventually tried the beer as well.[64] By January 2012, Serious Eats, the popular food website, reviewed CBS

Screenshot of Big Red Liquors CBS announcement

and found it "staggeringly impressive."[65] The Imasofat husband and wife reviewing pair paid $22 for a bottle and posted a review on YouTube that includes the comment, "It smells just like chocolate syrup."[66] All That Ales You posted a video review, noting the beer's "good marriage between the chocolate and coffee."[67] Among all this conversation and telling, I found myself within the network as well. In Lexington, Kentucky, I made several phone calls to a local liquor chain, Liquor Barn, and its many stores in town and inquired on the chain's Facebook page about the beer's release. I received promises of arrival that were not accurate, received denials that the chain had received any bottles that later were found to be untrue, and was told on the phone that they had no idea what the beer was. Eventually, I camped outside the store closest to my house until it opened at 9:00 A.M., and a Facebook update said the beer would be available. Not finding the bottle on the shelf, I asked if any had arrived. A salesperson went into the back and brought me a bottle. "One bottle limit?" I asked. "Of course," the sales person responded. I made my own comments on October 12 at my *Make Mine Potato* blog.[68] I saved the empty bottle for some reason that was not clear to me. It still sits on a shelf in my beer cellar. On October 13, 2011, I posted my review of CBS to RateBeer. In that review, I used the word "hype" four times.

My usage of social media to locate a bottle was not unique. In April 2013, John Thompson recalls the CBS release as a digital one where the beer's footprint was tracked for him by Untappd.

CRAFT TRACINGS

My RateBeer review of CBS

I recall in October of 2011, soon after Founders Backstage Series release of CBS (Canadian Breakfast Stout) and I saw one of my Untappd friends was drinking a bottle at Al's of Hampden.

I had never heard of Al's of Hampden, and how were they serving Founders, much less a very rare release? I immediately opened Google Maps to find where this Al's of Hampden was.[69]

In June 2013, the MyBeerCellar auction site listed a bottle of CBS that sold, along with a bottle of Founders' Better Half, for $204.99.[70] Two years after its release, CBS is still part of a narrative regarding distribution, access, and relationships. This narrative unfolds across social media spaces as well as on auction sites or on a shelf in a home in Lexington, Kentucky. The narrative moves through availability issues, public response, repetition of experience, and, finally, taste. The collective building of this network does not present a common interest beyond desire ("I want that beer"), and yet the collective tells the story of CBS as a force and not as an individual.

This brief tracing captures the building of a series of responses and participation around a special release, moments where consumers become a type of producer as they collaboratively network an object through moments of textual and visual communication, without such collaboration being foregrounded as an intentional gesture. In this version of carpentry, agency occurs through social interactions more than it occurs through intention. That the narrative of agents, human and nonhuman, build together without realizing their joint efforts suggests that networks are objects-as-relationships—relationships that join together a variety of forces whose networking constructs what could not be done individually.

Empty CBS bottle in my basement cellar

This tracing I present is not complete, but rather it shows a small example of carpentry as a networked activity. This tracing, as well, leaves out the popular beer website Beer Advocate's message board threads; the website's 2012 crash pulled all of the posts offline (though the site's owners claim the threads have been backed up).[71] The tracing extends one object (a 750-milliliter bottle of CBS) so that it becomes another object (the threads, discussions, videos, personal moments), which, in turn, consists of many objects in relationship with one another. As a result, more than one network is built, but I focus here on a quick tracing of the release day moment as an example of what might have been made. If the release day does have an aesthetic, and if that aesthetic is more than the taste of stout, maple syrup, or chocolate, then the aesthetic is this tracing. And if there is a philosophy here—as carpentry calls for—it involves questions regarding relationships among digital spaces.

Tracing Delivery

Once a portion of a craft network is traced (as I've done with these two examples), what does the information gained from this tracing allow for? An improved release date? A better method of distribution? Shorter lines? Alternative consumption habits? Better mad rushes to the store to buy limited bottles? Self-awareness of my own position in this network so that I finally refrain from such silly behavior like waiting in a liquor store's parking lot at 9:00 A.M. to buy a bottle of beer? Or none of the above? "But that's just the point," Latour has Norbert say toward the end of *Aramis* about the tracing of the failed transportation system and what its demise might mean. "It doesn't get us anywhere" (281). To reach a conclusion at a tracing's end is possible to the extent that invisible relationships are made visible. The various sites, blogs, videos, news releases, and experiences I trace have invisible relationships until the moment (the details) the relationships are made visible. Nothing in the delivery examples I began with made invisible relationships visible. These failed moments of delivery remained invisible overall; we only witness the failure in action and not the various agents that came together to cause Mrs. Roper to mock Mr. Roper's beer or the Three Stooges to overferment a wort.

I am not tracing the CBS release day in order to find resolution or an opportunity for policy/behavior change. The tracing does not reveal a larger critique or cultural phenomenon or even intervention. If I were to explain a reality based on this tracing, I would be guilty of what Latour calls the problem with explanation: "Social explanations run the risk of hiding that which they should reveal since they remain too often 'without object'" (*Reassembling* 82). Latour recognizes that reducing tracings to an explanation (the inevitable grand narrative) results in "the temptation to overreact and to turn matter into a mere intermediary faithfully 'transporting' or 'reflecting' society's agency" (84). Explanation is the temptation to write a grand narrative. Craft delivery, as understood via release day networked interruptions, does not reflect society's agency as though there were one singular force driving the day such as "capitalism" or "consumption" or "silly beer drinkers." If all a tracing revealed were the problems of capitalism (scarcity creating need or desire for superficial goods), then it would not be a tracing. It would be a retelling of a grand narrative. Grand narratives attempt to resolve interactions.

Instead of a resolution, I offer the insight of relationship complexity as central to craft delivery. Relationships, the tracing teaches me, and the complexity that constructs them, allow for a specific type of carpentry. The release day (at the brewery or in the distribution network), as these brief tracings demonstrate, extends across space, actors, movements, media, tellings, Connectors, and moments because of the relationships created. As Bogost writes,

> The experience of things can be characterized only by tracing the exhaust of their effects on the surrounding world and speculating about the coupling between that black noise and the experiences

internal to an object. Language is one tool we can use to describe this relationship, but it is *only* one tool, and we ought not feel limited by it. (*Alien Phenomenology* 100)

I am also not limited by relationships. I have a relationship, regarding CBS, with actions I take such as waiting in a parking lot, documenting my purchase, reviewing the beer, saving my bottle, photographing it, and eventually writing about the day. What might feel like a useless moment within a larger exchange is actually an agent participating in an overall carpentry as it uses language (speaking with liquor store employees, blogging, responding on message boards, writing this chapter) and doesn't use language (waiting, drinking, feeling anxious, getting angry, being satisfied, spending money). Remove the agent (or what Latour calls the mediator), and the network may still exist, but it is no longer the same network. Nor is it the same aesthetic experience as Barthes draws attention to, since without my trivial interaction I have no consumption pleasure in the network. If I am not in the network, it is not built the same way. It is still built, just without me and, thus, is built differently. In turn, I embrace this pleasurable aesthetic. Still, to present that embracement, I have to write it, or detail it, as Latour might argue. Without doing so, the network cannot be traced so that others might see its current existence or the revelation of its relationships. And without doing so, I cannot see the network either. Or to be more precise, the network cannot be traced as it currently is without being written (with me as one of the actors present). Writing, Bogost argues, limits the potential of carpentry. Latour agrees at the level of explanation or appreciation:

> In all domains, to say that something is constructed has always been associated with an appreciation of its robustness, quality, style, durability, worth, etc. So much so that no one would bother to say that a skyscraper, a nuclear plant, a sculpture, or an automobile is "constructed." This is too obvious to be pointed out. (*Reassembling* 89)

One might write, instead, that a painting or website or novel is constructed or built in a way to appreciate or admire. Writing can be the expression of appreciation ("this beer tastes good, like chocolate"; "I sure am grateful I scored a rare bottle"). If "I Am a Craft Brewer" is only a video about appreciation, then it does little more than explain an appreciation (I am a craft brewer; my product is artisanal; its value is in the craft). I don't understand the video accordingly; I see how it contributes to one part of the overall network of relationships. But I do understand carpentry making similar assumptions about appreciation. Carpentry, Bogost suggests, is a robust activity that extends what writing could not generate when limited to appreciation or critique (making is an act better than explaining). Carpentry sticks with an object as object, as if writing, too, is not an object. But carpentry exists in writing, in the detailing, tracing, and writing of the relationships, as much as it exists in the relationships that built the network or its traces. Otherwise, it explains an appreciation (i.e., presenting a toaster oven is better than writing about a beer). Writing, too, is craft or a way to reflect craft experience.

There is a network called release day that I trace. And there is a network called release day in which I am an object among objects in that network. But there is also the network called release day built in my writing, in my descriptions, in my tracing, in my narrating, in what I share here. It may seem "too obvious" to point out a network of a beer release. It may feel as if there is too much "admiration" when I recognize myself as in that network; that I am being self-indulgent. Or it may be the construction of that network that appears robust. And while Latour argues that "for any construction to take place, non-human entities have to play the major role" (*Reassembling* 92), I find that the construction can include at least one specific nonhuman, writing, and one human, me, as well. This construction, as I continue to see, is my craft obsession.

The position Bogost takes regarding carpentry, that it "seeks to capture and characterize an experience it can never fully understand, offering a rendering satisfactory enough to allow the artifact's operator to gain some insight into an alien thing's experience," extends to include the personal and writing itself, what I earlier called "personal weaving" (*Alien Phenomenology* 100). Within the networks called Dark Lord Day and CBS release day, I am as alien as the tweet or blog post or beer bottle or line or warning or stout or retail clerk selling a beer. I don't necessarily "understand," but I gain some insight as part of the network I trace and that I helped to build as well as imagine. I gain insight into my own consumption—to some extent—by identifying my relationships not previously revealed, but not at the level of critical awareness or habit change (as a cultural studies position might declare). My writing, another alien thing present, gains possible insight into me, into another piece of my overall craft obsession. My story, interrupted in this chapter, is also carpentry. Tony Sampson writes that the network tracing allows for "a generative process recursively reproducing itself—the character of organization it produces is always a product, an effect, a consequence, not an event" (44). Or the tracing is not, we can add, a single event or a single event without me as well, and without my own and others' reproducing of the releases. With an understanding of craft delivery, I will still drink beer; I will still hunt down CBS if another release day occurs (or another beer is released by Founders, as I have done with each of the Backstage releases). I, however, understand better the ways my work within the network affected others' work and helped build the network overall, a network that is still alive and functioning as other actors enter into it and leave. I understand how things make the world. Or I don't. In a networked tracing where delivery is complicated by all of these factors I've drawn attention to, comprehension's role is not the same as relationship revelation or, in Bogost's words, "insight into an alien thing's experience." In the previous chapter, I cited Bogost's declaration that carpentry reveals how things fashion one another. Network tracing, as I do here, performs likewise. "The object itself become[s] the philosophy," Bogost writes (*Alien Phenomenology* 93). Craft is one such carpentered philosophy. I fashion. I am fashioned. Craft is the philosophy, but I am part of that philosophy as well. Craft obsession is also a philosophy.

I am now ready to explore in the final two chapters my overall obsession. Obsession allows me to discover how my network comes together as a whole and is shared even further than the networks I trace here allow for. Obsession, or the image of obsession I project throughout the network, is the movement through what I have written about so far. Obsession is about relationships. Relationships entail sharing. With this sharing, obsession is also the movement through photographs, trades, and a concluding parental beer tale I eventually will share in the epilogue.

CHAPTER 7
Craft Sharing

> I get the party started with Arrogant Bastard.
> —People Under the Stairs, "Beer"

On February 19, 2013, beer blogger Jay Brooks posted a 1950 ad from Schlitz Brewing. Brooks often posts historic beer ads, each portraying some ideological or temporal perspective on how beer has been viewed or understood over time. His weblog, *Brookstone Beer Bulletin*, functions as a beer archive, preserving forgotten ads and modern infographics in order to document snapshots of beer history and to share that history with a readership. This particular ad, as part of a larger Schlitz campaign, featured a series of snapshots taken by travelers. The snapshots, unlike normal travel photographs, focused on Schlitz and not the places traveled to. As Brooks writes of the Schlitz ad,

> It's part of their "I was curious" series that always features three panels. This one features a scrapbook that, despite the fact that it would appear to be from a picturesque location, shows the person on vacation and his beer, but not the vistas they would have been looking at. Good thing whoever he was travelling with captured the moment he first saw Schlitz, and then the moment he first tasted it. Funny, that's what my vacation shots look like, too. (Brooks, "Beer in Ads #805")

The first panel of the ad features the caption "I was curious . . ." and the second panel features the caption "I tasted it . . ." The speaker does not express curiosity about the mountains or the area the snapshots show him visiting; he was curious, it seems, about the beer in his hand at the moment the photograph was taken. His narrative, or possibly retold anecdote, is of becoming aware of Schlitz—much as I and others tell stories about becoming aware of beer in general. The rest of his social landscape (or terroir) is blurred by his attention to the *now* moment, the beer being enjoyed.

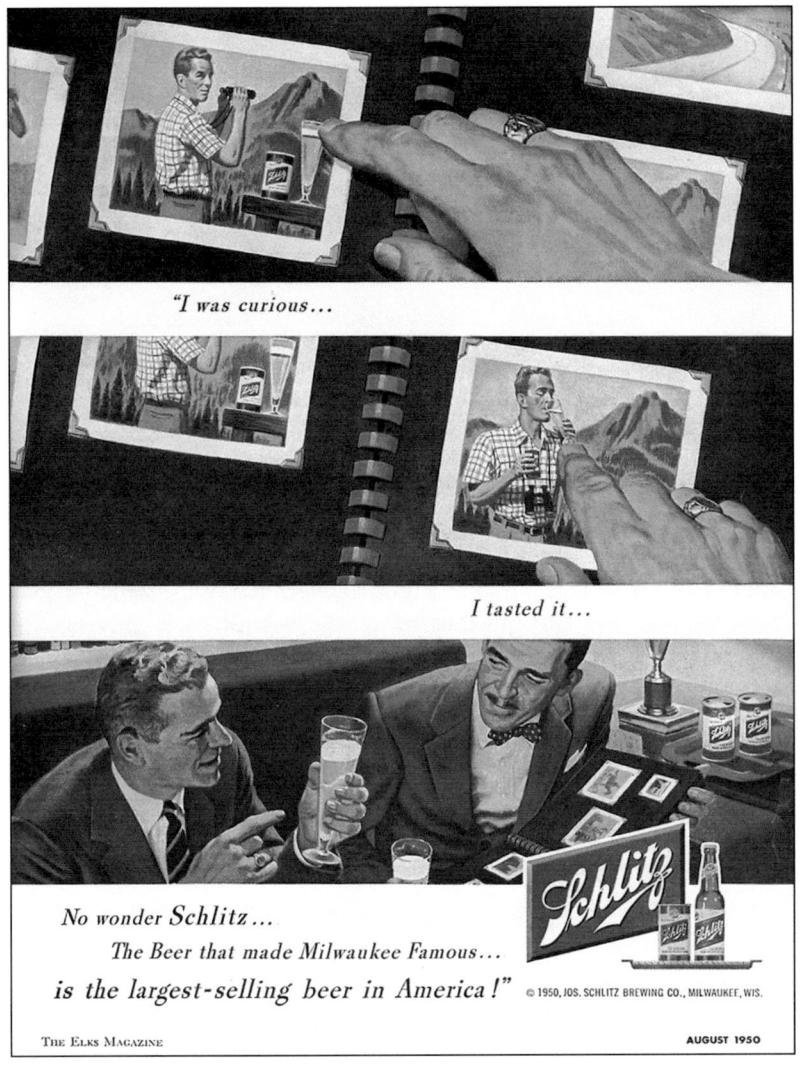

Schlitz's "I was curious . . ." campaign ad, August 1950

In the Schlitz ad, I identify the very familiar and aggregated associations of travel, taste, experience, beer, and photography. These associations exist in other beer advertising, such as a 1978 Schlitz commercial that features beer drinkers who are white-water rafting. "Making the most of now," the narrator declares in order to promote Schlitz's potency to viewers, "from the life you live to the beer you drink" ("1978 Schlitz Commercial"). Travel, we are to assume in either ad, is meant to be juxtaposed with beer. I, too, make that juxtaposition. In my phone or on my laptop's hard drive are stored travel pictures. These photographs mostly show my kids sitting in front of beer sampler trays at various brewpubs we have visited around the country. At Against the Grain, a sampler tray in front my child. At Revolution, a sampler tray in front my child. The sampler tray, of course, does not mark my children's curiosity; it marks *my* curiosity (tasting six small beers in order to get a better idea of the brewery's output and to get six ratings on RateBeer, rather than to drink one sixteen-ounce beer and get one rating). The sampler tray reduces my traveling experience to four to six glasses of four-ounce pours of beer set before me, which I, in turn, photograph so that I can share via Instagram or Facebook my experience of being curious. I have traveled, the photograph says to my imagined and shared digital audience, and here is a picture of a sampler tray in front of my child to prove this point. My child may be curious, too, as to what all that beer is doing in front of him or her, but that curiosity is altogether different from what I experience.

Against the Grain, 2012

Against the Grain, 2013

Most people who travel take pictures. For those of us interested in food or beer, we often photograph what we eat and drink. We do so because of the pleasure of the text. "By citing, naming, *noticing* food," Roland Barthes writes of this pleasure, the writer "imposes on the reader the final state of matter, what cannot be transcended" (*Pleasure of the Text* 45). The sharing of snapshots from travel is not, though, a final state (or grand narrative) but a networked state, a place of connection, with visited places and with the people one shares with. "Large numbers of people regularly travel out of their habitual environments for short periods of time," Susan Sontag offers. "It seems positively unnatural to travel for pleasure without taking a camera along" (9). When we travel with cameras, we find or create stories, even tiny, inconsequential stories, that we want to share, and we do a great deal of that sharing over social media spaces. "The story of beer in America is a story about travel," photographer and writer Michael Kiser writes. A sampler tray. A brewpub. What is the story here? I ask. What am I trying to share about my travels? "People imagine the storyteller," Walter Benjamin writes, "as someone who has come from afar" (84). In our efforts to tell the story of how far we have traveled as craft enthusiasts, we make visual our daily consumption experiences not just to cite or to notice, as Barthes contends, but *to be noticed*. I have come from or been afar. This is my experience. Notice me.

In this public noticing, the practice of everyday consumers photographing food and drink has become so prevalent that some chefs, such as Momofuku Ko's David Chang, ban patrons from taking pictures of their meals in their restaurants (Stapinski). Some beer bloggers, like Alan McLeod, have found themselves repeatedly asked not to take photographs of beer in shops and bars ("What Is the Etiquette"). Others, like *MustLoveBeer* bloggers, are unaware of or unconcerned with these bans; they post exquisite photographs on Google+ of poured beers next to bottles or cans. Some enthusiasts find photography closer to home; beer writer Brain Yaeger began a short series of "portraits of beer left in yard" to document craft littering near his house ("Portrait of Dead"). Michael Donk's Brew Bokeh site features stunning photographic portraits of breweries and the brewers who run them. Donk's photograph of Three Floyds' "Back off, you hippies" drawing (Donk), which can be found on the wall across from the brewpub's men's room, acts as a contagion of my own photograph taken in March of 2011. When I see Donk's photograph, I notice that I took the same photograph while having lunch with my family in the brewpub, a usual stopover on our six-hour drive from Lexington to Chicago. The photograph I took, shared on Facebook, and eventually turned into my profile picture on the site allowed me to tell the story of my distaste for hippies alongside (what I assume is) Three Floyds' similar distaste. The photograph allowed me to ask my Facebook and Instagram followers to notice me *as someone against hippies* but who also likes Three Floyds. That this photograph also functions as a contagion (in addition to its shared message) doesn't mean that Michael Donk and I know of each other's image, that we wanted our image to tell the same story, that one of us copied the other, or that we both dislike hippies. Instead, the photograph suggests that we have tapped into a similar interest or experience while traveling and then shared it, the way travelers often share their photography or the way craft beer enthusiasts share stories about their first beer or the way

My photo of the "Back off, you hippies" drawing, which can be compared to Michael Donk's professional image

drinkers of Pliny the Elder share similar tasting notes. I'm sure many other beer enthusiasts visiting the taproom in Munster have photographed the same image. And if so, they may, as well, have opted to photograph the mural in order to notice and be noticed.

Similar to these photographic moments I list, Beertography celebrates the art of photographing beer in order to tell a story, posting photograph contests as well as examples of exceptional images. While the site features a variety of imagery reflecting travels, I don't believe I've seen a photograph of a sampler tray in front of a child yet featured. Stan Hieronymus evokes a fascination with the unknown that travel evokes by often posting a photograph on his blog, asking where in the beer world the photo is from ("Where in the Beer World"). When Brandon Evans decided to spend a month forgoing water for beer (drinking BrewDog's Nanny State, .5 percent alcohol by volume), he shared his monotonous drinking experience on Instagram; given Nanny State's limited distribution, we might assume that his images did not reflect extensive travels to accomplish his goal.[1] On Flickr, Thijs Brabander shares rare photographs from inside the Westvleteren Abbey, where he visited in 2009, 2010, and 2011.[2] On Instagram, over forty-six thousand shared images, many of which include travel, are tagged #plinytheelder. The partial story, in this case, might be that, for some of us, travel ends with the networked terroir of Pliny.

This social sharing experience resembles Henry Jenkins's anticipation of consumer critique; consumers have been coopted within social media spaces so that they will advance companies' agendas by sharing photographs or experiences in lieu of the role that traditional advertising typically plays in this endeavor. Sharing beer photography, then, is either succumbing to such influence or reshaping such influence. Taking a photograph of Pliny the Elder while traveling, the argument would claim, serves the economic interests of Russian River and not the consumer's well-being, because the image freely advertises the product Russian River sells. Or, as Jenkins also writes in contrast to this idea, such a photograph, in fact, is not a cooptation, but instead it generates a conversation between producer and consumer. The photograph of a consumed product shared over a social network is a mode of discussion. Contagions, as I've shown throughout the previous chapters, too, are modes of discussion. They indicate shared ideas across platforms or across time. In Jenkins's words,

> One can see such behavior as cooptation into commodity culture insofar as it sometimes collaborates with corporate interests, but one can also see it as increasing the diversity of media culture, providing opportunities for greater inclusiveness, and making commodity culture more responsive to consumers. (*Fans, Bloggers, and Gamers* 151)

That responsiveness Jenkins alludes to, for me, does not reshape consumerism in ethical or nonmanipulative ways (as a typical critical stance might demand of those who make products we buy) but rather facilitates the sharing of obsessive behavior so that the behavior is mutual and not one-sided. The consumer and the producer share obsession. The producer, as part of this network of sharing photographs, is not only an object being conversed with but, within a travel experience, is communicating back (take my picture, share the snapshot, put your child in front of my product, tell the world about our mural in front of the men's room). Beer photography dominates a great deal of the craft experience and the obsessive experience I've been narrating throughout this book. Beer photography, like other craft features—distributed network releases, terroir, or anecdotes—is also a visual conversation. Helen Liggett writes that with photography in general, "images have more profound uses than to illustrate thought. They are capable of thought" (133). A beer image that thinks—produced by a brewery or by a beer enthusiast—might say to me or any other person sharing an image, "I am the product of someone's obsession. I am that obsession."

Even if the image speaks, beer photography discourse may not always claim for itself "obsession"; it may posit image sharing as the capture of proper composition in order to demonstrate appreciation (as I previously cited Latour dismissing the importance of appreciation). Few of us, it seems, would want to be known as obsessive. We prefer balance. Craft versus crafty suggests balance (we need to know who is legitimate and who supposedly is not). Appreciation, like being curious, can be the quest for balance in one's life. Balance is ideological, and it can offset obsession and the compulsion to consume or to rationalize obsession. But with photography, balance is still a key principle of composing, a way to illustrate thought while countering the amateur status often attributed to craft enthusiasts (as I noted earlier regarding reviews). The image, in the rhetoric of composing balance, conveys the thought of stability and professionalism. Even the Schlitz ad I began with offers such balance: its message is offered over three parallel panels, each balanced by the other. Offering beer photography advice, Beertography's John Kleinchester's defines quality beer photography as having a sense of equivalence and balance: "One simple rule is to never display mismatching glassware. If you're drinking a Carton Brewing beer out of a Brooklyn Brewery pint glass, hide the Brooklyn logo. It just doesn't feel right when you have another brewery's logo prominently displayed" (Page).

With all the beer glassware I own, I seldom follow such a rule. My craft beer anecdotes began with a sense of unbalance—the misrating. My craft enthusiasm, in word and image, has always been unbalanced, it seems. When I earlier wrote about ratings and associated them with the overall craft anecdote, I didn't note that most of the ratings I compose are accompanied by my own photography or, as the Schlitz ad displays, snapshots. I didn't note the lack of balance in my photography. In order to be noticed, I don't post my images to RateBeer (or even submit them to Beertography's contests) but instead, like many others, share them elsewhere via social media: on Instagram, Google+, Twitter, and my blog. I write a rating, and I take a picture. This is my routine. Typically, the photography I engage with is nothing more than an iPhone-captured image of the beer on our kitchen counter as kids' toys, books, odds and ends, counter cleaner, and other items become caught in the frame. On a more literal level of achieving balance, I often don't match glassware to the beer being consumed since a Bruery snifter, a Schlafly snifter, a Lost Abbey Teku tulip, and a Russian River glass are my go-to options regardless of what I am drinking. It feels fine with me to mismatch beer and glass. It feels fine to lack balance.

Whatever I may say about the iPhone's ability to take a beer picture of a mismatched beer and glass, I might settle on the likely adjective "crappy." When it comes to photography, I'm no Ansel Adams or Cindy Sherman or John Kleinchester, but my beer photography has its own unique style of identifying the image's thought: beer on the counter, near something my kid might have put there, next to an unused diaper, in front of a food processor, in front of my mortar and pestle, or on another counter where the bad lighting causes the flash to streak a hot spot across the image. We are messy! my images say. I share this point with the world.

When I use my ten-year-old Canon digital camera instead of the iPhone to photograph beer I am drinking, I act as if my photography is artistically informed by my ability to turn the setting knob on the camera to the picture of a person's face and not to the picture of a mountain, even though I am photographing a beer bottle and not a person. Thus, I act as if I have a secret trick I am sharing for other amateur beer photographers to use when they are taking pictures of beer bottles. When photographing a beer bottle you are drinking, switch the setting to the picture of a person's face, not the mountain. I'm not sure which picture Cindy Sherman turns her camera's settings to, but she and I share a specific way of staging the photograph. Sherman's canonical work photographed herself in an iconic pose in order to challenge popular representations of women and assumptions regarding the roles they play in society; I have positioned a beer bottle next to a can of baby formula because the can was there, and I did not bother to move it. And I have positioned the beer on a counter. These are not necessarily canonical poses (though their nightly repetition might suggest as such), and they do little to challenge cultural representations of beer or those who drink beer or those who are obsessed with craft. For instance, I can offer the example of a photograph of Rivertown's Lambic, which I bought at Jungle Jim's in Cincinnati not long after we moved to Kentucky. The photograph highlights the cork that broke off in the bottle. The photograph also highlights an open toaster oven and a bag of coffee from the co-op we frequent in Lexington. I challenge photography convention by creating a sense of balance (messy kitchen in a crappy rental house). The camera setting was also turned to the picture of a person's face when I photographed this bottle.

My photo of Rivertown's Lambic on the counter in our Lexington home

Shared Imagery

Just as the Schlitz snapshots focus on the beer and not the travels, my photography tends to focus on the beer as well, ignoring the travels as the focal point of any storytelling I might perform. My photography also interrupts; it focuses on blurry moments (my inability to focus properly), my children in breweries or brewpubs (the parental tales I want to tell), open toaster ovens (ignorance of bottle placement), and diapers on our kitchen counter. (When I began writing this book, my then two-year-old boy was not yet potty trained.) This photography allows me to participate in a larger social conversation regarding the snapshots of generic beer consumption that, according to the Brewers Association, amounted to over twenty-one million barrels of beer in 2014 (National Beer Sales). But how do my photographic contributions add to the overall discussion focused on craft beer, discussion that stretches from a Schlitz ad to beer sampler trays in front of my children to contemporary images? Is a photograph of Rivertown's Lambic in front of the toaster oven—shared over a social media space—as inconsequential as my first Weyerbacher rating—shared over another social media space? Neither one adds to the wisdom of crowds. Neither contributes to overall knowledge in the social sphere regarding photography or beer. Neither makes shared beer photography glamorous or even acceptable as a genre of social-media-based communication. Neither extends social media theory observations, such as those made by Clay Shirky. Both my photographs and my ratings share the same networked terroir of craft obsession. As inconsequential as they are to crowd-based knowledge, these photographs help build a larger network.

Why should I share an image of a beer in front of the toaster oven? Prior to the advent of digital photography, Pierre Bourdieu called such image taking *bourgeois* because it disregards the waste of film on trivial matters (such as a beer in front of a toaster oven) and lacks artistic sincerity (as any discussion of photographic balance and composition suggests). As many discussions of composing and balance dictate, such photography, he claimed, is useless within a greater hierarchy of class values:

> Since all it takes is the simple pressing of a button to liberate the impersonal aptitude by which the camera is defined—the hope is that the photograph will be justified by the object photographed, by the choice made in taking the photograph, or in its eventual use, which rules out the idea of taking a photograph simply in order to take a photograph as either useless, perverse, or *bourgeois*. (164)

Other than potential perversity, what thoughts (as Liggett asks) does an image express when shared across the social network? That I am bourgeois? Maybe. That I travel? Maybe. That all of this sharing is useless? Maybe as well. Maybe I have no higher value (or grand narrative) to express than such mundane or small-story points (like an anecdote). Communication, after all, can be banal. Writing in the *New York Times*' Bits section, Nick Bilton frames photographic sharing as communication:

> While it might seem that Yahoo's Flickr, Facebook, which also owns Instagram, and Twitter are fighting to become the ultimate online photo album or video vault, these companies are really fighting to provide the service for the newest way to communicate. ("Disruptions: Social Media Images")

I share because I want to communicate the useless or the supposed bourgeois practice of photographing without artistic contemplation. I want to communicate this concept via the image instead of only using words.

This communication sentiment (bourgeois or not) has long been a practice for disseminating ideas. One Reddit post on beer offers a nineteenth-century photograph to the site's readership and proclaims it to be

My wife's response to my beer photos on Instagram

"the earliest known photograph of men drinking" (Reddit). Tagged "Edinburgh Ale, 1844," the photograph shows three men (James Ballantine, George William Bell, and David Octavius Hill[3]) enjoying beers served in long glasses. In 1844, then, the desire to share beer photography existed. Three men share a beer and ask, or are asked, to be photographed. The desire to participate in photographic communication existed, even when the medium was extremely young. In the twenty-first century, this 1844 image, too, has been shared. Reddit shares it off the Wikimedia Commons site. The National Galleries of Scotland Commons' Flickr page, too, shares it.[4] Jay Brooks shares it on his *Brookston Beer Bulletin* as well ("History's First Photo"). A banal event that should be forgotten to time—three men gathered for a beer in the mid-nineteenth century—becomes a larger, distributed event communicated *over time*. The photograph remains with us because it was preserved but also because—like the Schlitz snapshot—it was shared. That sharing communicates the feeling of being together, of having a beer, of wanting to know someone had a beer, and of wanting to know that people drank beer in the nineteenth century in acts of camaraderie. Once this photo is shared, the message we receive may be the surprise of recognition: people drank beer and photographed it even back then! A moment of surprise (as I expressed in my Zoigl-Star anecdote) formulates. A moment of identification formulates (they are like us!). A moment of appreciation formulates. My drinking beer is not novel but is part of a larger tradition of beer consumption that can be traced to acts of friendship in the nineteenth century. The event of Edinburgh, 1844, therefore, is also the event of today. Events are contagions as well. Sharing is part of a larger network of meaning. Sharing is a contagion.

Events and occasions invite into their network photography and the sharing of images. This sharing speaks to an aspect of craft obsession, resembling Richard Benson's remark that many photographers "fail to understand that the best work might come from an obsession with the medium rather than the personally oriented choice of what might be done with it" (374). Beer photographers may not know what will become of their snapshots beyond the initial share. Beer photographers, instead, practice an obsession associated with one aspect of social media, the role photography plays in online communication of moments, people, objects, emotions, and, of course, events.

For me, one such event is not only sitting with friends and having a beer, as in the Edinburgh representation, but attending the Great American Beer Festival (GABF) in 2012 with my two regular beer traveling friends (broventurers and fellow academics Bradley Dilger and Thomas Rickert). Like the Edinburgh photograph's notion of camaraderie, GABF offers my own take on the banality of drinking beer with friends and capturing that moment via a shared image. I interrupt this discussion of sharing with another craft anecdote. The three of us had traveled previously to St. Louis and Portland on beer trips; GABF would mark a major moment in our beerventures; it is the largest American festival focused on beer. *The Oxford Companion to Beer*'s entry on GABF is fairly short, noting that it has become the "Super Bowl of Beer" (Laur 406). The year we attended GABF, forty thousand tickets to the event sold out in less than one day, echoing the contagion effect of release day delivery I noted regarding Dark Lord Day ("40,000 +"). During our trip, we traveled a familiar path that GABF attendees take (much as I once repeated Trubek's travels through San Francisco), making our way throughout Fort Collins, Boulder, and Denver, along with attending the festival. While in Fort Collins, one of us opened the drawer to our hotel's dresser and found a bag of medical marijuana inside. For some time, I had told myself that if I ever found myself far from home and my kids, somewhere where parental responsibility was not an issue, I would smoke weed again (I stopped when my wife was pregnant with our first child). Yet, there we were, three men in their forties with a bag of pot and none of our kids nearby, and none of us were interested. One of us turned the bag in to the front desk, where the attendant was only happy to make sure it was "well disposed of" when she got off shift.

The detail of finding marijuana in a hotel room and turning it in stands out for me within the larger narrative of attending GABF. I photographed the bag of marijuana and shared it on Facebook, displacing attention away from our beer trip to an otherwise unimportant detail. The detail the anecdote offers stands out more than other anecdotes I could possibly draw on to illustrate the experience. A typical GABF contagion (as retread grand narrative) description would include beers sampled, the crowds, meeting new people, meeting famous brewers, sampling rare beers. With me, the *detail* interrupts the topos of GABF stories. It displaces my attention, even as I write this chapter. A conversation regarding photographic sharing and beer is disrupted by a detail not focused on beer. This point will return shortly.

Despite the importance of this anecdote to our several days of beer sharing and to my memory, the only salvageable image that I can find among my iPhone photos from the afternoon that we spent at GABF (beyond a photo of the marijuana) has nothing to do with our camaraderie; it is one I took of the taster glass participants received. The anecdote of discovering marijuana or a separate anecdote of attending GABF is not captured in the image I have, but they exist around the image as socially related fragments or details that I connect—photographic terroir. The taster glass—itself a detail—anchors the hotel incident as an associated memory ("oh right . . . that occurred") and the tasting as a physical artifact (I used the tasting glass during GABF two days after the hotel incident). Before the crowds settled in, I set the small glass up on a table, in the first few minutes of the Saturday afternoon session, and took a picture. My final trip to GABF was an event. Via my obsession with the medium of iPhone photography, I wanted to remember GABF via this tasting glass set upon a table the way the men photographed in Edinburgh in 1844 likely wanted to remember their event. In taking the picture, I assumed that I would later share it and that someone would participate in the sharing through recognition, commenting, or reposting.

Throughout the event, I balanced a tasting glass, my notebook, a pen, and my iPhone while watching my broventure partners vanish from time to time among the other drinkers. When I did take other pictures, I didn't capture too much beyond a yellow haze and a big space of people. Like the Schlitz photographer, I was curious as I moved from booth to booth. I was curious about what I was experiencing and how I might remember the afternoon in saved imagery. I was not, as my few photographs remind me, a capable recorder of the event. My glass was not, as a National Public Radio reporter claimed of the tasting glasses, made of plastic (Chappell). My taster was made of glass, but the object, glass or photograph, contained more than beer. It contained interactions and the sharing of these interactions.

Even without creating many images to remember GABF, I depend on the photograph to record and communicate experience within my overall craft life. Images make my experience memorable. Snapshots matter. Pixels grant materiality to my experiences in a way the glass doesn't. My memory makes my experience temporary. For this reason, as I wrote earlier in this book, I rate beers. If I didn't do so, I would never remember what I have consumed. For this reason, I suppose, I take photographs.

I could summarize many of our beer experiences similarly. Two trips to Dark Lord Day or a summer in Portland, for instance, could be described as merely the photograph as event (rather than the event itself). Or these trips could be described as the obsession with a medium. Two trips to Dark Lord and a trip to Portland hardly constitute excessive beer traveling with friends (and for most craft enthusiasts would hardly constitute obsessive traveling). When I recorded our experience in Portland, an experience many others have had in communal beer tourism, I posted a series of photographs to my blog.[5] When I revisit those photographs as snapshots

Snapshot of my tasting glass at the 2012 Great American Beer Festival

to share, as in the Schlitz ad, I notice that—beyond the contagion images of sampler trays (with or without children) and chalkboard beer menus that most people visiting bars and brewpubs capture—the notebook and tasting glass focus have been part of our previous travels. My GABF moment, then, is not an isolated moment of obsession but an aggregated one of obsession (a terroir) consisting of various details over time. My moment has appeared before GABF, and it will appear again at some point. It is an aggregated contagion as much as an anecdote might be one.

My photographs, by being uploaded and shared through these aggregated experiences that others share as well, extend the general database of beer information that is delivered as a network among a multitude of actors (as I described craft delivery). This database grows with user contributions; it becomes, borrowing Henry Jenkins's phrase, spreadable. "In this emerging model," Jenkins writes, "audiences play an active role in 'spreading' content rather than serving as passive carriers of viral media: their choices, investments, agendas, and actions determine what get valued" (*Spreadable Media* 21). Spreadable content results from the relationship between consumer (GABF attendee, purchaser of sampler tray) and producer (brewer, bar). The relationships spread over photography (as in the Edinburgh image) and in other media by users like me, Michael Donk, John Kleinchester, or others. Facebook's Paul Adams calls contributions that spread out via users "permission marketing." As Adams

My notebook and glass at Tugboat Brewing, July 2010

My notebook and glass at a Lexington beer tasting, December 2014

writes, "Permission marketing happens when people give marketers permission to send them messages. Clicking the Like button on a brand's Facebook page is an example of permission marketing" (134). Clicking the like button generates an implicit acceptance of what the liked page opts to share. In social spaces, others see what I clicked like for, and they, too, may eventually like the same page or post. Likes allow images or texts to become spreadable. Clicking a like button, unlike Bourdieu's distaste for trivial clicking of a camera's shoot button, indicates a shared status. It indicates some form of relationship.

Seth Godin, who often exaggerates social media's economic effects amid hyperbole and enthusiasm, also emphasizes permission marketing amid the culture of online sharing and offers a definition relevant to how likes affect sharing. "Permission Marketing lets you turn strangers, folks who might otherwise ignore your unsolicited offer, into people willing to pay attention when your message arrives in an expected, appreciated way" (50). These messages, Godin tells us, depend on repeated contact or frequency: "Frequency led to awareness, awareness to familiarity, and familiarity to trust" (91). The more one engages with liking, the more one gains trust via such likes. With trust, images spread and sharing becomes frequent. Frequency builds relationships, transforming the contagion into more than repetition. Novelist Jonathan Franzen has, however, bemoaned the emergence of a culture of like, particularly for the ways it fosters relationships between individuals and consumerism at this level of implicit and repeated acceptance that Godin and others favor. The like for Franzen indicates superficiality, not a positive spreadable act:

> The striking thing about all consumer products—and none more so than electronic devices and applications—is that they're designed to be immensely likable. This is, in fact, the definition of a consumer product, in contrast to the product that is simply itself and whose makers aren't fixated on your liking it.

Craft is a consumer product, as Franzen laments regarding consumption. But its accessibility and meaning depend on liking and sharing. When I like an image or post on Facebook, I am permitting my like to be further shared. I am permitting my need for being liked (or even noticed). This sharing allows for marketing of my interests to occur without explicit permission from me. The makers of the product that captures my interest may, indeed, be fixated on my liking their product. But what does that matter? As a beer blogger remarks, "Sites like Beer Advocate or Rate Beer [sic] and apps like Untappd provide us with a constant stream of what everyone else is drinking (so does this blog) and when you see something good, you want it" (Roth, "Beware the Green Eyes of Envy"). Writing in the *New Inquiry*, Robert Gehl argues that liking (in ads or on Facebook status updates) "promises to encode brands into our bodies as pre-cognitive desire." In this encoding, Gehl argues, we not only express interest in a brand (such as a brewery or beer); we become an expression of that brand. Liking or sharing, in this case, also establishes identity, or what I have called the aggregation of craft identity. Unlike Franzen, I like having this identity. A hazy, yellow photograph of a GABF taster glass aggregates the brand (GABF) and me as one identity. As Gehl puts it,

> The choice to like an ad or brand in Facebook is seen as an affirmative interaction with that brand—and an agreement to have one's profile image associated with that brand and to have that approval follow you across the Web.

There has been a history of user anger expressed at Facebook and other sites for allowing permission marketing to override privacy concerns with liking as a marketing gesture. Angry or not, concerned or not over privacy, we share our likes—photographic or textual—and allow those likes to be used elsewhere, whether for personal or professional application. Privacy does not overshadow the generic, public desire to like and let others know what one likes. Secrecy, in certain situations such as social media, has its limitations. Product interest, it seems, is one area we have little desire to keep secret. "I am a craft beer drinker" is more than a video meme declaration; it is a desire to make public a consumer and lifestyle choice. Making one's identity public is not novel, but making one's craft identity public might very well be. With Facebook and other social media platforms, we are interested in letting others know what we like or don't like, who we are or who we are not. One marketing executive explains the importance of liking and being a fan of a product:

> Advocacy—the probability of a customer recommending a product to others, and the probability of that recommendation to affect sales—is another key metric [for measuring purchases]. Another area that is more difficult to measure is brand affinity—that is, the emotional draw that a customer feels towards a brand because of the relationship that develops between brands and fans over Facebook. If positive brand affinity tends to be a powerful sales indicator on other channels, it may be worth cultivating on Facebook, too. (Indvik)

Positive brand affinity is also a focus of liking and sharing, particularly with breweries who have limited advertising dollars to spend and craft enthusiasts who do not have complete access to the breweries they enjoy because of distribution limitations. This sense of affinity taps into what I previously called the importance of telling within delivery. Telling and its proliferation, for whatever secret reason, often has little financial payoff for the person sharing the news or photograph. If I tell you what I am interested in by clicking like on a given brewer's Facebook status update or sharing my GABF photograph or my sampler tray photographs, what do I gain from doing so? I gain nothing monetarily if you eventually like what I like or go to GABF or buy the Rivertown's Lambic I once posed in front of an open toaster oven. Locally, I may gain less if suddenly everyone eventually wants what I want (and thus there will be fewer bottles for my obsessive interests). Yet, I tell. I tell a great deal. Former Stone Brewing communication specialist and current Modern Times brewery owner Jacob McKean observes that the motivation for stimulating likes or followers is not entirely monetary for the brewery either, or not easy to value in terms of dollars or how such updates encourage purchases. To like and follow, at the least, are interactions that create relationships:

> There's really no way to know how "Likes" or whatever else translates into sales, at least that I'm aware of. So we measure success by the growth of our followers and the feedback we receive in comments and retweets and such. We believe and hope it helps sales (I wouldn't have created regionalized Facebook pages for most of our sales reps if we didn't), and we keep growing at a break neck pace, so something must be working. (Hanson)

Friending, too, is a form of permission marketing. Being in a Google+ circle is a form of permission marketing. Following someone on Instagram or Flickr is a form of permission marketing as this approach establishes relationships across users and their interests. In 2008 Scott Brown dismissed such sharing by calling it "friendonomics," a digital sense of oversharing. "We've lost our right to lose touch," Brown complained about the amount of connectivity occurring on Facebook. Permission marketing speaks to the opposite affective experience: the desire to stay in touch by sharing. Sharing photographs of a lambic beer posed in front of an open toaster oven is a form of permission marketing that allows one to stay in touch (or be engaged), not with my toaster oven, but with others who drink lambic beer or who may want to drink lambic beer. My sharing is an implicit agreement to continue sharing the image or idea. While I am not selling beer (or any product), I am marketing—to an extent—a belief or image or idea or even product via my shared images and posts. I am marketing beer information (style, producer, new release, event, purchase, trade). I am marketing myself (look at what I drink!). I am also marketing—without necessarily wanting to—the beer whose image I share. A great deal of online activity regarding sharing resembles marketing: marketing ideology, beliefs, interests, or concerns. This marketing allows me to stay in touch with friends who may or may not care about my product choices but who will learn of them by participating in my sharing network. Craft is one form of shared marketing.

For Adams, sharing a brand contributes to success via imitation. If I see a brand shared or people see me share a brand, they become knowledgeable about that brand and may want it as well. If there is such a thing as "friendonomics," then, it may also include imitative knowledge (contagion) effects. "Information is more likely to be absorbed if it comes from friends," Adams writes (137). I am not friends with all of the people in my Google+ circle or on Facebook in a traditional sense; we may have never met face to face. But our bonding over photographs and "here's what I'm drinking" posts make us a different kind of friend from the one who remembers birthdays or comes to a dinner party. This virtual friendship relies on the willingness to share and be involved over an object (a beer, a trade, a purchase). Because we are this specific type of friend, we absorb information from one another in a fairly easy manner. "Everybody in the world," Marshall McLuhan wrote pre–social media, "has to live in the utmost proximity created by our electric involvement in one another's lives" (*Understanding Media* 47). Hundreds of people in my Google+ circle live in proximity to me via an app or website. They know that I have attended GABF. They know that because of a shared photograph of a tasting glass. They may have attended once as well (we are sharing an event); they may want to attend in the future (I am sharing the event for them); they may merely appreciate that someone, somewhere is enjoying the event (the overall shared craft experience).

For Rachel Botsman and Roo Rogers, permission marketing of information, what they call "Collaborative Consumption," taps into overall industry interest in "the idea of moving a brand from something you want to something you love to something you can participate in" (203). Once the participation extends from my single moment of sharing to an activity that is communal on an online site (beyond being merely prosumer in nature), the brand (beer, my identity, or otherwise) shapes community. The community—whether or not its members know one another—feels or believes it is part of a larger shared participatory moment much as a beer drinker today might feel a part of "Edinburgh Ale, 1844" when viewing the photograph. "As with many Web 2.0 brands," Botsman and Rogers write, "community is the DNA of Collaborative Consumption brands, so much so that users are not referred to as consumers but embraced as members" (204). When I participate in this community, I am a member of craft; I am a craft beer drinker. If, as we see in the "I Am a Craft Beer Drinker" video, multiple people proclaim, "I am passionate about what I drink," these individuals are demonstrating a community joined by a networked contagion (repeated) line. That line, established as an interest, aggregates across each person to form identity. My identity, whether via Zoigl-Star or a shared photograph, becomes aggregated across interests.

I am not only an aggregated craft beer drinker; I am also a member of a photographic network of craft beer drinkers that extends from the nineteenth century to today. Shared photography communicates by placing me within a community via my participation in liking and sharing.

Shared photography also allows me to communicate with myself. That I have photographed my notebook and a glass of beer more than once (a form of internal permission marketing) suggests that I am still sharing the same concept with myself, much as I continue to share photographs of my children in front of sampler trays. I likely do so because of an obsession with the medium. I want to know—on multiple occasions—that I do, indeed, belong within this community. I want to communicate with myself what my identity might entail (craft beer drinker sometimes as opposed to academic all the time).

In the Schlitz ad, the photographs are shared over a beer (the beer may or may not be shared). My photographs are shared because they are about beer and because I am not the only one who obsesses about beer. Just as vacationers have obsessed over making sure that the images of their experiences are shared—from vacation slides shown to unsuspecting evening guests to photo blogs scattered all over the Internet—so, too, do beer travelers feel the need to visualize their experiences. The visualization of our lives creates a sense of friendship. We can *see* each other's experiences. Our involvement in each other's lives, to paraphrase Marshall McLuhan, is visualized as we engage with a cool medium. The cool medium, because of what it doesn't show or demonstrate, demands participation; we fill in the details. For this reason, we easily grant permission marketing of our lives. We don't necessarily see everything that one has experienced; instead, we see details (small stories) that stand out, that generate associations, that evoke feelings, that allow us to fill in the gaps, that cause us to fill in details: I want that. That's me! We're the same.

Such items are not always represented in the bottle or beer itself; that is, as it is shared among friends, a yellow-tinted photograph of a tasting glass from GABF might evoke nostalgia (the time one went as well), jealousy (the wish to attend one day), anger (beer should not be consumed as an event), or some other response. "Whatever it grants to vision and whatever its manner," Roland Barthes writes, "a photograph is always invisible: it is not it that we see" (*Camera Lucida* 6). In my or others' photographs, I don't see the beer as much as I see the *moment* of beer consumption, a moment that I assume belongs within a given community I participate in. What I'm trying to share via the photograph is my own and the other's moments. These moments, as I explored via release days, are complex and distributed acts of delivery where no single items stands on its own as a message is understood or received. These moments are more than just *one thing* caught in a digital image.

Photographic Sharing

Photographer Nick Stern bemoans the type of beer photography I and others do via Instagram and deliver to social media sites because, even if the image is shared, it lacks the authenticity of professional photography, moment based or otherwise. Even if shared, Instagram images, Stern complains, are not community based, as I claim, but are too solitary; they are set apart from the professional network of photography that defines and qualifies the practice. "Hipstamatic, Instagram and other apps produce images that are equally unethical or perhaps even more so. The image never existed in any other place than the eye of the app developer," Stern writes. Stern objects to the filters and spontaneity of mobile photography because of how the app controls the framing of the moment. Stern argues that a camera with more settings than person or mountain—or better controlled than someone arbitrarily choosing either—more accurately captures an authentic representation. For me, the app—on my iPhone or otherwise—is merely the medium that frames my moment. Or my memory. Or my experience. Or my obsession. I am not a professional photographer; I am not a professional beer drinker. I am an amateur, an "of the moment" social media user dependent on an Apple phone or camera with mountain and person settings. The image I capture with my phone, of course, has existed in places other than my eye or the app developer's eye; contagion repetition demonstrates that prior existence (such as "Back off, you hippies"). As does sharing. A photograph of friends sharing beer (me or others) already existed in the mid-nineteenth century.

With my interest in Instagram, I follow Barthes's frustration with formalized, "authentic" photography and its institutional taxonomy as *the way* to capture an image, at least when it comes to beer photography. One could argue that such formalization—antithetical to the narrative of prosumers and user-generated content popularized in social media discourse—leaves craft enthusiasts like me outside a given community. My moment is not in need of an authentic taxonomy by some outside force; authenticity is found in the responses and likes I may or may not receive. Barthes writes,

> What did I care about the rules of composition of the photographic landscape, or, at the other end, about the Photograph as family rite? Each time I would read something about Photography, I would think of some photograph I lived, and this made me furious. (*Camera Lucida* 7)

When Barthes reads about Photography (with a capital P to emphasize its professional framing and supposed authenticity), he imagines the lived experience instead; his anger comes from the gap between lived experience (emotions, feelings, intensity) and professionalism (authoritarian, rigid, uncompromising, properly positioned and lit). I am not furious with authenticity. I am not furious with a desire to maintain levels of authenticity when pleasure is explored via aggregation or via photographic sharing. I am not furious when a beer photographer, such as Michael Tonsmeire, known online as the Mad Fermentationist, gives advice to his readers regarding authenticity. In a post titled "Intro to Digital Photography for Beer," Tonsmeire spells out more advanced methods of photographing beer than knowing how to turn to the setting of the person's face or put a beer in front of an open toaster oven:

> With the number of pictures on this blog I've had to become pretty creative finding new photo shoot locations in my house to avoid the feeling of looking at the same picture on every post. I've shot next to the barrels, in the attic, outside, and on just about ever [sic] table and shelf I own. Props, like ingredients, can be nice to add, but usually it looks a bit too staged for me.

My photographs capture not only an "of the moment" logic but a lack of creativity, as Tonsmeire desires for his own photographs. My photographs are unintentionally staged, or staged by the facts of my fatherhood: Diapers. Bottle of olive oil. Open toaster oven. Spray cleaner. In the larger scene of beer photography, my parental beer tale need not only shape my approach to narrative convention but also my "inauthentic" framing of the image. As such, I am an amateur sharer bounded to supposedly inauthentic sharing tales. I have no knowledge of composition. I am not creative. I only know the Instagram filters I repeatedly turn to (and that Stern bemoans): X-Pro II, Nashville, 1977, Hefe. And out of such photos, mine or others' digital images, I pick out those that stand out, that strike me, that confuse me, that make me want beer. Because, even if the app controls the moment, the details captured within the app's framing cause me to want as well. Sharing leads to my desire. "Through our digital experiences," say Botsman and Rogers, "we are recognizing that by providing value to the community, we enable our own social value to expand in return" (90). For Barthes, desire is central to the image and its relationship to viewer or photographer:

> This photograph which I pick out and which I love has nothing in common with the shiny point which sways before your eyes and makes your head swim; what it produces in me is the very opposite of hebetude; something more like an internal agitation, an excitement, a certain labor too, the pressure of the unspeakable which wants to be spoken. Well, then? Interest? (*Camera Lucida* 18–19)

If my obsession has been captured even partly by the social sharing of images and the value it expands, then a significant part of this process captures my interest as well. Sharing makes me interested no matter how professional or amateur the photographs on Instagram may be. I still find the professional, or Photography with a capital P, images surrounding beer wonderful. My amateurism does not negate my appreciation of the professional. In fact, the two aggregate. These professional images, when shared with me, allow for my affective branding and identification with the product in ways that do not bother me but enthrall me. Professional images tell other kinds of small stories. Schlafly's Instagram account features images more carefully posed than I can create: a six-pack of Schlafly Yakima Wheat Ale or Summer Lager cases rolling down the assembly line, the menu of the downtown Tap Room.[6] Bell's Instagram account features beautiful images of barrels, the Eccentric Café, a pint of Oberon with a slice of orange in the glass.[7] Stone's Instagram account reveals brew master Mitch Steele at a tasting, a dog enjoying Enjoy By, a beautiful shot of several bottles of Dayman Coffee IPA neatly arranged.[8] A scan through Flickr images tagged "beer," unveils the nonprofessional as well: a photograph of a bottle of Drie Fonteinen surrounded by trinkets and awards,[9] a neatly arranged sampler tray from Lucky Labrador in Portland,[10] and a photograph of a bottle of Squatters' Outer Darkness taken at the 2013 Great Vegas Festival of Beer.[11] These are, for me, professional or amateur, moments of narrative interest.

These moments appear on other platforms as well. On Facebook, beer groups share photographs on the League of Extraordinary Beer Drinkers,[12] the Facebook Beer Group,[13] Head: the Craft Beer Group,[14] Bluegrass Beer Geeks,[15] and Honest Craft Beer Reviews.[16] A photograph accompanies each post made. These photographs brag (rows of purchased or traded for "whales"), show the mundane (a bottle of Sierra Nevada Pale Ale on a countertop in someone's home), review (comments on the beer pictured), show hauls (look what I just bought), and do more. These photographs, including a blurry yellow-haze image of a local tasting I hosted that I posted in June 2013,[17] receive likes (permission marketing), which, in turn, activate further interest, community, and engagement. These photographs are contagions; they repeat for circulation common experiences the way that anecdotes of a first time or tales of revolution do. One expects likes when posting to Facebook or Google+ (where the like is a mere + sign) because one feels a part of the social media site's community. My Google+ circle, creatively called "beer," includes 520 people, most of whom are posting photographs of their daily beers. One Google+ community attached to "beer" that I belong to is Craft Beer Exchange, where 44 members post photographs of beer trades they've completed. In another Google+ community I belong to, Craft Beer Enthusiasts, 449 members post photographs of what they are drinking and trading for. Interest? as Barthes asks. Yes, I am interested. Others are interested as well. Every day someone is drinking a beer and communicating that consumption via an image because that person feels others will be interested.

My photographs also tap into the Schlitz snapshot logic: I was curious. I tasted it. I want to taste it. Curiosity is a basic component of the social nature of sharing: interest. "The attention to detail has another name," Lennard Davis writes regarding obsession, "curiosity" (64). We assume the audience we share with is curious (they want to see what we consume), and we express our own curiosity (I found this beer and am sharing it). In fact, out of the thousands of saved photos on my iPhone, most are based on this simple premise: I was curious. I tasted it. The Instagram logic is not the logic of what Barthes calls "the shiny point," or the carefully arranged

My Instagram account

image. It is not the logic of authenticity or Photography with a capital P. It is the moment of instant interest. And 1950 Schlitz logic is contemporary Instagram logic, a belief in capturing the moments of curiosity and taste we encounter daily. An Instagram logic saves more than twenty-five photos and ninety likes every second.[18] That means at least twenty-five people every second share curiosity and taste, thus giving permission to each other to view and further share these moments. Photos are the new killer app, a *Fast Company* headline declares (Manjod). The "killer" status attributed to digital photography is based in the "of the moment" logic that I and others follow where we bombard each other with interests every second. This logic makes *now* the most meaningful experience imaginable. Now I am drinking. Now I am experiencing pleasure. Now is *being with* (as I note in the introduction regarding my daughter). Paul Ford, writing for *New York Magazine*, opines about Instagram as a now type of pleasure:

> It barely has a website; all the action happens on mobile devices. Thirty million people use it to pass time in the bathroom. You can add some fairly silly filters to the photos to make the pictures look like they were taken in the seventies, but that's more of a novelty than a requirement. So that's Instagram. It's not a site, or an app. What it is, really, is a product. ("Facebook and Instagram")

As a product, Ford claims, Instagram is "a thing that lets other people make things" (i.e., carpentry, as Bogost claims for his aesthetic of objects). What do I make with a photograph of a beer that is meant to reflect "of the moment" or the feeling of now? I make relationships. Those relationships are between people (those who click "like" or who follow me or whom I follow), and they are between objects. These photos aggregate (as in terroir aggregation) all of this beer-related activity into a sense of something called "craft beer." Each beer is put into relationship with another beer. Interest and curiosity drive these visual relationships. The overall aggregation is what we might term the feeling of *now having a beer*. This feeling communicates a conversation. We discuss what we are having, when we are having, how we are having. Of course, such sentiment extends to other experiences beyond drinking beer, but it is a focal point of online beer discourse. "I don't like the idea of Instagram as a photo sharing service, and I don't think it is," Instagram's cofounder Kevin Systrom says. "It's very much a communication tool, it's a visual communications tool" (qtd. in Honan). *Now* is a form of visual communication. In the final chapter and epilogue, I explore *now* in more depth regarding trades and a final parental beer tale.

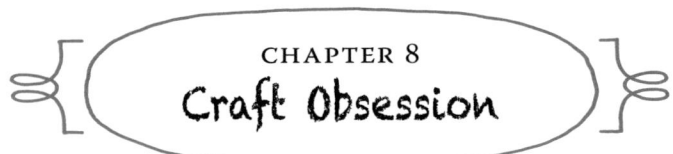

CHAPTER 8
Craft Obsession

> Though it received an outstanding rating by BeerAdvocate, this insulting beer alienates customers with the slogan "You're Not Worthy."
>
> —*Jeopardy* question in the form of an answer

Now is a marker of obsession. Now I am drinking a beer. Now I want a beer. Now I will find a particular beer. Now I am on RateBeer looking through the forums. Now I am reading RSS updates about beer. Now I am heading out the door because Lexington Beerworks posted on Facebook that it has a new Against the Grain on draught. My daughter, flipping through my iPad's camera roll, asks me, "Why do you take so many pictures of beer?" Why, in the moment of now, when drinking a beer, do I photograph it? The screen saver on my iPad is a photograph of my son sitting behind a just filled growler at Wicked Weed, twirling his hair as he drinks from a sippy cup. That was a now moment. I felt the need to photograph it. By sharing this image on Instagram, and by following other photographs shared, I am trading my now moments for others' now moments.

One photographic genre of obsession—and partial answer to the question of now—might be trading (and not just taking) photographs in order to participate in a communal, shared experience. Trading, too, taps into the curiosity and relationship characteristics of craft obsession. Sometimes, image trading involves the photographs taken after a box arrives from a beer trade. Unpacking the newly arrived box of beer, ignoring bits of packing popcorn and Styrofoam that form a mess on the floor, the recipient lines up the beers on a table or countertop, takes a picture, and shares that picture via Flickr, Instagram, RateBeer forums, Google+ circles, or elsewhere. The beers are first traded; the photos are traded afterward. My evenings often begin—after the kids have gone to sleep—with such a photo, either a beer I've traded for or one I've opened to enjoy.

What motivates me to line up beers in a row and share them with people whom I want virtual relationships with? Is this an obsessive practice of the now? Lennard Davis calls obsession "a singular attention to a particular thing or things, which in effect is the definition of specialization—itself an acknowledged feature of modernity" (81). For Davis, obsession networks specialization and a specific temporal moment, if not now. With such specialization, informed by the industrial age that the Arts and Crafts movement objected to, we practice "obsessive attention to detail" (Davis 84). A box of beer arriving in the mail is one such detail, as is a single bottle positioned on a table or a taster glass in a convention center, as is the detail Barthes isolated in imagery in order to practice a form of invention he called the *punctum*. These details, though, do not necessarily represent the specialization Davis associates with obsession. Even in specialization, which focuses attention on a specific task or topic like trading for or photographing a beer, there is aggregation, as I have written in the previous chapters.

I do not call my obsession a specialization (a focus on singular details) but rather identify it as an assumed aggregation over an ambiguous moment I call *now*. My attention is now. *Now* is my displaced attention. *Now* is the displacement of detail (the punctum) Barthes identified as sparking interest in photography. The second level of photographic meaning Barthes recognized as outside the detail is time: "I now know that there exists another *punctum* (another 'stigmatum') than the 'detail.' This new *punctum*, which is no longer of form but of intensity, is Time, the lacerating emphasis of the *noeme* ('that-has-been'), its pure representation" (*Camera Lucida* 96).

Now is this other level of photographic meaning, a temporal level of meaning, not a grand-narrative-focused attempt at meaning (*what are the larger consequences of this meaning*). *Now*, therefore, is not definitional. *Now* is a response to my daughter regarding my numerous beer photos stored on an iPad, computer, and phone: at one point, I felt that *now* I am drinking this beer, and I must photograph that moment. My feeling was not tied to the specific beer or the specific image or a specific time period, but rather to the moment of now. I suggested such a moment when I introduced the parental beer tale's *being with* quality at the beginning of this book. Now is the sense of social media I have been exploring throughout this book. My obsession belongs to the time of the shared "Edinburgh Ale, 1844" photograph and to now. I am 1844 and 2014 simultaneously because sharing extends beyond the limitations of time. I can list all of the photographs I've shared, but they would not disrupt this sense of shared time.

Now is the overall logic of craft obsession I will conclude with in this chapter.

Lists

Now is the social media moment of attention. By displacing attention to now, moments aggregate across a variety of spaces, interests, and time periods without specializing in any of these items. If one of the 170 members of the Bluegrass Beer Geeks Facebook group shares a recent beer purchase or drinking moment, that person displaces my attention from what I am doing (sitting in my home office, yelling at the cat to shut up, drinking coffee, writing) to his or her listed experience. The experience is listed in the Facebook group for me to read and interact with.

In addition to shared photographs, lists, as well, mark this sense of now by displacing attention that belongs to different times, spaces, or grand movements onto a shared media space. The beer list displaces my attention from the object (the beer) to some other experience (a best of, what to drink in the summer, where to drink, etc.) Lists, like photographic details, capture attention while displacing attention. "Most shared lists have a powerful ability to shape public discourse," Jonah Berger writes (97). My RateBeer profile lists characteristics about me: where I'm from, how many beers I've rated, when I joined the site, my favorite style. In this aggregation, a fellow user perceives a representation of me that is displaced from how I act or appear off the board. Such lists are what many Facebook critics object to: the data captured in a list can be removed from its social context (Do you like what I like? Who am I?) and used for marketing. A mainstream publication offers its readership a service by posting a best of beer list, or it pitches a product, or it shapes discourse by displacing attention from one aspect of daily life to another. Just as I was not convinced by the rigid nature of terroir as a taxonomy of place, I am not convinced by rigid distinctions regarding sharing—paid or nonpaid—as it exists in online spaces (such as lists). Craft, as I noted in the beginning

drfabulous
Lexington, Kentucky
Joined: Oct 16, 2004
Last seen: Aug 27, 2015
Good until: Thursday, September 24, 2015

4904 beer ratings · 99 place ratings
Avg Score Given: 3.61 · Avg Beer Rated: 3.55 · Favorite style: Sour/Wild Ale

upload your pic

My RateBeer profile as a list

of this book, is not a state of purity (it is neither artisan nor industrial). Craft displaces attention, categories, expectations, and, in this book, a linear narrative via interruptions.

When I read in the *Huffington Post*, for instance, that Kentucky is not among the top ten states for craft beer ranked in the publication's list, my attention is displaced. If the list claims Wisconsin to be number nine because it receives the top-twenty brewery Three Floyds, why isn't Kentucky, a state that also enjoys Three Floyds distribution, listed? (Satran, "States with the Best Access"). The list displaces my attention from now (where I am) to somewhere else that the list prompts me to want to be (Wisconsin) via information sharing. And in that displacement, I notice a contradiction (Wisconsin versus Kentucky distribution) demonstrating the hybridity of a beer's status. This spatial displacement is not uncommon at the *Huffington Post*, where readers have previously been directed to a list of the best local beers from each state ("The Best Local Beers"). The *Huffington Post*'s 2012 best local beers list, aggregated from the list-based website First We Feast, calls Pliny the Elder California's best beer and Lexington Brewing's Kentucky Bourbon Ale, a beer once unnecessarily traded to me in Kentucky, Kentucky's best (First We Feast, "The United States of Beer"). This arbitrary naming of "best of" lists, too, displaces attention.

In his book *Craft Beer World*, Mark Dredge introduces beautifully displayed lists of beers as "a snapshot of the world of craft beer" (7). Whereas Schlitz proposed its beer via snapshots, and whereas I share snapshots of daily drinking, Dredge's list displaces attention to a snapshot of "best of" or "top ten" or "must have" or a moment that can be categorized by a few beers arranged in an order based on an author's or website's taste. The ways we order, however, extend beyond basic expectations or categorical agreement as to how a given beer should be arranged according to "it's the best." There is no shortage of beer lists proclaiming "best of" beer moments. Best cities. Best summer beers. Best barrel-aged beers. Best new beers. Dredge's list of greatest beers, ordered by style, promises one devoted to the more esoteric concept of "the evolution of beer" (40). Dredge does not give a greatest beer of all time, then, but a list based on "evolution, creativity, and interpretation" (41). In this version of "it's the best," there is a method or, at the least, a series of categories to guide taste, a terroir.

The list, historically an early form of writing, organizes obsession by displacing attention away from the banal and everyday (what an anecdote emphasizes) to something exceptional, something worth remembering, or the best (the grand narrative approach). Twitter supports lists. Facebook uses lists. My RateBeer profile is followed by a list of rated beers. In online publications, we find endless lists regarding beer, contagions of texts like the one Dredge offers. Even as it displaces, the list repeats. Marcy Franklin introduces a list of the five best breweries in America with a contagion anecdote of first times:

> There's that moment when you try a better beer, a beer that's not your average Coors/Bud/Pabst/Enter One-Syllable Beer Name Here, and you're hooked. Not everyone may remember exactly where, or when. You may not even remember what beer it was. But much like a 1-year old who tries his first bite of birthday cake and has his first real taste of sugar, you know you're never going back to that other beer again. ("Top 15 Craft Beer Breweries")

Dogfish Head, Yahoo tells us, is the best brewery in America, a point repeated by the food and beverage website the Daily Meal ("The 25 Best"). The website Travel + Leisure lists America's best beer cities; Portland is number one (Hunt). CNN lists the eight best beer towns; Portland is number one (Burchette and Passell). *USA Today* offers the ten best craft beer states in America. California, this time, is number one, and Oregon is number four (10Best editors). Online, we discover the twenty most coveted beer releases (Berg), the best beer in America (Hendricks), the twenty most influential beers of all time (First We Feast, "The 20 Most"), the fifteen things craft beer fans think (but nobody says) (First We Feast, "15 Things Craft Beer"), the eleven strange beers you'll actually want to try (Fox News Magazine), the best beers of winter (Schaap), the 125 places to have a beer before you die (Lyke), the 100 best places to drink beer in America (Imbibe, "100 Best Places"), and the 100 best beer bars. Portland has the top three of four listed bars, and I visited two of these four in 2011 ("America's 100 Best"). Evan Benn lists for *Esquire* the best new beers of spring and summer (Benn). Even the Weather Channel has created a beer list; it recommends eight beers to try this summer (Jess Baker). All of this listing, indeed, displaces my attention. My thoughts wander from list to list regarding craft beer. At some point I may forget that Lexington Brewing supposedly produces the best beer in Kentucky.

Lists are the snapshots highlighted in the Schlitz ad: they offer fragmented moments as *the* moments of *now*. Lists are obsessive efforts at categorizing the world into top tens or best ofs, the spaces that organize our desires and pleasures. Lists are assumptions regarding what is valuable or worth sharing. A list, Jack Goody writes, "is a kind of inventory of persons, objects, or events" (80). An early form of writing, lists, Goody argues, allowed for a change in "terms of the formal, cognitive and linguistic operations which this new technology of the intellect opened up" (81). Since its inception, the list has taught ways to organize economics, experience, and taste. A best of list teaches assumed value, for instance, and how to organize one's self around that assumption.

Obsession encourages the *checking off the list* gesture. "Anyone else go through beer overload?" one Beer Advocate thread begins regarding overpurchasing habits where new releases become items acquired from an imagined list of needs and wants, special releases and rarities ("Beer Overload"). A list, as Goody notes, does not fulfill (historically or now) "a hidden 'need'" but instead affects thought patterns (81), that is, how we organize our thoughts around craft. If I believe I want or need some beer, a list contributes to this obsessive thought. When "Session #76" of the beer bloggers carnival (an online beer discussion distributed over various blogs and centered on one topic) asks about compulsion, the question regarding assumed need as an organizational principle is posed accordingly: "What lengths do you go to hide this compulsion? For instance, do you try and sneak beer into the house so your other half doesn't see it? (Not saying that I've done this. Oh, okay, I have done this" (Beer Is Your Friend). I have done this sneaking, too, regardless of actual need. I can trace this sneaking into a series of listed moments that organizes a given day: I know that when I leave work at a certain time, I can stop at the beer store; my wife will still be at work by the time I get home, and she will not see the purchase. I, thus, can retell my compulsion as an anecdote-based list.

Compulsion as anecdote means planning a family vacation to Charleston, South Carolina, where, after listing ahead of time on my iPhone's Evernote app what I want to find, I purchase and consume many new beers, only to later lament that two days after we leave, Westbrook will hold a sale for barrel-aged Mexican Cake Stout (a beer, at that time, on my list of wants). Compulsion is fretting over every Facebook/RateBeer announcement of rare bottle releases at Three Floyds just three weeks before I am planning to visit or a week after I have visited. Compulsion is not just the feeling of acquiring—as in the guy who stops for one bottle and ends up with a bill over $100—it is working through a list (wants) (Beerbecue). Compulsion is the narrative told by beer blogger the Fuj whose "innocent beer run" to Night Shift Brewing ended up as a seventeen-hour, seven-hundred-mile trip—to Hill Farmstead, Lobster Brewing, Rail Trail Flat Bread Company, and Allagash—"12 and half of those hours on the road" (Fuj). In telling his story, he lists each place he stops at. The experience is organized as a compulsion list.

Compulsion is discovery. Compulsion is acquiring. Compulsion also is the fear of not acquiring, of not filling out or completing the imaginary list of rates I want to add. It might appear that compulsive beer-oriented people like me or the Fuj are mere collectors, gathering whatever they can to fulfill their obsession and tick off items from their checklist of wants. If that were true, however, I would leave the beer unconsumed the way that action figure collectors leave toys in the packaging, and I would merely list my possessions for others to see. "It seems the length in which we delay draining a bottle increasingly erodes our certainty of a special moment," Christopher Staten writes ("Just Drink It"). I don't purchase beer only to look at it or because I believe it will maintain for me a special moment. I buy it. I drink it. Then, as a grown man who is forty-five years old, I catch a note on the Beer Advocate forum—where threads list current trends and activities in my region—that Founders' Doom is at the Liquor Barn down the road from where I live. I leave my unfinished lunch on the table, race to the store, and buy it. The obsession is partly driven by a fear of not acquiring, of not experiencing an object on a list (physical or mental) that connects to *now*. If there is a way to express this fear, it is sometimes done via the list, for the shared list anchors any displacement I may have (sneaking beer into the house, rating) in a present moment. The way I account for this fear is by keeping my own lists of consumption. I externalize what I want to consume and what I have consumed via the list. The list is not bound to a period of time but rather to an aggregated feeling or craft terroir shared over a social network.

Trading from the List

When I log in to my RateBeer account, I find a list of beers I either supposedly want or supposedly have. These lists are kept in my metaphoric Rate-Beer beer cellar. The beer cellar is a list of beers that RateBeer members

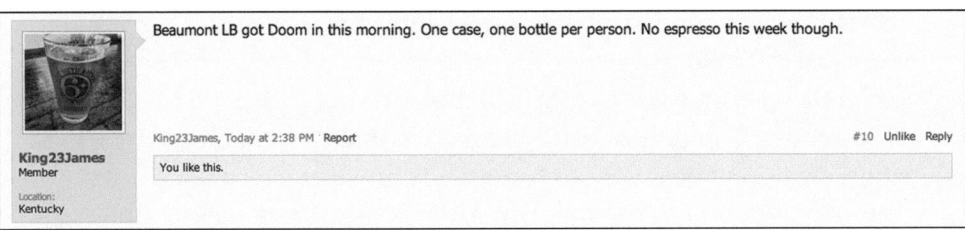

Beer Advocate's update of Founders Doom

make public. These lists are used for trading; I can search for people who want what I have and vice versa. The list shares desire, if not need. In secret Santa trades—blind trades organized by the RateBeer "Santa" and held every winter and summer on RateBeer—traders try to "hit" others' listed wants. The excitement of receiving a want often equates the excitement of locating another trader's wants. While there is a monetary value to the blind trade ($55, for instance), the overall goal is to knock items off the recipient's want list. One California blogger using Beer Advocate's system for listing wants and haves (a system similar to RateBeer's) expresses this excitement over a trade, a trade based on Pliny being someone else's want:

> After I snatched up Pliny the Elder, I quickly added it to my gots list. Within a few hours someone in Michigan had contacted me looking to make a trade. As I mentioned in several previous posts, Pliny the Elder is like gold to most beer enthusiasts. If you have a bottle, you can essentially trade for anything on the site. (Beers for Fears)

Food Republic's Jon Katz, too, describes using the Beer Advocate forums to locate beers unavailable where he lives:

> Brews you've been dying to try that you simply can't get where you live. For me, those beers were from Jester King, Karbach, St. Arnolds and No Label, all unavailable in my homestate of New York. Through a message board, I found a fellow beer trader in Texas who had access. In exchange, I sent him some local Northeast favorites like Ithaca Flower Power and Tröegs' Nugget Nectar. Though none of these are particularly rare, they're desirable because of their relative unavailability.

For some traders or enthusiasts, Pliny the Elder is a major want because of its relative unavailability. Even though it can be found in Whole Foods stores across parts of California for $5 to $6 per 500-milliliter bottle, it is not available for those of us who live far from the West Coast, Colorado, or Philadelphia (Russian River distribution markets). For me, Alltech's Bourbon Barrel Stout is not a want; it's brewed in Lexington, where I live. In one secret Santa trade, my Pennsylvania assigned trading partner shipped me a bottle for some reason (apparently, it didn't register that he was shipping to Lexington even though the brewery's official name is Lexington Brewing).

Beyond inexpensive though widely desirable beers like Pliny the Elder or despite receiving beers we can buy down the street like Bourbon Barrel Stout, many craft wants border on the unobtainable; these wants maintain a rarity described by traders as a "whale." *Whale* is a keyword for the almost impossible beer to acquire: Cantillon Blåbær Lambik, Bullfrog Beekeeper, Lost Abbey Cable Car, Hill Farmstead Ann, the mythical Midnight Sun M, Hair of the Dog Dave, and others. Danish beer reviewer Master of Hoppets noted that the bottle of Blåbær Lambik featured in his shared YouTube video came from Copenhagen; after tasting the beer, Master of Hoppets concludes that the beer was not worth the hype (Master of Hoppets). Ryan Reschan filmed a Cable Car vertical tasting at San Francisco's Tornado, noting, "I don't know if this is worth a $100 a bottle" ("The Lost Abbey Cable Car"). I have had none of these whales via trade, purchase, or share. Even if they are on my lists of wants, I doubt I will experience one of these beers at some point. I know I cannot trade for them. I lack the rhetorical power of persuasion or actual material possession of another whale to make such a trade possible. RateBeer trading advice takes whales into consideration for how they can dominate trade desire, recognizing that my predicament is common and often confused for an ability to make such an acquisition. That is, a user confuses possession (have) with desire (want). One such piece of advice follows:

> When asking for something, do not post that you want Barrel Aged Alesmith Speedway Stout for some local beer that—while it may be quite good—does not live up to the rarity of something that is sold once every two years, only at the brewery, and in numbers lower than 300 bottles. (Ross)

Beer Advocate members define a whale as a brewery-only release, a beer difficult to trade for over time, and as a beer one chases (as in Ahab chasing the whale) ("How Would You"). In 2012 Beer Advocate members compiled their White Whale List, placing Hair of the Dog Dave at number 1 and Fantôme Santé X! at number 177 ("The White Whale List"). At number 99 was Russian River's Duck Duck Gooze, which I once owned two bottles of (purchased through Lost Abbey's now defunct Sinners club). I shared the Duck Duck Gooze with one of my broventure buddies and drank the other on my forty-third birthday. I did not trade either for other whales.

When it comes to trading for whales, I either lack the required big beer to send out or I lack the desire to search for whales to acquire. "What is the personal whale that let you down and what lived up to the hype?" a Beer Advocate thread asks ("Hybrid Beers"). The answers offer no wisdom of crowd consensus: Rare was a let down / Rare lived up to the hype; Canadian Breakfast Stout was a let down / Canadian Breakfast Stout lived up

drfabulous' Beer Cellar			
Wants		**Haves**	
Find 10 Barrel Rye'm or Treason		Find Alaskan Pilot Series: Perseverance Ale	
Find 3 Fonteinen Armand'4 Oude Geuze Lente		Find Anchorage Galaxy White IPA	
Find 7venth Sun Overhead IPA growler for growler?		Find Anchorage Love Buzz Saison	
		Find Arcadia Hopmouth Double IPA	
Find 7venth Sun Summer Overhead IPA American White Oak growler for growler?		Find Avery Hog Heaven if available	
Find Alchemist Heretic		Find Avery Mephistopheles Stout	
Find Alchemist Luscious		Find Avery Salvation	
Find Ale Industries Anniversary IPA		Find Avery The Czar Imperial Stout	
Find Ale Industries Fysus		Find Avery The Maharaja Imperial India Pale Ale	
Find AleSmith Evil Dead Red		Find Avery The Reverend	
Find Allagash Vagabond		Find Bells Batch 10000 Ale	
Find Almanac Autumn 2011 Farmhouse Pale		Find Bells Batch 9000 Ale	
Find Almanac Farmers Reserve 1 would like to try their sours		Find Bells Cherry Stout	
		Find Bells Expedition Stout	
Find Alpine Beer Company Gouden Vallei		Find Bells Hopslam When it's out, I'll get it fresh.	
Find Alpine Beer Company Great			
Find Amsterdam Tempest Imperial Stout		Find Bells Java Stout most Bell's can do	
Find Arbor Sodibo Barrel Aged Blond Ale			
Find Avery Barrel-Aged Series 7 - Dihos Dactylion		Find Bells The Oracle DIPA Ale when available and fresh	
Find Barrier Evil Giant IPA			
Find Beachwood System of a Stout		Find Bells This One Goes to 11 Ale	
Find Berkshire Bourbon Barrel Imperial Stout		Find Bells Two Hearted Ale	

Part of my RateBeer beer cellar, June 2013

to the hype. The assumed meaning of these experiences is not homogenous. Some writers chronicle their trades for whales noting the pleasure and frustration the experiences deliver. Jay Hillman, both dismissing the whale and wanting the whale, writes that these types of trades tap into the feeling of both absence and need. Thus, just as there is no consensus on the effect of hype, there is no internal consensus on need and lack of need:

> I continually suffer from a low-grade feeling that I'm missing out on some of the greatest beers on the planet, and if only I searched a little harder, traded a little more intensely, proactively stockpiled a cellar full of rarities for trading, I'd get to taste all the amazing beers that are being made right now, rather than feel like I'm barely skirting the edges of what's good. ("On #Whalez and Whaling")

Hillman's discussion focuses on a series of Instagram photographs taken by Corbett Griffith, a craft enthusiast from Ann Arbor, Michigan, who shares photographs online of his collection and of his drinking moments (C. Griffith). Photography, as a shared network experience, often accompanies whale acquisitions. Corbett's posing of twenty-seven mostly rare beers on his carpeted stairs—and publicly sharing this image—prompts Hillman to question the relentless beer quest that accompanies craft, referring to it as "this wallet-busting corner of the beer dorkisphere—the collecting, hoarding and trumpeting of the uber-rare and unique" ("On #Whalez and Whaling"). Among Corbett's displayed beers are barrel-aged variations of Dark Lord, some Tired Hands growlers, Bourbon County Vanilla, an Upland Sour Reserve, and some Hill Farmstead. In October of 2013, Jay sent me Sante Adairius Rustic Ales' Love's Armor, a beer I considered a whale since I had yet to drink anything from that brewery, and all of my attempts to trade for Sante Adairius had failed.

We see similar collections of whales to Corbett Griffith's assemblage in TheCiderchick's (the handle of Grant Curlow) 2010 YouTube video of an almost seven-minute tour of a massive storage of beer in what appears to be his basement (Ciderchick). A hand moves along the various bottles, picking up an Alesmith 2005 Barrel Aged Wee Heavy, a Firestone Walker twelfth anniversary, a Southampton Double Ice Bock, and a Lost Abbey Veritas, batch 4, among others, some of which we might assume were acquired in trades. Pete Bochek's December 2013 posting to the Facebook group Beer shows eighteen boxes of Bruery Society allocations and a photo album featuring images of each beer lined up neatly on a large table in a collection of what looks like two hundred bottles of beer. "Show Us Your Beer Collection," a *Chicago Reader* story begins with a photograph of a hand holding up a bourbon-barreled Dark Lord variation ("Show Us"). In a video interview with Louisville.com, Schlafly regional representative Scott Schreffler holds up his prized whale, a bottle of the Bruery's Black Tuesday, which he obtained in a trade (Louisvillebeer). To his 694 views, YouTube vlogger Chad9976 announces in 2011 that he has a bottle of Founders Canadian Breakfast Stout, and "I'm hoping to trade that for a Vanilla Bean Three Floyds Dark Lord" ("2011 Vlog"). A whale for whale trade. A Beer Advocate thread titled "Post a Picture of Your Latest Haul" begun in early 2012 runs over five hundred pages ("Post a Picture"). Each posted picture outdoes the previous with a rare or hard-to-find beer acquired in a trade or purchased locally. One picture from February 24 features four Pliny the Elders, among others, acquired by user Turfy (Turfy). A picture posted three days later by user WesM63 shows six Pliny the Elders, among others, acquired via trade (WesM63). Rate-Beer regular Adam Jackson documents his hauls on his blog (Chandler). July 2013 for Jackson highlights ninety-three bottles of mostly rare and hard-to-find beers including Peg's G.O.O.D. Rare Dos, various Cantillons,

Bruery Reserve Society acquisitions, several bottles of Cascade Figaro, and others. That's just one month of trading. In the September/October 2013 issue of *Draft Magazine*, RateBeer member Dakine Beckman (with the handle Daknole) is featured as someone whose whale quests are summed up and represented in a day he follows the Cantillon distributor around Phoenix so that he can buy up allotments before others do (Staten 40). I once traded with Dakine when he responded to an ISO that I had posted on RateBeer.

Blogger Bryan Roth's research on the RateBeer database reveals that imperial stouts are among the site's most wanted beers (Roth). Writing in *Beer Advocate* magazine, Martin Cizmar describes his quest to drink through the Beer Advocate top one hundred (a list!) beers, which includes many whales:

> I began my quest to try the Beer Advocate top 100 at my 30th birthday in September 2010. Two and a half years and several thousand dollars later, I'm still a dozen beers short, but I've already learned far more than I'd dreamed I would. (53)

Goose Island Bourbon County Brand Stout is number four on Beer Advocate's "Top 250 Beers" list ("Top 250 Beers"). I assume that, thousands of dollars later, Cizmar checked the beer off on his quest. On November 27, 2013, Goose Island sponsored a Black Friday sale of Bourbon County Brand Stout and its variants (Barleywine, Backyard, Coffee, and Coconut). By limiting the sale of Bourbon County Brand Stout to a one-day Black Friday release, Goose Island transformed the beer into a whale. Limited release equates a rhetoric of scarcity and need. Posters announcing the sale, online discussion and hype, the barrel aging of beer in general, discussions of how many cases would be available in which markets, the connotation of Black Friday sales regarding other products, the beer's overall scarcity—all of these networked moments rhetorically made a whale out a beer that, while typically is in demand and not produced on a large scale, only a few years earlier could be easily bought months after its release. (I would often see it in the Columbia, Missouri, Hy-Vee supermarket cooler for some time after its release.) All of these networked moments created lines outside retail stores across the country, where consumers waited to buy beer the way others wait to buy marked-down toys and appliances on Black Friday. I, too, waited in line.

When a normally distributed beer, such as Bourbon County Brand Stout, transforms into a one-day release, photographic sharing occurs as enthusiasts make public their purchases. For many social media theorists, this desire reflects permission marketing (continuing the hype that has made the beer now rare) and is also the basis of weak-tie connections, connections not based on strong family, professional, or other fairly intimate relationships. "It is these weak ties that allow messages to move from one cluster of people to new audiences, where it might be further propagated," write Nahon and Hemsley (32). I discovered many of these described images via weak ties: Facebook groups, retweets, postings on message boards. I don't know any of the people who have shared these photos, purchases, or other information with me.

Tweets marked with the hashtags #gooseisland, #bourboncounty, and #bcbs demonstrated some of this sharing among weak ties regarding Goose Island Black Friday. Facebook did as well. In one thread on the Facebook forum ISO: for trade (FT), the poster asks ironically, "Is this stuff good" and posts a picture of a pickup truck's bed full of over $1,000 worth of Bourbon County Brand Stout beers (Metcalfe). Another thread in the same forum posts a haul of at least eight twenty-two-ounce bottles and several four packs in front of Christmas decorations (Tippett), an image similar to that posted by a Twitter user who also used his Christmas tree to frame his haul (Van Dyk). As the Facebook thread unfolds, the original poster notes that he has been overwhelmed with e-mail requests for trades. If Goose Island's networked terroir has been reduced to the taxonomy of "crafty" as opposed to the supposedly more desirable label of craft (as I noted earlier regarding terroir and taxonomy), then Black Friday in 2013 showed no indication of such a label's negative consequences regarding this want. While some notable critiques surfaced, such as Evil Twin Jeppe Jarnit-Bjergsø's tweet "Scary how the whole craft beer world go crazy over an Anheuser Busch release . . ." (Evil Twin Brewing), consumption—which motivates networked terroir—was not affected by the supposed negative connotation of being crafty. People lined up to buy the beer. People hoarded. People took pride in their hoarding by posting photographs of hauls. People celebrated the now moment of a purchase or even of waiting in line. People disseminated information about their purchases among their weak and strong ties. No one cared who owns Goose Island.

It is easy to critique Goose Island for participating in the contagion effects of Black Friday consumerism that have already overshadowed the day after Thanksgiving. It is easy for me to make this critique, but I, too, was a part of this day's purchasing. I was a part of what Philip Montoro, two days before Black Friday, referred to as the craft-beer boom's grossest bullshit: nerds with more free time than sense queuing up outside a liquor store before dawn, for instance, or shadowing a delivery truck from one stop to the next, or buying a shop's entire bottle allotment to sell or trade online.

While I did not do any of these activities, I'm not outside this network. I can't pretend that I didn't contribute to Goose Island's networked terroir as much as anyone or anything else did leading up to and including that Friday. Whatever I have observed regarding Dark Lord Day or Founders Canadian Breakfast Stout's release, I can apply the same observations to Goose Island Black Friday. As soon as I lined up, I helped foster networked terroir and its delivery. I announced on Twitter my presence in line at the local Liquor Barn. I publicly commented about buying the beers. If I were to post a picture of my haul or line up my beers for an Instagram now moment, which I eventually did on *Make Mine Potato*, I would become a part of this networked delivery through photographic sharing, too. My shared photograph, like the ones I draw attention to circulating in various online forums, builds current and future hype when viewed as part of the same influential network (much as I note regarding other releases) where the

My Black Friday haul, with the previous year's haul slightly visible in the background

ties among nodes (participants, viewers) need not be strong. "To get new information, we have to activate our weak ties," says Barabási (*Linked* 43). Such is how networks work. They aren't built because they are ever-moving connections and disconnections, many of which we are a part of whether we know the connections we interact with or not. We are always sharing our presence in a given network, via images and via text. The photograph must be shared even if I am embarrassed to do so (my shame at being part of the superficial celebration of Black Friday and rampant consumerism I am helping to perpetuate). I share because I already feel the emotional lure of being part of a community, a community where boasting and showing off play as much of a role in identity formation as liking or aggregating interests does. Once shared, the photograph furthers networked terroir via emotional emphasis ("I want that, too!" the photograph evokes in its audience). Black Friday haul pictures generate additional interest in quests. They list for a general public what whales we've tracked down.

Craft Trades

In 2010 Brian Yaeger documented for *All about Beer* his whale quest, which did not include Bourbon County Brand Stout nor did it involve waiting in a line. Instead, he traded beer. "By any means possible," he stated, "I set sail to land the following whales in a one-month period: Flossmoor Station Wooden Hell, Cantillon Blåbær Lambik and Iron Hill Ring of Fire" ("Gray Market/White Whale"). In his quest to land a Blåbær Lambik (a trade with well-known RateBeerian Papsø) Yaeger writes,

> We were close to striking a deal—basically exchanging a smattering of bottles involving a total of 26 from my end for six from his including, I kid not, the 2005, 2007 and 2009 Blåbær vintages. That's like catching Moby Dick, Mrs. Dick and Moby, Jr. with one harpoon. Papsø suggested I do a vertical of three batches. "I'm pretty sure that would be a popular tasting to attend :-)." ("Gray Market/White Whale")

Trading beer, for whales or even for off-the-shelf beers, involves negotiations. Trading involves the rhetoric of capturing attention and convincing someone of a worthwhile deal to engage in. To lure in a trade that will excite and motivate the online audience, one often offers keywords of "lambic," "sour," "barrel aged," "one off," "bottle count," and "brewery release." To perform this rhetorical work, trading also involves being in the now moment, the kairotic period where wants and haves converge so that a trade may occur, even if it is not directed at these specific keywords. A posted ISO or FT may receive numerous responses or zero responses depending on the day, time of year, attention of other forum members, and momentary (now) interest. While ratings offer stable user-generated systems of measuring either obsession or taste (aggregated rankings produce top-beers lists and alert readers to overall quality), trades are unstable and unpredictable. At one point a bottle may generate great interest and at another moment little or no interest depending on which craft actors (people, but also hype, desire, releases, best-of lists, etc.) become involved in the trading network. At one point Alpine and Captain Lawrence beers were in high demand. When I first started trading, Captain Lawrence beers dominated ISO requests. My 2009 trade of a growler of Flat Branch Brewing's chili beer for Captain Lawrence Cuvee de Castleton (and a few others) was, for me at the time, a huge win. Today, I find few Captain Lawrence requests. What is or is not a whale depends on the moment, the feeling of now, when a beer captures its audience's attention. That attention may be directed by a release day, limited release, sudden interest, cost, online discussion, high ratings, and other undetermined factors. Trading involves the rhetorical concept of audience.

By the summer of 2013, there were no Captain Lawrence requests on the RateBeer forum; instead, Peg's G.O.O.D. Rare Dos imperial stout was in demand as were bottled Toppling Goliath beers. By the end of summer 2013, Lost Abbey had rereleased Duck Duck Gooze, and it returned to its status as a highly sought beer. In 2010 a friend and I struggled to find a serious taker for Goose Island Rare, despite its already rare status (a $40 and limited-release version of Bourbon County Stout aged for twenty-four months in twenty-three-year-old Pappy Van Winkle barrels). In 2013 Rare ISO requests surfaced, including the Facebook post I noted earlier. In June 2013, while writing this chapter, I posted a FT for a fresh bottle of Three Floyds Dreadnaught (number seventeen on RateBeer's "Best Top 50" list), which I picked up locally off the shelf, and received no response. If I had known Derrick from Winston-Salem a few months earlier, I might have talked him into trading for it, but alas, our paths never crossed; we shared no kairotic moment. Eventually, he blogged about receiving a Dreadnaught in a trade from Dave in Wisconsin at that time (All the Same Beer). After spending almost a year trying to trade for Block 15 beers, I easily landed two different bottles in a trade for a locally available Prairie Artisan Puncheon and a Kuhnhenn Fourth Dementia I had in my cellar—all by answering a FT request at the right moment with the right person.

Writing in *Bon Appétit*, Lucy Burningham observes one day's transaction from her perusal a few years earlier for trade requests. She lists the available beers: "On today's forum, one trader wants to swap a bottle of De Dolle Stille Nacht Reserva 2010 for a selection of desirables, which includes 3 Fonteinen Oude Geuze (pre-2008) and Captain Lawrence Barrel Select Gold" ("Inside the World"). A year later Burningham found herself at a Portland, Oregon, bottle share where she partook in "seven vintages of Goose Island Bourbon County Brand Stout, four of Roots Epic Ale—a coveted strong ale from a now-defunct Portland brewery—and seven years of He'Brew Jewbelation, plus He'Brew's blend of those seven beers aged in whiskey barrels" ("Bottle Shares Spread the Beer"). Gatherings such as these, Burningham declares, occur because of social media, where information spreads and lists are written:

> Following an explosion in craft brewing around the country and the rise of social media, many bottle shares are organized through popular beer websites or on Twitter. They happen around beer festivals and brewery bottle releases, in hotel rooms or beer bars. Sometimes strangers meet at these events for the first time. In advance, participants often list the beers they plan to bring on shared online spreadsheets, which ramps up anticipation. ("Bottle Shares Spread the Beer")

Bottle shares also occur because of social media and trades. On Flickr, Candianghetto_ut posts the results of a trade that include a bottle of Canadian Breakfast Stout and two Pliny the Elders.[1] On one day's RateBeer forum, I notice a FT offer of twelve 2011 Jackie O's sours, a FT Cigar City Gates of Hell / ISO Hill Farmstead Madness and Civilization number 1, and ISO Avery's Uncle Jacob / FT Chicago stuff. These, too, indicate whale or whale-ish trade requests whose results may have ended up in a bottle share somewhere in the country. Sometimes, trade requests for the rare and difficult overshadow what is available off the shelf and what is local. Often, these two taxonomies of value clash. Even if it is only distributed in a few states and is a top-fifty beer, Three Floyds Dreadnaught may not be deemed worthy of one's attention on a given day of trading since I bought it off the shelf and did not acquire it as a one-time brewery release.

There exists a terroir-induced politics to trading, one whose rhetoric is as much based on perception (must be from a special release or brewery beer club) as it is on quality. Three Floyds Dark Lord, the subject of my discussion of networks and release days and once a much desired beer for me as well as a major whale, was being dismissed on the Facebook forum

Beer at about the same time as these 2013 moments of whale-searching occurred. While other whale trades were circulating and generating their own kairotic moment, one trader no longer qualified Dark Lord as a whale. Its taxonomy, in this instance, had vanished. Trading emotions affect the kairotic moment as much as other influential factors such as number of bottles released, style, availability, and the barrel used to age the beer. A Dark Lord diminishment does not stand for a change in Dark Lord's trading value; it only represents one moment (a now) of perceived change. An April 2013 FT post on RateBeer sought out 2013 versions of Surly Darkness, Cigar City Hunahpu, or Bruery Black Tuesday in exchange for Dark Lord and reported accepting offers (1971hemicuda). Dark Lord still occupies the number one spot on RateBeer's Most Wanted Beer list (Pliny the Elder is number eight) ("Most Wanted Beer"). I opened a 2013 Dark Lord at a bottle share during the same year and heard no complaints. Whale is not a permanent taxonomy.

My trading began in June 2009, when I sent from Missouri to Michigan a Lost Abbey Devotion with Brett and a number of other beers for some Shorts, Dragonmead, Kuhnhenn, and Dark Horse. In retrospect, the trade makes little sense to me because only two years earlier I had left Michigan—where I often drank these breweries' beers and visited Dragonmead and Kuhnhenn at times—and moved to Missouri. Why my first trade was not to a state for beers that I had never had is not clear to me, much in the way that my first bad review is not currently clear to me. I was new to trading and anything unavailable in Missouri seemed novel and unique; thus I settled on the familiar, or the topos, of beer drinking. Newness, as I've noted regarding ratings, often means not being acclimated to the practice of new media logics such as crowd sourcing, engagement, and participation. Newness prevents the sharing or contributing that social media are supposed to encourage. Since I had yet to engage in trading, I was not sure what I wanted or why. I merely felt the need to participate in this part of online exchanges. My trade request was my first posting of a FT thread on the forums, and I reached an agreement with the first and only response I received. "I have a bottle of Devotion with Brett up for trade. Can also thrown in Boulevard Smokestacks, Schlafly bottle conditioneds—including new Quad—and I'm sure other stuff" (Drfabulous). On RateBeer I've completed over ninety trades since that first one. Two boxes have been damaged out of all my trades. One time, after a box sent to Seattle broke and the surviving bottles were returned to me, I received a note from FedEx admonishing me, not for sending beer, but for not checking "Adult Signature Required" as required by the company's ground shipping policy. Even with significant RateBeer trading (not counting trades I have done with friends, on Google+ and even from Twitter), I have completed sixty fewer trades than the fiftieth best trader on RateBeer's "Top Traders" list (RateBeer compiles a list for almost every statistic of its site's activity) ("Top Traders"). Even with contemporary knowledge regarding participation, I am still not among the most active participants.

Letter from FedEx about selecting the "Adult Signature Required" service

New traders often announce their status and introduction to the community (beyond my FT post, I did not) on the forum. Sometimes, Pliny the Elder, the subject of my initial terroir discussion, is the announcement's focus. One new trader starts a thread by noting how desire for Pliny the Elder has influenced a desire to trade. Shared and circulated discussion of a detail (a hard to find Russian River double IPA) prompts a trade: "I am new to trading . . . I have been working with a few people on the other site in regards to getting some Pliny (while searching on how to find this I discovered the 'world' of beer trading)" (AJDePaul). Another new trader is told that Pliny the Elder can be sent as an introduction to trading (Ray101). An October 2013 new trader introduction is met with user Bytemesis's response that

> things like Pliny the Elder, Fat Heads IPA, Marshal Zhukov, New Glarus Serendipity are all shelf beers in some part of the country, and you should be able to find somebody who is willing to pick them up in exchange for your shelf beers. (Bytemesis)

One blogger's advice regarding getting started in beer trading includes the following:

> Someone across the country in a far away state is not going to send you Pliny the Elder in exchange for some crappy, mass produced swill. You'll need beers that are unavailable on the west coast, yet also in demand if you're going to try and land some Pliny. (Beer and Stuff)

Even the NBC News website offers Pliny-based trading advice to newbies: "Want a bottle of Pliny the Elder and have a lovely Captain Lawrence Imperial IPA laying around? Hit up the beer trading boards on RateBeer, Beer Advocate or Reddit and find someone to swap with" (Galligan, "How Do You Score"). In the rhetoric of introductions to trading, Pliny is the contagion, the repeatable item circulated from exchange to exchange, "triggered by anybody connected to the network, dependent on her stumbling into chance encounters," as Tony Sampson notes (112). Trading introductions stumble into one another in the forum's network as each introduction or response to introduction triggers the Pliny mention, or the sense of trading terroir where lists play a role in aggregation.

If I were to search out the first trade by a well-known RateBeerian, such as the Danish member Papsø, whose over 25,000 ratings and 210 trades dwarf anything I've done on the site, I would not learn much about his first time trading via the shared database, nor would I learn if Papsø first traded for Pliny. My communal knowledge of Papsø is limited to his filled-out lists left as traces on the site. I know that his first recorded trade was to Tbone in 2005, and it has been documented by the following list of items he sent out:

> Anchor Our Special Ale 2005 Brooklyn Christmas Ale Cimes Piste Noire Fuglsang Julebryg Fur Julebryg Gourmetbryggeriet Jingle Ale Harboe Årgangsbryg 2005 Pokal Julebryg Serafijn Celtic Angel Sterkens Julemandens Trøst Svaneke Bryghus Julebryg Svaneke Bryghus Julebryg (COOP) Søgaard Julebuk Thisted Overgæret Julebryg Willemoes Jule Ale. ("Papsoe's Trade History")

Most of these beers are unknown to me; they are not in my network of terroir. The list tells me a partial story of the first-time trading experience. Danish beers were shipped to another Danish location; reciprocal trade feedback is found when I click on Tbone's account and discover what Papsø sent out. Unlike the other lists I discover, this list does not promote beers for summer or an idea of what the best beer bar in America might be. The list describes an exchange that supposedly ended positively; I make that assumption from feedback left in the network. I infer from this list that European trades mirror American trades. I infer the feeling of success. I infer from the over two hundred follow-up trades Papsø has completed that he, like others, now is "addicted" to trading—a point I will expand upon shortly. Addiction, too, is a narrative of the trading experience that stems from the list. Once one starts to trade, the narrative explains, one cannot stop. I have felt that addiction many times. My story is that I first traded for beers from a state I had lived in only a few years earlier. My anecdote is about a failure to seek out the new. *My addiction* followed as I sought out unavailable and new-to-me beers over time. Of course, Papsø may not be addicted to trading. But what are Papsø's or other traders' stories? I can list a few things I know: In November 2007 he traded with Ken Weaver. In 2010 Yaeger gave Papsø feedback regarding the trade he narrated in *All about Beer*, noting the amount of beer exchanged: "My 26 bottles to him for 12 of his to me." These stories include relationships (as do most social media stories). These stories include lists of what was sent and what was received. What other stories can be found in the list of trades that constitute a significant part of the RateBeer database?

Trading encourages storytelling. Anecdotal retellings. Landing whales. Taking photographs and sharing the photographs to tell a story of excitement or pleasure. Listing what one wants and has. Bragging about acquiring multiple bottles of a special beer. Posting hauls. Sharing. The stories, exemplified in Yaeger's narrative and others, are tales of acquiring the impossible. The stories are grand and confident in gesture. The stories are about making one's way through lists—Top 100, Best in State, 100 Bars to Visit Before You Die, Beers of Summer, etc. Achievements. Surprise Results. Rarities. Unbelievable Finds. Newness. These might serve as keywords of trade narratives whose listing builds a larger tale. A Wisconsin writer tells his story about acquiring a bottle of Goose Island's Rare by referencing trading: "I was able to secure a bottle behind the scenes from Discount Liquor in Milwaukee's storage room, but reaching out to the craft beer community's excellent trading market could possibly yield the goods as well" (Ivanovic). "I can honestly say that I have no regrets about any of the beers I traded away," Georgia bartender Keith Dion writes online. "Except for a couple of CCB Hunahpu's Stouts and about a six pack of Founders KBS all of my boxes contained fairly common things I put little effort into finding" (Dion). Blogger Suzy Six Pack states,

> I first joined the beer trading world last spring, when I posted a message on Beeradvocate's [sic] Trading Forum in search of New Glarus Raspberry Tart and Wisconsin Belgian Red, two fruity and highly desirable beers only distributed in the Mid-West. As it turned out, once I actually tried these brews, I didn't care for them. But that's not the point: once I opened that package up and saw beers inside, I was hooked. (Suzy Six Pack)

Writer Ken Weaver's trading story begins with a flight to San Diego to acquire what was impossible to find in a trade, and then shipping

> out approximately $125+ in rare beer, including two of the aforementioned BA Alesmiths, Fish Tale's Barrel Aged Poseidon, 3 Fonteinen J & J Blauw, 1.5 liters of 2001 HOTD Doggie Claws, and some Michigan rarities that have since been lost to the annals of time. ("The Things")

These beers, in turn, were posted for trade on RateBeer in order to land a 2000 De Dolle Stille Nacht Reserva (Kmweaver). I considered buying the 2010 version of the same beer when I saw it locally but balked at the $40 price tag even though the possibility of acquiring something rare in return was tempting. Reading through a March 2009 thread on the Beer Spot titled "What'd You Get in the Mail Today," I discover stories about trades (a growler of Surly 16 sent for a collection of Grand River and Kuhnhenn, for instance) but also stories about traders' relationships with each other: Gator and Beagle, Nuclear George picking on Gator, members saving beer for an upcoming Upper Peninsula beer geek weekend, members receiving very rare Bullfrog bottles, one member receiving a Captain Lawrence DIPA growler; and as the threads move into April, members anticipating drinking received beer over Easter ("What Did You Get"). Two years later in the same thread, the traders have changed, but the overall stories regarding acquisition, generosity, and sharing continue on as contagion moments.

Forum or blog posts tell stories. Sometimes I catch myself skimming through trade lists, not to see who has positive feedback to trade with, but to see who sent what to whom, and if those received beers were rated and enjoyed. In that sense, I am reading trading stories. Did the trade, in other words, deliver satisfactory results at the moment of eventual consumption? I assume, based on his narrative, that Ken Weaver was satisfied with his documented trade. I assume, based on the online banter that I've read, that Nuclear George and Gator are satisfied with their trades. I will check the ratings of people I've traded with (did they like that can of West Sixth IPA I threw in as an extra?), and I will make assumptions based on the ratings they write. In addition, I'll also browse ratings and trades of people I have never engaged with on the site. I want to know their stories as well. I want to know what they are sending and what they are receiving. I want to be socially engaged even if my engagement is based on assumptions.

One popular narrative that traders share about their engagement is that of addiction. One blogger begins a post by stating, "My name is Josh, and I have a problem. I've become addicted to beer trading" (Christie). One RateBeer thread is titled "1-800-number for beer trading addiction."[2] When a newbie thread is begun in February 2013, DalzAle advises, "Stop before you start. Otherwise you will meet incredibly generous people along the way who make it a harder habit than heroin to quit . . ." (DalzAle). At 106 trades, RateBeer member DietPepsican declares he has to take a break. His explanation is that it is time to appreciate local beer:

> About a year after I started trading I looked back through my fedex [sic] account and I have over 150 packages I've sent off. Good lord that is a lot of beer shipped! At that point I knew I had to take a bit of a break aka cut back as much as I can and start revisiting the amazing beers the midwest [sic] has to offer. (DietPepsican)

Almost four years after he made that remark, he has over two hundred trades. The initial point he makes, though, is important to the story of trading. Even with local options, we trade. We may declare that we need to stop because of certain variables (cost, time, and energy playing major roles in our need to stop trading) that reflect a grand narrative of meaning, but we often come back to trading at some point (often, for me, a mere few weeks later) because of the small story (pleasure). This part of the narrative justifies itself by being told as sharing (experiences, local options), ticking (checking off the beers one's had), variety (getting new beer), and making relationships (interacting with other RateBeer members). At some point, a trader arrives at the epiphany that—after spending thousands of dollars shipping boxes across the country—there exist worthwhile beers closer to home. As one beer blogger declares after Goose Island's Black Friday event in 2013, "I am giving up on chasing rare beers" (N. Miller). The local topos, we learn, breaks addiction and overcomes the exhaustion of endless whale hunting. Matt of the *Hoosier Beer Geeks*, a collaborative blog, expresses that appreciation in a May 2012 post:

> I've been drinking better beer for about a decade now. I would say that I've been trading beer for probably seven of those ten years, but in the last six months I've almost quit trading cold turkey, and I've found out a great deal about beer and myself along the way. I haven't pursued rare beer, trading beer, or worried about when a beer was going to hit the market. It has been very easy and very satisfying. (Hoosier Beer Geek)

Even as he documents his whale hunt, Yaeger acknowledges a similar position regarding the local, noting that it always provides enough craft to satisfy one's enthusiasm. Trading, Yaeger argues, may be pleasurable, but it is not necessary:

> Procuring beer—by hook or by crook, or at least by beer trading or an online auction—that is not ordinarily available to you, either because it is not sold in your market or no longer commercially available, is not necessary. That is said from the standpoint that beer is necessary. But in this day and age, no matter where you live in the United States and most of the industrial world for that matter, a reasonably locally brewed, well-made beer is available to you. This is why sought after beers are called "wants" and not "needs." ("Gray Market/White Whale")

For the last two years, I've given up on chasing Founders' KBS (a barrel-aged version of the breakfast stout). After hours of waiting in line, running from store to store, all to acquire one or two twelve-ounce bottles, I've since opted for other purchases. Except, of course, for my Black Friday Goose Island moment.

In Kentucky, trading is one of two ways I can acquire out-of-state beer. The other is traveling. Most retailers won't ship to Kentucky. Before I moved to Kentucky, shipping allowed me to acquire out-of-state beer. While a CNBC article declares that beer shoppers will not pay more for shipping when ordering online, I often did pay more without much of a thought for the extra dollar or two per bottle in shipping costs produced (Sandholm and Rotunno). I mentioned my first purchase from South Bay Drugs and Pharmacy for Pliny the Elder. My obsession returns as memory when, while writing this final chapter, I discover, on another laptop I own, an e-mail order I placed to South Bay for Pliny the Elder on August 11, 2008. The South Bay e-mail declared,

> Beer—Joey@South Bay Drugs wrote: > *South Bay Drugs Newsletter—August 11th, 2008* > * > _/Russian River Pliny the Elder:/_ It's finally here! First time > available in bottles! Only 3 cases arrived so I have to put a 2 bottle > per-person limit. Just like Blind Pig, if you don't score any from this > wave don't worry, it should be a very consistent release soon and you > should be able to land many more eventually. 8.0%abv, $4.50per 500ML > bottle, limit 2 per-person.

What I don't remember until I read this saved e-mail is that Pliny would have been available in bottle for the first time in 2008, and that from Columbia, Missouri, I would have secured two bottles of this first-time event. In May 2013, I traded (again) for Pliny, answering a FT request on the RateBeer trading forum. For three bottles of Pliny, I sent a bottle of Three Floyds' Behemoth. The local does not break my addiction or my quests. The local (or the somewhat local Three Floyds), instead, provided me with a bit of California. Black Friday provided me with a bit of Chicago, by way of its Belgian conglomerate owners (whose own locality is summed up, as I note, in the disingenuous "where is your beer brewed" campaign). Locality does not, in the end, prevent trading for me; it fosters it. In this way, trading establishes a connection not unlike the connection that I experience with a photograph of three men sharing a beer in 1844. I am local, but I am away as well. I am displaced in place (terroir), time (release/trade), and consumption (the beer itself). I am here and then and now at once. I am an aggregated identity shared across trades.

EPILOGUE
Father-Son Stories

In food culture, local often aggregates family: family farms, family-oriented activities, family artisanal practices, families who live near one another. I began this book with the most memorable craft moment aggregated within beer storytelling and most local to my experience as a father—the parental beer tale. Such a moment is memorable for how it anchors experience with one's children and allows craft to be a part of the family experience. My own parental beer tales revolve around my daughter, whom I have shared beer experiences with since she was two weeks old. Stories of a first time drinking beer (as I noted in chapter 1), however, often revolve around sons and fathers (not fathers and daughters). These stories, like the Schlitz ad I began chapter 7 with, are snapshots. They reveal fragmented moments of sharing in which parental bonding over an object supposedly occurs. My physical snapshots (like a Great American Beer Festival photo taken in the event's early minutes) can be blurry or framed improperly; they are fragments of what should be larger, more properly framed and positioned images. My beer memories, as informed by my own parental beer relationship, can be blurry as well. As I noted in the introduction, I may only remember the minor details (the small story) of the parental beer tale, not the grand, important narratives memories often evoke. Such is how anecdotes work when they are neither beginnings nor even clear depictions of larger stories. The parental beer tale, like the list or the interruption, is a sharing of displacement—the detail removed from the larger story of importance. Displacement, in this case, is not a bad thing. My daughter and I remained bonded over beer. The story is what displaces us—a banal moment overpowering a larger, supposedly more important narrative.

Father-son stories, unlike father-daughter stories, are often told as stories of displacement (fathers and sons typically do not get along). To that I add the element of beer. When I tell a beer anecdote (as a father), it may involve my son or daughter sitting in front of a sampler tray at a brewery. When my father, whom I have alluded to throughout this book, tells a beer anecdote, he shares two anecdotes he has mentally stored regarding beer, stories that are blurry fragments of his internal beer narratives, one of which also involves a sampler tray. Neither anecdote is about handing me a Heineken on a hot Miami summer day. Because he is not a beer drinker, he clings to these two stories (which are not about me) as ways to anchor his experience in brief moments of sharing. One anecdote involves touring New Belgium years ago and marveling over the sampler of beer (a novel idea to him) put in front of him. The other anecdote involves a tour of Highland Brewing, near his North Carolina home, where "pitchers of beer" were poured for visitors. No other details follow. These contagion anecdotes, repeated at every get-together or holiday, whether in my home in Lexington or my parents' home in North Carolina, anchor his beer experiences into two repeated, social moments. They are not parental beer tales, however, because unlike any of the anecdotes, details, social media moments, aggregations, and images I have presented in this book, they are not about sharing, even though they are repeatedly shared. In the repetition of the story, nothing is actually shared other than the repetition. His anecdotes are repeated yet fragmented memories, without terroir. They are not told in order to connect to my anecdotes. They are not told in order to recognize larger sharing experiences. They are not told to aggregate experience. They are simply told. Such a point is important to the story I have been trying to tell all along about social media and craft beer. Rather than return to the parental beer tale I began with as an effort to wrap up or neatly tie together my anecdotes and blurry storytelling as a narrative might do, I conclude with this interrupted father story, and then with another interrupted father-son beer anecdote, one that my father never repeats.

 One early beer anecdote I locate as a snapshot among other mental photographs I've taken involves my father and me almost twenty years ago. At that point I was not yet into craft beer or, apart from an occasional Moosehead, much into beer in general. One afternoon in downtown Hendersonville, North Carolina, not far from where my parents live in nearby Flat Rock, my sister and I walked into a homebrew shop. As we walked around the shop looking at the various ingredients and brewing kits for sale, we thought about our father, who we felt needed a hobby to invest his time in. Because he liked making things (furniture, paintings, decks), we bought a homebrewing kit for him, believing that even if he wasn't a big beer drinker, he would enjoy "making" something for himself, and he would take pride in the accomplishment that typically accompanies building a table or deck. Instead of trying out the kit, he waited until we left North Carolina, returned the kit, and kept the money. Over twenty years later in the summer of 2011, I had just moved to Lexington, Kentucky. My parents were coming to visit us in our new, crappy rental home (where the Rivertown photo was taken in front of a toaster oven) three days before Father's Day. On the phone before their trip, I told my dad I would take him for a beer at The Beer Trappe, a local shop and bar in Lexington that specializes in craft beer. The day before my parents were to arrive, he had a massive heart attack and almost died.

Beer joins these two anecdotes. Beer transforms these brief stories into something social; I share them here at this book's conclusion as a form of media sharing. The anecdotes are fuzzy, not sharp in detail or complete in their overall meaning to me, but they situate my own obsession in two moments that otherwise might not stand out as related to my craft obsession. They don't help create my obsession, and I have not previously considered them as part of my craft obsession. I now identify them—in retrospect—as part of my overall craft network the way I once discovered the Star of David on a Cantillon bottle. The anecdotes anchor me, for a moment, in a displacement from the moment of now (writing this epilogue) in a way that my father's own beer-related anecdotes of visiting two breweries do not (his anecdotes are not distractions but simply repeated topoi). These moments frame another kind of parental beer tale that does not reflect a traditional narrative of bonding associated with stories about parents and children, one I've come to assume must accompany tales of father and sons drinking beer, one which I wish I could conclude this book with.

In issue number 77 of *Beer Advocate* magazine, Wil Wheaton narrates this traditional tale I desire when he shares anecdotes about brewing beer with his son, stories that *do* demonstrate bonding experiences. Unlike my narrative, Wheaton does not return a beer kit given to him but cherishes the shared experience of father and son brewing together that the kit offers. Even with minimal experience brewing, Wheaton identifies the possibilities of brewing with his son as positive no matter how good or bad the beer they brew tastes: "I thought, even if it was a spectacular failure, it would still be something we did together, something we could bond over, and something that would stay with us—success or failure—for the rest of our lives" (48). Wheaton's story is a story about sharing. Wheaton's story is a variation on the parental beer tale as well as on the photographic or trading narrative I've been describing. What unites these stories is sharing. Sharing homebrewing with his son, sharing the homebrew with his own dad, sharing time together, Wheaton enters into this contagion network. The contagion is a shared experience, sharing the same story. If there is one contagion that, for me, stands out among craft obsession, it is the fairly commonplace (and possible cliché) one of sharing. Sharing might mean photographs, or it might mean lists, or it might mean trading.

But for me, it has not meant a parental tale where I am the child. I have often thought about my father returning the beer kit we bought him and the ways it shut down any sense of possible sharing. We lost that *now* moment I currently attempt to preserve and share with others via social media experiences. If I had not developed a sense of craft obsession, that moment might not return to me as a painful snapshot. It might have been forgotten as other father-son experiences would gain importance in my memory. But that moment, long before my interest in craft beer, is with me *now* because of how my current interests are shaped by various forces online and offline, and how these forces aggregate. That moment is with me now because of my overall craft network terroir. That moment is delivered to me via this network. For that reason, I share it here.

Where my parents live, there is a brewery, Southern Appalachian, that I have yet to visit even though it is located in the town they live in. Forty miles to the north is Wicked Weed, a brewpub we visit every time we pass through Asheville on the way to Flat Rock. This metaphoric travel narrative, a small, quintessential story interrupting this epilogue, and having a brevity equal to that of a status update or tweet, speaks to a lack of sharing present in my jealousy of Wheaton's narrative. We visit the distant brewery, not the one close to my parents' house. The local, my family's local, is distant to me; it feels displaced. It is outside my network of terroir moments even though I have a long-standing personal connection with the town. This distance feels like an error in judgment.

In the Hendersonville newspaper my parents receive daily, the *Times-News*, I read about how public sharing of beer information can be erroneous because of distance. Writing at a time before the Internet, syndicated columnist Lewis Grizzard used his column to retract a previous statement he had made that Paul Newman drank Coors. Apparently, Anheuser-Busch wrote to Grizzard and rebuked him for this claim, showing him a letter from Newman claiming the opposite. Grizzard corrects himself with these words:

> Paul Newman DOES NOT drink Coors beer. He drinks Budweiser. Sometimes—and I've got a letter to prove it—he even drinks it two cases at a time while hunkered down in the men's room of the Beverly Hills Hotel and what I'd give to know the rest of that story. (3)

Erroneous reporting. Inconclusive story lines. Bad sharing of information. Distance (Grizzard does not ask Newman what he drinks; he does not even know Paul Newman). Frustration (Grizzard's ironic tone suggests that he does not want to make this retraction). Exaggeration (two cases at a time). A syndicated story located far away from the author's original location or the original site of publication. An anecdote that does not fulfill its promise. These are old media problems retained in social media. These are old social problems retained in the era of craft obsession, where sharing can never be a totalizing experience; where despite the inordinate amount of online sharing one does regarding beer, one might still lack a sense of the personal (Grizzard does not know Paul Newman's drinking habits) and a lack of parental sharing (I have never visited a brewery near my parents' home; my dad returned the beer kit). I read a syndicated article about beer in a local city (where my family has lived for some time), and I return to the syndicated moments of this book, the aggregated emotional and physical craft beer moments I've incorporated into a story about craft beer, social media, and me via various interruptions and displacements. I return with these anecdotes in order to conclude.

Aggregation is at the heart of sharing. When friends visit Lexington, we try to share our places of interest: restaurants, parks, breweries. In this sense we engage with the physical aspect of being social. That I still have not visited the brewery near where my parents live speaks not to taste (who does or does not drink beer) but to this sense of sharing that I have been tracing throughout the previous chapters; it speaks to the missing part of a larger emotional aggregation, of a personal terroir that marks craft. In the case of Hendersonville, I am not physically sharing with its beer culture even though I have a very physical connection to the city I have been visiting since I was ten. In these moments of beer-based, aggregated openness, I perform the ultimate self-sharing: the selfie. These very personal stories I share about craft beer and myself—throughout this book—are textual selfies, outward projections of an image of me. *Craft Obsession* is a selfie, a projection of my academic, beer self distributed over a virtual social media space.

In the later chapters concerned with photography, in a book that has been mostly a giant selfie—a projection of the author onto the beer world through details and small moments—I have only this final selfie about family, parenting, place, beer, and sharing to give. The father-daughter tale is the selfie I began this book with. The father-son tale is the selfie I conclude with. My own son, too, is shared in this photographic, contagion beer moment that repeats a father-son moment with another father-son image.

EPILOGUE

Selfie from Instagram with son at Blue Stallion Brewery, August 2013

One parental beer tale (daughter) is slightly displaced/interrupted by another (son). In that final observation, I notice a distance as well, one that keeps me from identifying with the totalizing narratives associated with the object I obsess over. I don't conclude with a tale of revolution, beer saving the world, beer that bonds me to my family, or beer that opens up new possibilities. I conclude a story of sharing with a story of not sharing, with an anecdotal father-son selfie that differs dramatically from these two photographic selfies of me and my son. In every textual experience, Roland Barthes notes, there is a contradiction. This contradiction, which is built into all texts, is what Barthes identifies as the pleasure of the text. Craft beer is my pleasure text, and it is a text of contradictions, as I've tried to show throughout this book. With these contradictions I am left where I began: with small-story-based observations regarding social media and craft. Despite their lack of "grandness," my observations are still meaningful. Paul Ford writes that social media reinforce the observation as a site of connection:

Social media has no understanding of anything aside from the connections between individuals and the ceaseless flow of time: No beginnings, and no endings. These disparate threads of human existence alternately fascinate and horrify that part of the media world that grew up on topic sentences and strong conclusions. This world of old media is like a giant steampunk machine that organizes time into stories. I call it the Epiphanator, and it has always known the value of a meaningful conclusion. ("Facebook and the Epiphanator")

I have no such meaningful conclusion, no print-based epiphanies about my beer life, no final comments on the selfie narrative of my father or on the photographic selfie of my son, much as I had no meaningful anecdote to begin with regarding my daughter. No tales of craft saving me. No stories of craft overcoming the sterile world of fizzy beer. No obsession awakenings that have changed my life. No realizations other than I am a craft beer drinker. No realization, just details. I am an academic. I am obsessed. I have two kids. I buy too much beer. I share much of this information online. I learn a great deal about this world and develop my beer terroir via social media. That is my story. My Epiphanator. My conclusion.

Selfie from Instagram with son at Three Taverns Brewery, April 2014

NOTES ~ WORKS CITED ~ INDEX

NOTES

Introduction: Craft Parenting
1. <https://www.flickr.com/photos/cog_nate/2099146265>.

1. Craft Introductions
1. Full thread at <http://beeradvocate.com/community/threads/roots-of-beeradvocate.12813/>.

2. Craft Interruptions
1. <https://twitter.com/lagunitasT/status/268496774224809984>.

3. Craft Networks
1. See, among others, <http://www.sodakbeer.com/beer-reviews/odell-footprint-regionale/>; <http://www.focusonthebeer.com/2012/02/beer-thoughts-odell-footprint.html>; <http://www.brewbound.com/Reviews/Odell_Brewing_Co/Region_Ale_Foot_Print>; <http://nebraskabeer.blogspot.com/2012/02/review-footprint-from-odell-brewing.html>.

4. Craft Terroir
1. See some RateBeer responses: <http://www.RateBeer.com/forums/budweiser-a-local-beer_235882.htm>.
2. Tweet to Roger Baylor: <https://twitter.com/StoneGreg/status/328879587431960577>.
3. See the Beer Advocate debate among some users: <http://beeradvocate.com/community/threads/american-lambics-or-gueuze.19295/>.
4. <https://plus.google.com/115804671673356875620/posts/bjHFBEb1Soc>.
5. Once located at <http://beerinator.com/beerfeeds2/>.
6. <http://makeminepotato.ydog.net>.

7. <http://paper.li/NateDawg27/1315900391>.
8. <http://makeminepotato.ydog.net/?p=181>.

5. Craft Delivery

1. "I Am a Craft Brewer" influenced a spinoff video, "I Am a Craft Beer Drinker" <http://www.youtube.com/watch?v=Xh20DdTHXQU>.

6. Craft Tracings

1. While the citation style of the Modern Language Association does not encourage the placement of URLs in endnotes, in this chapter and the next I have done so for a specific reason. Placing the referenced Web pages in a works cited list would not let readers easily follow the tracings I am performing of release days. Placed as notes, these URLs can be easily accessed and identified, and thus readers can move through the variety of posts, images, videos, and comments I trace. If I were to list only the name of the reference and not the URL, readers would likely not be able to find the references. At press, these links worked. Even if they are later broken, Web cache can help locate them again.
2. <http://beeradvocate.com/community/threads/hunahpus-release.266/page-3>.
3. <http://www.tampabay.com/things-to-do/food/spirits/craft-beer-lovers-go-to-extremes-for-shot-at-tampa-brewerys-rare-offering/2108031>.
4. <http://beeradvocate.com/community/threads/next-jackie-os-release.49520/page-3>.
5. <http://www.charlestoncitypaper.com/Eat/archives/2013/07/15/westbrook-barrel-aged-mexican-cake-draws-a-crowd>.
6. <http://www.thebeerspot.com/forum/index.php/topic,640.0.html>.
7. <http://beernews.org/tag/dark-lord-day/page/3/>.
8. <http://www.RateBeer.com/event/6824/>.
9. Beer Advocate links are to the links that existed prior to the site's crash in 2012. Site administrators say the content exists, but it has not been restored.
10. <http://beeradvocate.com/forum/read/1207861#1213876>.
11. <http://www.youtube.com/watch?v=FI2vY3gyeeo>.
12. <http://hoosierbeergeek.blogspot.com/2008/04/darklord-day-2008.html>.
13. <http://chicagoist.com/2008/04/28/chicagoist_at_d.php>.

14. <http://www.flickr.com/photos/fejnation/3457958266/in/photostream/>.
15. <http://www.flickr.com/photos/bgramer/sets/72157604788989211/with/2450257341/>.
16. <http://beeradvocate.com/forum/read/1346047>.
17. <http://beernews.org/2008/04/dark-lord-day-2008-troubles-overshadow-spirit-of-the-event/>.
18. <http://www.thebeerspot.com/forum/index.php/topic,640.msg38068.html#msg38068>.
19. <http://www.flickr.com/photos/jmichael/2447231466/in/set-72157604768283039/>.
20. <http://www.thebrewbros.com/2012/04/is-three-floyds-dark-lord-day-really-worth-it/>.
21. <http://www.RateBeer.com/forums/2010-dark-lord-day-how-was-it_138832.htm>.
22. <http://www.RateBeer.com/forums/dark-lord-day-2010_129965_2.htm>.
23. <http://www.3floyds.com/2010/03/17/two-trending-topics-on-twitter/>.
24. <http://thatbeerguy.com/?p=21>.
25. <http://beeradvocate.com/forum/read/2620046>.
26. <http://www.RateBeer.com/forums/dld-trades-post-here_137455.htm>.
27. <http://beeradvocate.com/forum/read/2715271>.
28. <http://www.RateBeer.com/forums/dark-lord-day-thread_133764.htm>.
29. <http://www.RateBeer.com/forums/2010-dark-lord-day-how-was-it_138832_4.htm>.
30. <http://beeradvocate.com/forum/read/2731706>.
31. <http://www.youtube.com/watch?v=ZAq6QdSd5i0>.
32. <http://www.chicagonow.com/blogs/chicago-beer-travelers/2010/04/some-dark-lord-day-thoughts.html>.
33. <http://beernews.org/2010/04/beer-notes-fritz-talks-anchor-sale-lost-abbey-dilemma-duvel-tripel-hop/>.
34. <http://www.RateBeer.com/forums/dark-lord-day-2005_138871.htm>.
35. <http://www.examiner.com/examiner/x-9128-Chicago-Craft-Beer-Examiner~y2010m4d25-Dark-Lord-Day-memories-2005>.
36. <http://sixpacktech.com/2013/04/29/dark-lord-day-2005/>.
37. <http://makeminepotato.ydog.net/?p=354>.

38. Reviews start around <http://www.ratebeer.com/beer/founders-backstage-series-2-cbs-canadian-breakfast-stout/98973/1/50/>.
39. <http://www.ratebeer.com/RateBeerBest/bestbeers_012011.asp>.
40. <http://foundersbrewing.com/latest-news/2011/cbs-on-the-bottling-line/>.
41. <http://beerpulse.com/2011/09/just-bottled-founders-canadian-breakfast-stout/>.
42. <https://twitter.com/evanbenn/status/104256780003057665>.
43. <http://www.thebeerisgood.com/2011/07/founders-backstage-series-update.html>.
44. <http://beerpulse.com/2011/08/foudners-canadian-breakfast-stout-to-be-bottled/>.
45. <http://www.RateBeer.com/forums/canadian-breakfast-stout-release-press-release_179432.htm>.
46. <http://www.chicagofoodies.com/2011/09/founders-canadian-breakfast-stout-release.html>.
47. <http://beerpulse.com/2011/10/founders-canadian-breakfast-stout-a-very-incomplete-state-by-state-rundown/>.
48. <http://www.snobbybeer.com/blog/canadian-breakfast-stout-fail>.
49. <http://aleheads.com/2011/10/27/founders-cbs/>.
50. <http://beerpulse.com/2011/10/founders-canadian-breakfast-stout-reservations-crash-store-website/ and https://twitter.com/foundersbrewing/status/121224608178380802>.
51. <http://www.RateBeer.com/forums/cbs_180805_2.htm>.
52. <http://www.RateBeer.com/forums/cbs_181563.htm>.
53. <http://www.markandshaunbeer.com/2011/10/founders-canadian-breakfast-stout.html>.
54. <http://blog.hopbunnies.com/2011/10/founders-canadian-breakfast-stout-release/>.
55. <http://beyondthepour.com/2011/10/04/founders-canadian-breakfast-stout-tasted-alongside-founders-kbs-beyond-the-pour-beer-review/>.
56. <http://beerpulse.com/2011/09/new-york-liquor-store-releases-founders-canadian-breakfast-stout-early/>.
57. <http://beeravatar.blogspot.com/2011/10/founders-canadian-breakfast-stout.html>.
58. <http://boozedancing.wordpress.com/2011/10/10/craft-beer-poll-the-founders-cbs-dilemma-has-limited-release-craft-beer-pricing-gotten-out-of-hand/>.

59. <http://foundersbrewing.com/latest-news/2011/cbs-allocations-and-pricing/>.
60. <http://www.youtube.com/watch?v=7IoTuYBL5YE>.
61. <http://beermonger.net/2011/11/30/hype-and-hope/>.
62. <http://www.flickr.com/photos/24747481@N03/6217931865/>.
63. <http://www.flickr.com/photos/eatitdetroit/6255664798/>.
64. <http://www.thebeerisgood.com/2011/10/founders-canadian-breakfast-stout.html>.
65. <http://drinks.seriouseats.com/2012/01/founders-canadian-breakfast-stout-review-compared-to-kbs.html>.
66. <http://www.youtube.com/watch?v=DA6PAY_ZmsE&feature=related>.
67. <http://www.youtube.com/watch?v=_pvyhU341jk>.
68. <http://makeminepotato.ydog.net/?p=1306 and http://makeminepotato.ydog.net/?p=1328>.
69. <http://baltimorepostexaminer.com/untappdgamification-of-beer/2013/04/26>.
70. <http://mybeercellar.com/?itm=3617>.
71. <https://twitter.com/drfabulous/status/225295814132633600>.

7. Craft Sharing

1. <http://instagram.com/mansurvivesonhops>.
2. <http://www.flickr.com/photos/bethmasoch/sets/72157625974747146/>.
3. The image and full description are housed at <http://commons.wikimedia.org/wiki/File:Edinburgh_Ale_by_Hill_%26_Adamson_c1844.png>.
4. <http://www.flickr.com/photos/nationalgalleries/>.
5. <http://makeminepotato.ydog.net/?cat=111>.
6. <http://instagram.com/schlaflybeer>.
7. <http://instagram.com/bellsbrewery>.
8. <http://instagram.com/stonebrewingco>.
9. <http://www.flickr.com/photos/travlr/4126636154/>.
10. <http://www.flickr.com/photos/afagen/3002609890/>.
11. <http://www.flickr.com/photos/photofmdotcom/8729282583/>.
12. <https://www.facebook.com/groups/478820775478881/>.
13. <https://www.facebook.com/groups/hopheads/>.
14. <https://www.facebook.com/groups/craftbeerhead/>.
15. <https://www.facebook.com/groups/425537837459905/>.

16. <https://www.facebook.com/groups/236495823109087/>.
17. League of Extraordinary Beer Drinkers Facebook forum, <https://www.facebook.com/photo.php?fbid=10152904594510401&set=gm.634144979946459&type=1&theater>.
18. <http://instagram-engineering.tumblr.com/post/10853187575/sharding-ids-at-instagram>.

8. Craft Obsession

1. <http://www.flickr.com/photos/28252926@N03/7270103224/in/photostream/>.
2. <http://www.RateBeer.com/forums/1-800-number-for-beer-trading-addiction_234272.htm>.

WORKS CITED

Acitelli, Tom. *The Audacity of Hops: The History of America's Craft Beer Revolution*. Chicago: Chicago Review Press, 2013. Print.

AdamJackson. "Post Your First Ever Review and Critique It!" *Ratebeer.com*. 26 Oct. 2013. Web.

Adams, Paul. *Grouped: How Small Groups of Friends Are the Key to Influence on the Social Web*. Berkeley: New Riders, 2012. Print.

Adclassix. "1984 Heineken Beer." 12 June 2014. Web. 4 Apr. 2016. <http://www.adclassix.com/a6/84heinekenbeer.html>.

AJDePaul. "New to Trading . . . How to Value Cellar." *Ratebeer.com*. 5 July 2012. Web. 4 Apr. 2016. <http://www.RateBeer.com/forums/new-to-trading-how-to-value-cellar_207699.htm>.

Alexander, Bryan. *The New Digital Storytelling: Creating Narratives with New Media*. Santa Barbara: Praeger, 2011. Print.

All the Same Beer. "Beer Trade with Dave #1." *All the Same Beer*. 17 Mar. 2013. Web.

Alström, Jason, and Todd Alström. "Beer 3.0." *Beer Advocate* 37 (2010): 1. Print.

Alworth, Jeff. "Why Americans Don't Make Lambics." *Beervana*. 9 Aug. 2013. Web.

"America's 100 Best Beer Bars: 2012." *Draft*. 16 Jan 2012. Web.

Anderson, Will. *The Beer Book: An Illustrated Guide to American Breweriana*. Princeton: Pyne Press, 1973. Print.

Aristotle. *On Rhetoric: A Theory of Civic Discourse*. Trans. George Kennedy. Oxford: Oxford UP, 1991. Print.

Arthur, Tomme. Foreword. *Farmhouse Ales: Culture and Craftsmanship in the Belgian Tradition*. By Phil Markowski. Boulder: Brewers Publications, 2004. vii–x. Print.

Asimov, Eric. "Beers Worth Waiting For." *Diner's Journal: New York Times Blog on Dining Out*. 21 Aug. 2007. Web.

———. "Sampling American Pale Ales." *New York Times*. 28 June 2010. Web.

"AT&T Brewery Celebrate." *Spendadd.com*. n.d. Web.

WORKS CITED

"August Schell Brewing to BA in Response to 'Craft vs. Crafty': 'Shame on you.'" *Beerpulse.com*. 14 Dec. 2012. Web.

Avant, Jason. "Dad, Can I Try a Sip of Your Beer?" *All about Beer* 33.1. 1 Mar. 2012: 88. Print.

Baker, Jeff. "Craft Beer vs. Crafty Beer." *Burlingtonfreepress.com*. 17 May 2013. Web.

Baker, Jess. "8 Beers to Try This Summer." *Weather.com*. Weather Channel, 28 June 2013. Web.

Barabási, Albert-László. *Bursts: The Hidden Pattern behind Everything We Do*. New York: Dutton, 2010. Print.

———. *Linked: The New Science of Networks*: Cambridge: Perseus, 2002. Print.

Barbera, Greg. "Dad's Favorite Beer." *All about Beer*. 30.2. May 2009. Web.

Barham, Elizabeth. "Translating Terroir: The Global Challenge of French AOC Labeling." *Journal of Rural Studies* 19 (2003): 127–38. Print.

Baron, Stanley. *Brewed in America: A History of Beer and Ale in the United States*. New York: Little, Brown, 1962. Print.

Barthes, Roland. *Camera Lucida*. New York: Hill and Wang, 1981. Print.

———. *Mythologies*. New York: Hill and Wang, 1972. Print.

———. *The Pleasure of the Text*. Trans. Richard Miller. New York: Hill and Wang, 1975. Print.

———. "The Rhetoric of the Image." *Image—Music—Text*. Trans. Stephen Heath. New York: Hill and Wang, 1977. Print.

———. *Roland Barthes by Roland Barthes*. Berkeley: U of California P, 1994. Print.

Bauerlein, Mark. *The Dumbest Generation: How the Digital Age Stupefies Young Americans and Jeopardizes Our Future*. New York: Penguin, 2008. Print.

Baylor, Roger. "Wednesday Weekly: As They Say, Think Globally and Drink Locally." *Potable Curmudgeon*. 20 Oct. 2010. Web.

———. "Wednesday Weekly: To the 'Craft' of the Matter." *Potable Curmudgeon*. 23 June 2010. Web.

Beard, James. *Delights and Prejudices*. 1964. Philadelphia: Running Press Book Publishers, 1992. Print.

Beaumont, Stephen. "It's Not 'Belgian,' It's 'Belgian Style.'" *Blogging at World of Beer*. 20 Aug. 2014. Web.

Beeradvocate. "Drink Local Beer." *Beeradvocate.com*. 3 Aug. 2003. Web.

Beer and Stuff. "Thoughts on Trading." *Beer and Stuff*. n.d. Web.

Beerbecue. "The Session #76: But I'm Just Getting One Bottle, Dear." *Beerbecue.* 7 June 2013. Web.

Beer Culture. Free Mind Productions, 2013. Film.

Beer Drinker Rob. "Pliny the Elder." *Daily Beer Review.* 3 Mar. 2011. Web.

Beers for Fears. "Beer Mail #1: My First Trade." *Beers for Fears.* 6 Apr. 2011. Web.

Beer Is Your Friend. "The Session #76 Announcement: Compulsion." *Beerisyourfriend.org.* 9 May 2013. Web.

"Beer Overload." *Beeradvocate.com.* 12 Nov. 2013. Web. 4 Apr. 2016. <http://beeradvocate.com/community/threads/beer-overload.129634/>.

Beer Pioneers. Beer Guppy Multimedia, 2013. Film.

"Beer Review #500: Russian River Pliny the Elder." *Gregsbeerviews.* 13 Dec. 2011. Web.

Beer Wars. Dir. Anat Baron. Ducks in a Row Entertainment Corporation, 2009. Film.

Benjamin, Walter. "The Storyteller." *Illuminations: Essays and Reflections.* Trans. Harry Zohn. New York: Shocken, 1968. Print.

Benn, Evan S. "The Best New Beers of Spring and Summer." *Esquire.* n.d. Web.

Benson, Richard. Afterword. *In the Picture: Self Portraits: 1958–2011.* By Lee Friedlander. New Haven: Yale University Press, 2011. Print.

Berg, Thomas. "20 of the Most Coveted Craft Beer Releases in America." *Matador.* 15 Apr. 2013. Web.

Berger, Jonah. *Contagious: Why Things Catch On.* New York: Simon and Schuster, 2013. Print.

Bernstein, Joshua. *Brewed Awakening: Behind the Beers and Brewers Leading the World's Craft Beer Revolution.* New York: Sterling Epicure, 2011. Print.

"The Best Local Beers from Every State." *Huffington Post.* 1 Dec. 2012. Web.

Bickerdyke, John. *The Curiosities of Ale and Beer: An Entertaining History.* London: Field and Tuer; Leadenhall Press, 1886. Print.

Bilger, Burkhard. "A Bitter Brew: The Rise of Extreme Beer." *New Yorker* 24 Nov. 2008. Web.

Bilton, Nick. "Disruptions: As User Interaction on Facebook Drops, Sharing Comes at a Cost." *New York Times.* 3 Mar. 2013. Web.

———. "Disruptions: Social Media Images Form a New Language Online." *New York Times.* 30 June 2013. Web.

Bland, Alastair. "As Craft Beer Starts Gushing, Its Essence Gets Watered Down." *NPR.org.* National Public Radio, 9 May 2014. Web.

———. "Forget Barley And Hops: Craft Brewers Want a Taste of Place." *NPR.org*. National Public Radio, 6 Nov. 2013. Web.

"Blind Beer Tasting." *Celebrator.com*. Feb.–Mar. 2008. Web.

Bocheck, Pete. Beer. *Facebook Groups*. Dec. 2013. Web.

Bogost, Ian. *Alien Phenomenology: Or What It's Like to Be a Thing*. Minneapolis: U of Minnesota P, 2012. Print.

———. "The New Aesthetic Needs to Get Weirder." *Theatlantic.com*. 13 Apr. 2012. Web.

Bostwick, William. "The Sour and the Glory: An Ancient Belgium Beer Style Blooms in America." *Wall Street Journal*. 10 Aug. 2012. Web.

Botsman, Rachel, and Roo Rogers. *What's Mine Is Yours: The Rise of Collaborative Consumption*. New York: HarperCollins, 2010. Print.

Bourdieu, Pierre. "The Social Definition of Photography." *Visual Culture: The Reader*. Ed. Jessica Evans and Stuart Hall. Thousand Oaks: Sage, 2002. 162–80. Print.

Bowen, Dana. "Our Daily Bread: Thank Heaven for Bakers." *Saveur*. 147. May 2012. Web.

Brewers Association. "Brewers Association Releases Top 50 Breweries of 2012." *Brewersassociation.org*. 13 Apr. 2013. Web.

———. "Craft vs. Crafty: A Statement from the Brewers Association." *Brewersassociation.org*. 13 Dec. 2012. Web.

———. "National Beer Sales and Production Data." *Brewersassociation.org*. n.d. Web.

———. "Zymurgy Magazine Announces 2015 'Best Commercial Beers in America.'" *Brewersassociation.org*. 18 June 2015. Web.

Bridle, James. About page. *The New Aesthetic*. Web. 4 Apr. 2016. <http://new-aesthetic.tumblr.com/about>.

Brooklyn Magazine. "25 Years of Brooklyn Brewing: An Interview with Garrett Oliver." *Brooklyn Magazine*. 13 June 2013. Web.

Brooks, Jay. "Beer in Ads #805: Schlitz Snapshots." *Brookston Beer Bulletin*. 19 Feb. 2013. Web.

———. "Beer in Ads #730: Waiting in Line to Vote." *Brookston Beer Bulletin*. 5 Nov. 2012. Web.

———. "Big Bottles Equals Wine?" *Brookston Beer Bulletin*. 5 Mar. 2013. Web.

———. "History's First Photo of People Drinking Beer." *Brookston Beer Bulletin*. 3 Feb. 2014. Web.

———. "New Pliny Elder the Video by the Famous." *Brookston Beer Bulletin*. 15 Mar. 2011. Web.

Brostrom, Geralyn G., and Jack Brostrom. *The Business of Wine: An Encyclopedia.* Westport: Greenwood Publishing Group, 2009. Print.

Brown, Bill. *Let There Be Beer.* New York: Harrison Smith and Robert Haas, 1932. Print.

Brown, Pete. *Three Sheets to the Wind: One Man's Quest for the Meaning of Beer.* London: Pan Books, 2007. Print.

———. "Wikio Rankings for April 2010—and a Call to Action." *Pete Brown.* 4 May 2010. Web.

Brown, Robert. *The Great Dionysiak Myth.* Vol. 2. 1878. Madison: U of Wisconsin P, 2008. Print.

Brown, Scott. "Scott Brown on Facebook Friendonomics." *Wired.* 20 Oct. 2008. Web.

Brummett, Barry. "Burke's Representative Anecdote as a Method in Media Criticism." *Critical Studies in Mass Communication* 1.2 (1984): 161–76. Print.

Bruns, Axel. *Blogs, Wikipedia, Second Life, and Beyond.* New York: Peter Lang, 2008. Print.

Brussels Sights: A Travel Guide to the Top 30 Attractions in Brussels, Belgium. Boston: Mobile Reference, 2010. Print.

Bryson, Lew. *Pennsylvania Breweries.* Mechanicsburg: Stackpole Books, 2005. Print.

"Buffalo Wild Wings TV Commercial: 'Weird Drink.'" *Ispot.tv.* 9 Feb. 2013. Web.

Burchette, Jordan, and Lauren Passell. "8 Best Beer Towns in the USA." *CNN.com.* 7 May 2013. Web.

Burgess, Jean. "YouTube and the Formalization of Amateur Media." *Amateur Media: Social, Cultural and Legal Perspectives.* Ed. Dan Hunter, Ramon Lobato, Megan Richardson, and Julian Thomas. New York: Routledge, 2013. 53–58. Print.

Burke, Kenneth. *A Grammar of Motives.* Berkeley: U of California P, 1969. Print.

———. *The Philosophy of Literary Form.* Berkeley: U of California P, 1973. Print.

Burningham, Lucy. "Bottle Shares Spread the Beer." *Wall Street Journal.* 1 Nov. 2013. Web.

———. "Inside the World of Black Market Beer." *Bon Appétit.* 18 Dec. 2012. Web.

Burns, Josh. "Why Storytelling Will Be Important to Business in 2013." *Inc.Well.* 31 Dec. 2012. Web.

Bytemesis. "New to Trading . . . Need Some Direction." *Ratebeer.com.* 19 Oct. 2013. Web. 4 Apr. 2016. <http://www.ratebeer.com/forums/new-to-tradingneed-some-direction_245757.htm>.

Calagione, Sam. *Brewing Up a Business: Adventures in Entrepreneurship from the Founder of Dogfish Head Craft Brewery.* Hoboken: John Wiley and Sons, 2005. Print.

Canham-Nelson, Meredith. *Teachings from the Tap: Life Lessons from Our Year in Beer.* Carmel Valley: Beer Trekker Press, 2012. Print.

Carlsen, William. "For a Success Story, Here's to Beer!" *New York Times* 9 Aug. 1978: C1. Print.

Castells, Manuel. *Communication Power.* Oxford: Oxford UP, 2009. Print.

Chad9976. "Chad Reviews Stuff." *YouTube.* 19 Sept. 2013. Web.

———. "2011 Vlog #19: Requests Recap; Upcoming Trades; My 'Beer Cellar'; October Reviews." *YouTube.* 8 Oct. 2011. Web.

Chandler, Adam. Blog. *Adamchandler.com.* Web. 4 Apr. 2016. <http://adamchandler.beer/?s=beer+haul>.

Chang, David. "My Name is David Chang and I Hate Fancy Beer." *Esquire.com.* Oct. 2014. Web.

Chappell, Bill. "At the Great American Beer Festival, Big Tastes Come in Small Packages." *NPR.org.* National Public Radio, 14 Oct. 2012. Web.

Christie, Josh. "Addicted to Beer Trading." *Blog about Beer.* n.d. Web.

Cicero. *De Oratore, Books 1–2.* Trans. E. W. Sutton. Cambridge: Harvard UP, 1996. Print.

Ciderchick. "Beer Cellar." *YouTube.* 3 Apr. 2010. Web.

Cizmar, Martin. "Beer Baggers." *Beer Advocate* 76 (2013): 52–56. Print.

Clemons, Eric K. "Harnessing Social Networks." *Forbes.com.* 23 Aug. 2007. Web.

Cochran, John. "Craft vs. Crafty." *John at Terrapin.* 18 Dec. 2012. Web.

Cohen, Rich. *Tough Jews: Fathers, Sons, and Gangster Dreams.* New York: Simon and Schuster, 1988. Print.

Coleman, Bill. "Salty Dog." Comic strip. 2008. Web. 4 Apr. 2016. <http://www.flickr.com/photos/saltydawg/2757264620/in/set-72157601508657713>.

"A Conversation with Bob Sylvester of St. Somewhere." *YouTube.com.* 27 Aug 2012. Web.

Cornell, Martyn. "So What Did Pliny the Elder Say about Hops?" *Zythophile.* 14 Mar. 2010. Web.

———. "The Woman Who Served George Orwell Pints of Mild." *Zythophile.* 11 June 2011. Web.

Cottone, Vincent. *Good Beer Guide: Breweries and Pubs of the Pacific Northwest, British Columbia, Washington and Oregon*. Seattle: Homestead Book Company, 1986. Print.

Cowan, Jeremy. *Craft Beer Bar Mitzvah*. San Francisco: Malt Shop Publishing, 2010. Print.

Crable, Bryan. "Burke's Perspective on Perspectives: Grounding Dramatism in the Representative Anecdote." *Quarterly Journal of Speech* 86.3 (2000): 318–33. Print.

Crouch, Andy. "Another Lament on the State and Future of Beer Writing and Blogging." *Beerscribe*. 6 Mar. 2011. Web.

———. "Celebrating the Success of Craft Beer." *Beerscribe*. 19 Mar. 2010. Web.

———. "Craft Beer Attitude Adjustment." *Beer Advocate* 66. July 2012: 18. Print.

———. "The Death of a Flagship." *Beer Advocate* 67. Aug. 2012: 18. Print.

———. *Great American Craft Beer: A Guide to the Nation's Finest Beers and Breweries*. Philadelphia: Running Press Book Publishers, 2010. Print.

Curtis, Matt. "In Search of a Pliny, Part I (the Elder)." *Total Ales*. 17 Mar. 2013. Web.

DalzAle. "Newbie." *Ratebeer.com*. 18 Feb. 2013. Web. 4 Apr. 2016. <http://www.RateBeer.com/forums/newbie_226209.htm>.

Davis, Lennard. *Obsession: A History*. Chicago: U of Chicago P, 2008. Print.

"Days of Beer and Weeds." *Three's Company*. 21 Feb. 1978. Television.

De Baets, Yvan. "A History of Saison." *Farmhouse Ales: Culture and Craftsmanship in the Belgian Tradition*. By Phil Markowski. Boulder: Brewers Publications, 2004. 95–128. Print.

DeBenedetti, Christian. "Royally Brewed." *Slate*. 3 Jan. 2013. Web.

De Keersmaecker, Jacques. "The Mystery of Lambic Beer." *Scientific American* Aug. 1996: 74–80. Print.

De Lesso, Angelo. "Pliny the Elder vs. Heady Topper." *Brewpublic*. 9 May 2013. Web.

DietPepsican. "Traders, Why Do We Do It?" *Ratebeer.com*. 13 Apr. 2009. Web. 4 Apr. 2016. <http://www.RateBeer.com/forums/traders-why-do-we-do-it_113897.htm>.

Dion, Keith. "Beer Trading: The Year in Review." *Beer Drink Run*. 6 Nov. 2012. Web.

Donk, Michael. "Three Floyds Taproom Hall." *Brew Bokeh*. 2012. Web.

Douglas, Jane Yellowlees. *The End of Books—Or Books without End? Reading Interactive Narratives.* Ann Arbor: U of Michigan P, 2001. Print.

Dredge, Mark. *Craft Beer World: A Guide to Over 350 of the Finest Beers Known to Man.* New York: Dog 'n' Bone Books, 2013. Print.

———. "I Rate Beer." *Hop Press International.* 27 Dec. 2009. Web.

Drfabulous. "FT: Lost Abbey Devotion with Brett." *Ratebeer.com.* 11 June 2009. Web. 4 Apr. 2016. <http://www.RateBeer.com/forums/ft-lost-abbey-devotion-with-brett_117777.htm>.

Duguid, Naomi. "Travelling with Kids." *Lucky Peach* 7. Spring 2013: 11–13. Print.

Eckhardt, Fred. "The Craft Beer Revolution, 30 Years On." *All about Beer.* May 2010. Web.

———. "Craft Beer: State of the Union 2010." *All about Beer.* 31.6. 1 Jan. 2011. Web.

———. *A Treatise on Lager Beers.* Portland: Hobby Winemaker, 1972. Print.

Edbauer, Jenny. "Unframing Models of Public Distribution: From Rhetorical Situation to Rhetorical Ecologies." *Rhetoric Society Quarterly* Fall 2005: 5–24. Print.

Ehret, George. *Twenty-Five Years of Brewing: With an Illustrated History.* New York: Gast Lithograph and Engraving, 1891. Print.

"8 Essential Craft Beers." *Draftmag.com.* 7 Oct. 2013. Web.

Ellsworth, Amy. "The Craft Beer Aesthetic." *The Craft Beer Girl.* 12 Jan. 2012. Web.

Eng, Dinah. "Jim Koch: Samuel Adam's Beer Revolutionary." *CNN Money.* 21 Mar. 2013. Web.

Erickson, Jack. *Brewery Adventures in the Big East.* Reston: Redbrick Press, 1994. Print.

———. *California Brewin': The Exciting Story of California's Microbrewing Revolution!* Reston: Redbrick Press, 1993. Print.

Esterl, Mike. "Craft Brewers Tap Big Expansion." *Wall Street Journal.* 28 Dec. 2011. Web.

Evil Twin Brewing. *Twitter.* Web. 4 Apr. 2016. <https://twitter.com/EvilTwinBrewing/statuses/406552411973910528>. Web.

"Facts." Brewers Association: A Passionate Voice for Craft Brewers. *Brewersassociation.org.* 17 Jan. 2010. Web.

Feinberg, Don. "Terroir, Beer and the Pleasures of Drinking or Why We Root for Rocky." *Belgian Experts.* 3 Oct. 2011. Web.

Ferretti, Fred. "A Brewmaster with a Ph.D. Now Makes the Beer in Brooklyn." *New York Times* 19 Dec. 1971: A8. Print.

"First Beer You Ever Tried." *Beeradvocate.com*. 29 Oct. 2013. Web. 4 Apr. 2016. <http://beeradvocate.com/community/threads/first-beer-you-ever-tried.126411/>.

First We Feast. "The 15 Things Craft Beer Fans Think (But Nobody Says)." *Firstwefeast.com*. 18 Apr. 2013. Web.

———. "The 20 Most Influential Beers of All Time." *Firstwefeast.com*. 10 Jan. 2013. Web.

———. "The United States of Beer: The Best Brew from Each of the 50 States." *Firstwefeast.com*. 5 Dec. 2012. Web.

Fisher, M. F. K. "How to Drink to the Wolf." *The Art of Eating*. Hoboken: Wiley, 2004. 329–34. Print.

Ford, Paul. "Facebook and Instagram: When Your Favorite App Sells Out." *New York Magazine*. 10 Apr. 2012. Web.

———. "Facebook and the Epiphanator: And End to Endings?" *New York Magazine*. 18 July 2011. Web.

Fortenbaugh, William. "Aristotle's Platonic Attitude toward Delivery." *Philosophy and Rhetoric* 19.4 (1996): 242–54. Print.

"40,000 + Great American Beer Festival Tickets Sell Out in Record Time." *Beerpulse*. 2 Aug 2012. Web.

Fowle, Zachary. "Odell Footprint Regional Ale." *Phoenix New Times*. 22 Feb. 2012. Web.

Fox News Magazine. "11 Strange Beers You'll Actually Want to Try." *Fox News Magazine*. 26 Mar. 2013. Web.

Franklin, Marcy. "Top 15 Craft Beer Breweries in the USA." *USA Today*. 26 Aug. 2013. Web.

———. "The 25 Best Craft Breweries in America." *The Daily Meal*. 29 July 2013. Web.

Franzen, Jonathan. "Liking Is for Cowards. Go for What Hurts." *New York Times*. 28 May 2011. Web.

Fredal, James. "The Language of Delivery and the Presentation of Character: Rhetorical Action in Demosthenes' *Against Meidias*." *Rhetoric Review* 20.3–4 (2001): 251–67. Print.

Fuj. "Epic New England Beer Trip." *The Fuj*. Blog. 18 Oct 2013. Web.

Fumari, Chris. "Video: A Craft Collision." *Brewbound*. 15 Dec. 2012. Web.

Galligan, Jim. "A Beer Geek's Quest to Hunt Down an Elusive Brew." *Today.com*. 22 Mar. 2012. Web.

———. "How Do You Score a Rare Beer? Pros Share Their Tips." *NBCnews.com*. 17 Jan. 2013. Web.

Galloway, Alex. *The Interface Effect*. Malden: Polity, 2012. Print.

Gehl, Robert W. "A History of Like." *The New Inquiry*. 27 Mar. 2013. Web.

Giard, Luce. "Plat du Jour." *The Practice of Everyday Life: Volume 2: Living and Cooking*. Ed. Michel de Certeau, Luce Giard, and Pierre Mayol. Trans. Timothy J. Tomasik. Minneapolis: U of Minnesota P, 1998. 171–98. Print.

Gladwell, Malcolm. *The Tipping Point: How Little Things Can Make a Big Difference*. New York: Bay Back, 2002. Print.

Godin, Seth. *Permission Marketing*. New York: Simon and Schuster, 1999. Print.

Goody, Jack. *The Domestication of the Savage Mind*. Cambridge: Cambridge UP, 1977. Print.

Gopnik, Adam. "Shining Tree of Life." *New Yorker*. 13 Feb. 2006. Web.

Grant-Davis, Keith. "Rhetorical Situations and Their Constituents." *Rhetoric Review* 15.2 (1997): 264–79. Print.

Griffith, Corbet. @*Corbet*. Web. <http://www.iphoneogram.com/u/4867>.

Griffith, Erin. "2013, The Year of Storytelling." *Pandodaily*. 31 Dec. 2013. Web.

Grizzard, Lewis "Paul Newman Does Not Drink Coors Beer." *Times-News* [Hendersonville, NC] 15 Feb. 1983: 3. Print.

Grossman, Ken. *Beyond the Pale: The Story of Sierra Nevada Brewing Co.* Hoboken: John Wiley and Sons, 2013. Print.

Hall, John. "New Albion Brewing." *Craftbeer.com*. 9 June 2010. Web.

Hanson, Arik. "Are Craft Breweries Doing Enough to Market Themselves Differently?" *Communications Conversations*. 18 June 2013. Web.

———. "Social Media Case Study: Stone Brewing." *Communication Conversations*. 9 May 2011. Web.

Harman, Graham. *The Quadruple Object*. Winchester: Zero Books, 2011. Print.

Heat-Moon, William Least. "A Glass of Handmade." *Atlantic* Nov. 1987: 75. Print.

Hendricks, Drew. "What is the Best Beer in America?" *Huffington Post*. 7 June 2013. Web.

Hieronymus, Stan. "The Dirt on Terroir." *Draft Magazine*. July–Aug. 2011. Web.

———. *For the Love of Hops: The Practical Guide to Aroma, Bitterness and the Aroma of Hops*. Boulder: Brewers Association, 2012. Print.

———. "'Native' Ales and 'Spokane Style.'" *Appellation Beer*. 24 Apr. 2013. Web.

———. "Where in the Beer World 09.24.14." *Appellation Beer*. 14 Sept. 2014. Web.

Hilman, Jay. "Beer Samizdat Manifesto." *Beer Samizdat*. 3 Aug. 2011. Web.

———. "On #Whalez and Whaling." *Beer Samizdat*. 2 Sept. 2013. Web.

Hindy, Steve. "Don't Let Big Brewers Win Beer Wars." *CNN*. 12 Dec. 2012. Web.

Hoffman, Maggie. "This Is What the Line for Pliny the Elder Looks Like." *Seriouseats.com*. 13 Feb. 2013. Web.

Honan, Matt. "Inside Instagram: How Slowing Its Roll Put the Little Startup in the Fast Lane." *Gizmodo*. 7 Feb. 2012. Web.

Hoosier Beer Geek. "Dr. Strangelove: Or How I Learned to Stop Worrying over Rare Beer and Love Regular Beer." *Hoosier Beer Geek*. 23 May 2012. Web.

"How Would You Define a Whale?" *Beeradvocate.com*. 27 Apr. 2012. Web.

Hunt, Katrina Brown. "American's 20 Best Cities for Beer Lovers." *Travel and Leisure*. 15 Aug. 2015. Web.

"Hybrid Beers That Didn't Live Up to the Hype." *Beeradvocate.com*. 12 Nov. 2013. Web.

"I Am a Craft Brewer." *YouTube*. 27 Apr. 2009. Web.

Imbibe. "100 Best Places to Drink Beer in America." *Imbibe*. 12 Jan. 2009. Web.

Indvik, Lauren. "Cost per Like: A Subjective Valuation of Your Facebook Fans." *Mashable*. 26 Apr. 2013. Web.

Ivanovic, Niko. "The White Whales of Craft Beer." *Daily Cardinal*. 30 Oct. 2012. Web.

Jabbloner, Amy. "Where the Wild Yeasts Are: Belgian Lambics." *Brew Your Own*. Feb. 1988. Web.

Jackson, Michael. "Appellations of a Different Nature." *Beerhunter.com*. 3 Apr. 2000. Web.

———. "Beer Chic." *Playboy*. Aug. 1983: 163–66. Print.

———. "Blue Collar Brews." *All about Beer*. 22.3. July 2001. Web.

———. "California Pilgrimage Part 1." *The Beer Hunter*. Discovery, 1989. Television.

———. "Farewell, Father . . . It's Beer War." *All about Beer*. 23.6. Jan. 2003. Web.

Jay, Paul, ed. *The Selected Correspondence of Kenneth Burke and Malcolm Cowley, 1915–1981*. Berkeley: U of California P, 1990. Print.

Jenkins, Henry. *Convergence Culture: Where Old and New Media Collide*. New York: New York UP, 2006. Print.

———. *Fans, Bloggers, and Gamers: Exploring Participatory Culture*. New York: New York UP, 2006. Print.

Jenkins, Henry, Sam Ford, and Joshua Green. *Spreadable Media: Creating Value and Meaning in a Networked Culture*. New York: New York UP, 2013. Print.

Johnson, Steven. *Where Good Ideas Come From: The Natural History of Innovation*. New York: Riverhead Books, 2010. Print.

Johnstone, Christopher Lyle. "Communicating in Classical Contexts: The Centrality of Delivery." *Quarterly Journal of Speech* 87.2 (2001): 121–43. Print.

Joyce, Michael. *Of Two Minds: Hypertext Pedagogy and Poetics*. Ann Arbor: U of Michigan P, 1995. Print.

Kahn, Jeffrey. "How Beer Gave Us Civilization." *New York Times*. 15 Mar. 2013. Web.

Kaplan, Andrew. "Arrogant? Not Really." *Beverage World*. 15 Mar. 2011: 22–26. Web.

Katz, Jon. "5 Steps to Mastering the Art of Beer Trading." *Food Republic*. 8 Aug. 2013. Web.

Keen, Andrew. *The Cult of the Amateur: How Blogs, MySpace, YouTube, and the Rest of Today's User-Generated Media Are Destroying Our Economy, Our Culture, and Our Values*. New York: Doubleday, 2008. Print.

Keller, Josh. "Studies Explore Whether the Internet Makes Students Better Writers." *Chronicle of Higher Education*. 11 June 2009. Web.

Kentucky for Kentucky. About page. Web. 4 Apr. 2016. <http://www.kentuckyforkentucky.com/pages/about-us>.

Kiser, Michael. Good Beer Hunting: Michael Kiser's Passport to the World Is through Its Beer." *Forma Collective*. Issue 3. Web.

Kmweaver. "ISO: De Dolle SNR 200; FT: Stuff." *Ratebeer.com*. 7 May 2008. Web.

Kobler, John. *Capone: The Life and World of Al Capone*. New York: De Capo Press, 1971. Print.

Koch, Greg, and Matt Allyn. *The Brewer's Apprentice: An Insider's Guide to the Art and Craft of Beer Brewing Taught by the Masters*. Minneapolis: Rockport Publishers, 2011. Print.

Koch, Greg, and Steve Wagner, with Randy Clemens. *The Craft of Stone Brewing Co.: Liquid Lore, Epic Recipes, and Unabashed Arrogance*. Berkeley: Ten Speed Press, 2011. Print.

"Krebs, Oklahoma." *Wikipedia*. Web. 4 Apr. 2016. <http://en.wikipedia.org/wiki/Krebs,_Oklahoma>.

Kriser, Michael. "3 Floyds' Dark Lord Day—The Monsters of Munster, Indiana." *Good Beer Hunting*. 3 May 2013. Web.

Latour, Bruno. *Aramis, or the Love of Technology*. Cambridge: Harvard UP, 1996. Print.

———. *An Inquiry into Modes of Existence: An Anthropology of the Moderns*. Cambridge: Harvard UP, 2013. Print.

———. *Reassembling the Social: An Introduction to Actor-Network-Theory*. New York: Oxford UP, 2005. Print.

———. *We Have Never Been Modern*. Trans. Catherine Porter. Cambridge: Harvard UP, 1993. Print.

Laur, Mike. "Great American Beer Festival." *The Oxford Companion to Beer*. Ed. Garrett Oliver. Oxford: Oxford UP, 2012. Print.

Leonard, Devin. "The Plot to Destroy America's Beer." *Bloomberg Business*. 25 Oct. 2012. Web.

Leppla, Brian. "Huge Surprise: Hops Still Popular." *Hop Press*. 13 July 2012. Web.

Lewis, Sean. "Brau Brothers Brewing Company." *Beer Advocate* 46. Nov. 2010: 30–32. Print.

———. "Throwback Brewery." *Beer Advocate* 77. June 2013: 38–40. Print.

Life with Beer. *YouTube*. Web. 4 Apr. 2016. <http://www.youtube.com/user/LifeWithBeer>.

Liggett, Helen. *Urban Encounters*. Minneapolis: U of Minnesota P, 2003. Print.

LinusStick. "Post Your First Ever Review and Critique It!" *Ratebeer.com*. 29 Oct. 2013. Web.

Logan, Tim. "Big Beer Moves into Small Batch Space." *STLtoday.com*. 18 Nov. 2012. Web.

Louisvillebeer. "Beer Hoarders Episode 2—Scott Schreffler." *YouTube*. 17 July 2012. Web.

Lyke, Rick. "Growler List: The 125 Places to Have a Beer before You Die." *All about Beer*. 1 Mar. 2008. Web.

Lyotard, Jean François. *The Postmodern Condition: A Report on Knowledge*. Trans. Geoff Bennington and Brian Massumi. Minneapolis: U of Minnesota P, 1984. Print.

Maffesoli, Michel. *The Time of the Tribes: The Decline of Individualism in Mass Society*. Trans. Don Smith. London: Sage Publications, 1996. Print.

Magee, Tony. *Twitter*. 13 Nov 2012. Web. 4 Apr. 2016. <https://twitter.com/lagunitasT/status/268496774224809984>.

MagicDave6. "Post Your First Ever Review and Critique It." *Ratebeer.com*. 29 Oct 2013. Web.

Manjod, Farhad. "Photos Are the New Killer App." *Fast Company.* 19 Nov. 2011. Web.

Markowski, Phil. "Farmhouse Ales: Bucolic Beers for the Modern Era." *All about Beer* 31.1 (2010): 24. Print.

Martin, Wallace. *Recent Theories of Narrative.* Ithaca: Cornell UP, 1987. Print.

Master of Hoppets. "TMOH—Beer Review 400#: Cantillon Blåbær Lambik." *YouTube.* 7 July 2011. Web.

Maytag, Fritz. Foreword. *California Brewin': The Exciting Story of California's Microbrewing Revolution.* By Jack Erickson. Reston: Redbrick Press, 1993. Print.

"May 24 : Zombie Dust : 3 Floyds Brewing Co : at Small Bar with the Hop Cast." *New Brew Thursday.* 25 May 2012. Web.

McCullough, Malcolm. *Abstracting Craft: The Practiced Digital Hand.* Cambridge: MIT Press, 1998. Print.

McFarland, Ben. "Russian River Brewing Company." *The Oxford Companion to Beer.* Ed. Garrett Oliver. Oxford: Oxford UP, 2012. Print.

———. *World's Best Beers. One Thousand Craft Beers from Cask to Glass.* New York: Sterling, 2009. Print.

McKean, Jacob. "Why Beer Ratings Are Great and Awards Are Overrated." *Beerpulse.* 16 Apr. 2013. Web.

McLeod, Alan. "Do Writers Have a Disproportionate Influence on Beer?" *A Good Beer Blog.* 22 Mar. 2010. Web.

———. "What Is the Etiquette of Beer Blog Photography?" *A Good Beer Blog.* 8 June 2011. Web.

McLuhan, Marshall. *The Gutenberg Galaxy.* Toronto: U of Toronto P, 1962. Print.

———. *Understanding Media: The Extensions of Man.* New York: Signet, 1964. Print.

McLuhan, Marshall, and Quentin Fiore. *The Medium Is the Massage: An Inventory of Effects.* Corte Madera: Gingko Press, 2001. Print.

Metcalfe, W. C. "Is this Stuff Good?" Beer Trade: ISO/FT. *Facebook Groups.* 29 Nov. 2013. Web. <https://www.facebook.com/groups/beertraderisoft/permalink/494722783977514/>.

MF Doom. "All Out of Ale." *The Prof. in. Convexed.* Nature Sounds, 2002. Music recording.

———. "One Beer." *MM . . . Food.* Rhymesayers Entertainment, 2004. Music recording.

Miller, Henry. *Black Spring.* New York: Grove, 1963. Print.

———. *Tropic of Capricorn.* New York: Grove, 1961. Print.

Miller, Norman. "Rare Beer? You Can Keep It." *Beer Nut.* 5 Dec. 2013. Web.

Moeckel, Jamison. "Jamisons Beer Review Russian River Brewing Pliny the Elder." *Beer Geek Nation.* YouTube Channel, 15 Apr. 2011. Web.

"The Moment You've All Been Waiting For!" *Brouwer's Café.* 18 Feb. 2012. Web.

Montoro, Philip. "Brace Yourselves: Here Come Goose Island's 2013 Bourbon County Variants." *Chicago Reader.* 25 Nov. 2013. Web.

Morris, Stephen. *The Great Beer Trek: A Guide to the Highlights and Lowlites of American Beer Drinking.* Brattleboro: Stephen Greene Press, 1984. Print.

Morris, William. *Art and Socialism.* Whitefish: Kessinger Publishing, 2004. Print.

———. "How We Live and How We Might Live." *The Collected Works of William Morris: Signs of Change.* London: Longmans Green and Company, 1915. 3–26. Print.

———. "Lectures on Socialism." *The Collected Works of William Morris: Signs of Change.* London: Longmans Green and Company, 1915. Print.

Morton, Timothy. *The Ecological Thought.* Cambridge: Harvard UP, 2010. Print.

Mosher, Randy. *Tasting Beer: An Insider's Guide to the World's Greatest Drink.* North Adams: Storey Publishing, 2009. Print.

"The Most Prolific Tweeting Brewery Owner Starts a Blog." *Beerpulse.com.* 25 Nov 2012. Web.

"Most Wanted Beer." *Ratebeer.com.* Web. 4 Apr. 2016. <http://www.ratebeer.com/Ratings/TopMostWanted.asp>.

Moyer, Michael. "Manipulation of the Crowd." *Scientific American* July 2010: 26–27. Print.

Murphy, Matt. "How Does Location Influence Beer Ratings?" *BeerGraphs.* 18 June 2013. Web.

Mustlovebeer. *Google+.* Web. 4 Apr. 2016. <https://plus.google.com/112371649878234903308/posts>.

Nah, Fiona Fui-Hoon. "A Study on Tolerable Waiting Time: How Long Are Web Users Willing to Wait?" *Behaviour and Information Technology* 23.3 (2004): 153–63. Print.

Nahon, Karine, and Jeff Hemsley. *Going Viral.* Malden: Polity, 2013. Print.

New Belgium. "Fat Tire Ale—Want a Beer?" *YouTube.* 15 May 2013. Web.

"1978 Schlitz Commercial." *YouTube*. 19 July 2010. Web.

1971hemicuda. "FT: Dark Lord 2013; ISO: Other Imperial Stout's." *Ratebeer.com*. 16 Apr. 2013. Web. 4 Apr. 2016. <http://www.ratebeer.com/forums/ft-dark-lord-2013-iso-other-imperial-stouts_231748.htm>.

"1977 Lowenbrau Commercial." *YouTube*. 12 Nov. 2009. Web.

"99 Bottles." *Imbibe*. No. 21. Sept.–Oct. 2009. Web.

"No-Li Receives Federal Approval for New Style of Beer: Spokane Style." *Nolibrewhouse.com*. 11 Apr. 2013. Web.

"Number of Breweries." *BrewersAssociation.org*. n.d. Web.

"Odell Footprint RegionalAle Debuts on February 11." *Beerpulse*. 31 Jan. 2012. Web.

Ogle, Maureen. *Ambitious Brew*. Orlando: Harcourt Books, 2006. Print.

———. "What Is in Your Beer? Or the Dangers of Dumbassery." *Maureen Ogle*. 18 Aug. 2013. Web.

Oliver, Garrett. *The Brewmaster's Table: Discovering the Pleasures of Real Beer with Real Food*. New York: HarperCollins, 2003. Print.

———. "'Wine-ification' of Beer Article Just Sour Grapes." *Craftbeer.com*. 11 Mar. 2013. Web.

Ong, Walter. *Orality and Literacy: The Technologizing of the Word*. London: Methuen, 1987. Print.

O'Reilly, Tim. "What Is Web 2.0: Design Patterns and Business Models for the Next Generation of Software." 30 Sept. 2005. Web.

Orwell, George. "The Moon Under Water." *Saturday Evening Standard* 9 Feb. 1946. Print.

Pace, Gina. "Beer Is the New Wine, and It's Hoppy Hour as Premium Brews Win New Respect . . . and Hefty Prices." *New York Daily News*. 16 Oct. 2013. Web.

Page, Jon. "Get to Know Our Guest Instagrammer." *All about Beer*. 14 June 2014. Web.

Palmer, Brian. "Pliny the Younger Is Supposedly the Best Beer in the World. What Does That Even Mean?" *Slate*. 16 May 2012. Web.

Papazian, Charles. *The Complete Joy of Homebrewing*. New York: Avon, 1991. Print.

———. Ed. *Zymurgy: Best Articles*. New York: Avon, 2010. Print.

Papazian, Charlie, Bob Peace, and Dan Kopman. "Craft or Crafty? Consumers Need to Know the Truth." *STL Today*. 13 Dec. 2012. Web.

"Papsoe's Trade History." *Ratebeer.com*. Web.

Pattinson, Ronald. "Sort of Zoigling." *Shut Up about Barclay Perkins*. 4 July 2012. Web.

Pepys, Samuel. *The Diary of Samuel Pepys*. London: George Bell and Sons, 1899. Print.

"Philadelphia Trio Held in Liquor Plot." *New York Times*. 16 Nov. 1928. Web.

Plato. *The Dialogues of Plato*. Introd. Erich Segal. New York: Bantam Books, 1986. Print.

———. *Gorgias*. Trans. Donald J. Zeyl. Indianapolis: Hackett Publishing Company, 1987. Print.

———. *Phaedrus*. Trans. Alexander Nehamas and Paul Woodruff. Indianapolis: Hackett Publishing Company, 1995. Print.

"Pliny, Homebrew Stouts and More." *The Barley Blog*. 24 Aug. 2009. Web.

Pliny the Elder. *The Natural History of Pliny*. Vol. 3. Ed. John Bostock. London: George Bell and Sons, 1892. Print.

Pollan, Michael. *The Omnivore's Dilemma: A Natural History of Four Meals*. New York: Penguin, 2006. Print.

Porter, James E. "Recovering Delivery for Digital Rhetoric." *Computers and Composition* 26 (2009): 207–24. Print.

Porter, John. *All about Beer*. Garden City: Doubleday & Company, 1975. Print.

"Post a Picture of Your Latest Haul." *Beeradvocate.com*. 22 Feb. 2012. Web. 4 Apr. 2016. <http://beeradvocate.com/community/threads/post-a-picture-of-your-latest-haul.136/>.

Pour Fool. "Craft Beer vs. Faux Craft: BudMillerCoors Go Stealth Route." *Seattle PI*. 12 Sept. 2013. Web.

Quintilian. *Institutes of Oratory*. Ed. Lee Honeycutt. Trans. John Selby Watson. 2006. Iowa State University. Web. 4 May 2010. <http://rhetoric.eserver.org/quintilian/>.

Raban, Jonathan. "The Getaway Car." *New York Times Magazine*. 10 June 2011. Web.

Rao, Hayagreeva. *Market Rebels: How Activists Make or Break Radical Innovations*. Princeton: Princeton UP, 2009. Print.

"RateBeer Best Top 50." *Ratebeer.com*. Web. 4 Apr. 2016. <http://www.RateBeer.com/RateBeerBest/bestbeers_012013x.asp>.

Ray101. "New to Trading." *Ratebeer.com*. 28 Nov. 2010. Web. 4 Apr. 2016. <http://www.RateBeer.com/forums/new-to-trading_157180.htm>.

Reddit. *HistoryPorn*. Web. 4 Apr. 2016. <http://www.reddit.com/r/HistoryPorn/comments/zlu5v/the_earliest_known_photograph_of_men_drinking/>.

Reschan, Ryan. "The Lost Abbey Cable Car 08-12 Vertical at Toronado San Diego on the Road Vol. 29." *YouTube*. 12 Nov. 2012. Web.

———. "A Response to Greg Koch." *YouTube.* 9 July 2013. Web.

Rice, Jeff. "My Archer Liquors Purchase Arrived." *Make Mine Potato.* 14 Sept. 2007. Web.

Riess, Steven A. "Sports and the American Jew." Ed. Steven Riess. *Sports and the American Jew.* Syracuse: Syracuse UP, 1998. 1–59. Print.

Risatti, Howard. *A Theory of Craft: Function and Aesthetic Expression.* Chapel Hill: U of North Carolina P, 2013. Print.

Risen, Clay. "Craft Beer's Larger Aspirations Cause a Stir." *New York Times.* 4 Mar. 2013. Web.

Rkuhnel. *Beeradvocate.com.* 24 Feb. 2008. Web. 4 Apr. 2016. <http://beeradvocate.com/beer/profile/863/21690/?ba=rkuhnel>.

Robertson, Blair Anthony. "Pliny the Elder Released. Fans Line Up for Limited Edition Beer." *Huffington Post.* 13 Feb. 2013. Web.

Ross. "Guide to Making Trade Requests: How to Do It and How Not to Do It." *RateBeer.* 23 Feb. 2007. Web.

Roth, Bryan. "Beerhavior: Rankings, Biases, and Our Changing Palate." *This Is Why I'm Drunk.* 28 Oct. 2013. Web.

———. "Beware the Green Eyes of Envy: Beer and Compulsion." *This Is Why I'm Drunk.* 31 May 2013. Web.

Rude, Carolyn D. "Toward an Expanded Concept of Rhetorical Delivery: The Uses of Reports in Public Policy Debates." *Technical Communication Quarterly* 13.3 (2004): 271–88. Print.

Ruhlman, Michael. "Artisan Butchers (Does Artisanal Even Mean Anything Anymore?)" *Michael Ruhlman: Translating the Chef's Craft for Every Kitchen.* 19 Aug. 2010. Web.

Russell, Don. "Heritage Breweries: Yesterday's Breweries Have Become Tomorrow's." *All about Beer* 33.1. Mar. 2012: 23–28. Print.

"Russian River Pliny the Elder." *The Perfectly Happy Man.* 4 Mar. 2010. Web.

Sachs, Adam. "Artisanal America." *Details.* 1 Aug. 2010. Web.

Sampson, Tony D. *Virality: Contagion Theory in the Age of Networks.* Minneapolis: U of Minnesota P, 2012. Print.

Sandholm, Drew, and Tom Rotunno. "Merchants Not So Bubbly for Postal's Alcohol Delivery Pitch." *CNBC.com.* 11 Aug. 2013. Web.

Satran, Joe. "The 50 Best Craft Beers in America in 2013 According to Zymurgy Magazine." *Huffington Post.* 17 June 2013. Web.

———. "The States with the Best Access to Craft Beer." *Huffington Post.* 1 Sept. 2013. Web.

Schaap, Rosie. "The Best Beers of Winter." *New York Times Magazine.* 14 Feb. 2014. Web.

Schank, Roger. *Tell Me a Story: Narrative and Intelligence.* Evanston: Northwestern University Press, 1990. Print.

Scheitrum, Kevin. "The Magic of Craft." *Beer Advocate* 28 (2009): 25–27. Print.

Schimke, Kim. "I Drink. I Take Pictures. What Instagram Has Taught Me about Beer." *Brewpublic.* 7 Dec 2012. Web.

Schroppfy. "Interview with Ron Jeffries of Jolly Pumpkin." *Rate Beer Weekly Magazine.* 22 Sept. 2005. Web.

Schuhmacher, Harry. "Change We Can Believe In." *All about Beer* 32.6. Jan. 2012: 70–71. Print.

Seidl, Conrad. "Beer Gardens." *The Oxford Companion to Beer.* Ed. Garrett Oliver Oxford: Oxford UP, 2012. Print.

Sennett, Richard. *The Craftsman.* New Haven: Yale University Press, 2008. Print.

Shaviro, Steven. *Connected, or What It Means to Live in the Network Society.* Minneapolis: U of Minnesota P, 2003. Print.

Shirky, Clay. *Cognitive Surplus: How Technology Makes Consumers into Collaborators.* New York: Penguin Press, 2010. Print.

———. *Here Comes Everybody: The Power of Organizing without Organizations.* New York: Penguin Press, 2008. Print.

"Show Us Your Beer Collection." *Chicago Reader.* 12 May 2011. Web.

Siciliano, Chris. "Is Craft Beer a Social Movement." *Siciliano's Market.* 18 Feb. 2013. Web.

Skilnik, Bob. *Beer: A History of Brewing in Chicago.* Fort Lee: Barricade, 2006. Print.

Snyder, Stephen. *The Brewmaster's Bible: The Gold Standard for Homebrewers.* New York: HarperCollins, 1997. Print.

Sommers, Brian J. *The Geography of Wine: How Landscapes, Cultures, Terroir, and the Weather Make a Good Drop.* New York: Plume, 2008. Print.

Sontag, Susan. *On Photography.* New York: Farrar, Strauss, and Giroux, 1977. Print.

Sparrow, Jeff. *Wild Brews: Beer beyond the Influence of Brewer's Yeast.* Boulder: Brewers Publications, 2005. Print.

Spector, Dina. "How Beer Created Civilization." *Business Insider.* 26 Dec. 2013. Web.

Standage, Tom. *A History of the World in Six Glasses.* New York: Walker and Company, 2006. Print.

Stapinski, Helene. "Restaurants Turn Camera Shy." *New York Times.* 22 Jan. 2013. Web.

Staten, Christopher. "Extreme Beer Collectors." *Draft* Sept.–Oct. 2013: 40–42. Print.

———. "Just Drink It Already." *Draft*. May–June 2014. Web.

———. "Native Ales: A New State of Beer." *Draft*. Mar.–Apr. 2013. Web.

Steele, Mitch. *IPA: Brewing Techniques, Recipes, and the Evolution of India Pale Ale*. Boulder: Brewers Publications, 2012. Print.

Stern, Nick. "Why Instagram Photos Cheat the Viewer." *CNN*. 22 Feb. 2012. Web.

Stevenson, Seth. "Nice Cans! Miller Lite's Bizarre New Campaign Is All about Beverage Containers." *Slate*. 3 May 2010 Web.

Stewart, Kathleen. *A Space on the Side of the Road*. Princeton: Princeton UP, 1996. Print.

Stoddard, W. O. "Bowery, Saturday Night," *Harper's New Monthly Magazine* Apr. 1871: 670–80. Print.

Strader, Eric. "Huge Line Waiting for Russian River Pliny the Younger." *The Elkhart Truth*. 3 Feb. 2013. Web.

Surowiecki, James. *The Wisdom of Crowds*. New York: Anchor, 2005. Print.

Suzy Six Pack. "Welcome to the Wonderful World of Beer Trading." *Suzy Six Pack*. 13 Sept. 2010. Web.

Swinchatt, Jonathan, and David Howell. *The Winemaker's Dance: Exploring Terroir in the Napa Valley*. Berkeley: U of California P, 2004. Print.

10Best Editors. "10 Best Craft Brew States in American." *USA Today*. 22 Aug. 2013. Web.

Tippett, Nick VanillaGorilla. "New to this Page." 29 Nov. 2013. Web.

Tonsmeire, Michael. "Intro to Digital Photography for Beer." *The Mad Fermentationist*. 13 May 2013. Web.

"Top Traders." *Ratebeer.com*. Web. 4 Apr. 2016. <http://www.RateBeer.com/Users/TopTraders.asp>.

"Top 250 Beers." *Beeradvocate.com*. Web. 4 Apr. 2016. <http://beeradvocate.com/lists/top>.

Trillin, Calvin. "Magic Bagel." *Feeding a Yen*. New York: Random House, 2003. Print.

"Trouble Brewing #80." Comic strip. *Beer Advocate* Sept. 2013. Print.

Trubek, Amy. *The Taste of Place: A Cultural Journey into Terroir*. Berkeley: U of California P, 2008. Print.

Trum, Matthias. "Historical Depictions, Guild Signs, and Symbols of the Brewing and Malting Handcraft." Thesis. Technical University Munich, 2006. Web.

Tucker, Joe. "What Is Craft Beer?" *RateBeer*. 12 May 2014. Web.

Turfy. 17 May 2010. Web. 4 Apr. 2016. <http://beeradvocate.com/community/threads/post-a-picture-of-your-latest-hau1.136/page-4#post-7848>.

Tutle, Brad. "Trouble Brewing: The Craft Beer vs. 'Crafty Beer' Cat Fight." *Time*. 27 Dec. 2012. Web.

Ulmer, Gregory L. *Avatar Emergency*. Clemson: Parlor Press, 2012. Print.

———. *Heuretics, or the Logic of Invention*. Baltimore: Johns Hopkins UP, 1994. Print.

Van Bree, Edo. "Bavaria's Best Kept Secret? Zoigl in Windischeschenbach." *RateBeer*. 25 Oct. 2007. Web.

Van den Steen, Jef. *Geuze and Kriek: The Secret of Lambic*. Tielt: Lannoo, 2011. Print.

Van Dyk, Matthew. Web. 4 Apr. 2016. <https://twitter.com/mattvandyk/status/406867311514365952>.

Vargas, Antonio Jose. "The Face of Facebook: Mark Zuckerberg Opens Up." *New Yorker*. 20 Sept. 2010. Web.

Verive, John. "Four Magic Words That Will Make You Sound Like a Craft Beer Expert." *Los Angeles Times*. 7 Aug. 2013. Web.

VideoBeerReviews. *YouTube*. 1 June 2009. Web.

"Vinnie Cilurzo—Russian River Brewing Company." *YouTube*. 22 Feb. 2010. Web.

Voight, Joan. "Big Beer Brands Are Fooling Us with Their Crafty Looks: Indie Brewers Want Transparency." *Adweek*. 31 Mar. 2013. Web.

Weaver, Ken. "The Future of Craft." *RateBeer Weekly*. 9 Jan. 2013 Web.

———. "The Things One Keeps in Empty Bottles of Rare Beer." *Hop Press*. 16 Oct. 2009. Web.

Webb, Tim, Chris Pollard, and Siobhan McGinn. *LambicLand: A Journey Round the Most Unusual Beers in the World*. Cambridge: Cogan and Mater, 2010. Print.

Weinberger, David. *Everything Is Miscellaneous: The Power of the New Digital Disorder*. New York: Times Books, 2007. Print.

Welch, Kathleen E. "Reconfiguring Writing and Delivery in Secondary Orality." *Rhetorical Memory and Delivery: Classical Concepts for Contemporary Composition and Communication*. Ed. John Fredrick Reynolds. Hillsdale: Lawrence Erlbaum Associates, 1993. 17–30. Print.

Wells, Ken. *Travels with Barley: A Journey through Beer Culture in America*. New York: Free Press, 2004. Print.

WesM63. 6 Nov. 2011. Web. 4 Apr. 2016. <http://beeradvocate.com/community/threads/post-a-picture-of-your-latest-hau1.136/page-6#post-14088>.

"What Did You Get in the Mail Today?" *The Beer Spot*. 6 Mar. 2009. Web.

"What Does 'Craft' Mean in Craft Beer Poll?" *Beeradvocate.com*. 7 Aug. 2013. Web.

"What? No Beer!" *YouTube*. 11 Nov. 2011. Web.

Wheaton, Wil. "Home Brewing Bridged Three Generations." *Beer Advocate* 77. June 2013: 46–56. Print.

"Where Your Beer Is Brewed." *Ispo.tv*. 24 Aug. 2014. Web.

"The White Whale List: 2012." *Beeradvocate.com*. 24 Dec. 2012. Web. 4 Apr. 2016. <http://beeradvocate.com/community/threads/the-white-whale-list-2012.57581/>.

Willett, Megan. "Beer Experts Say These Are the 20 Best Beers in the World." *Business Insider*. 18 Sept. 2013 Web.

Williams, Raymond. *Keywords: A Vocabulary of Culture and Society*. New York: Oxford UP, 1983. Print.

Willijschidmt. *Beeradvocate.com*. 30 Apr. 2007. Web. 4 Apr. 2016. <http://www.beeradvocate.com/beer/profile/863/7971/?view=beer&sort=&start=3225>.

Wilson, Denis. "Big Beer Dresses Up in Craft Brewers' Clothing." *CNN Money*. 12 Nov. 2012. Web.

Wilson, James. *Terroir: The Role of Geology, Climate, and Culture in the Making of French Wines*. Berkeley: U of California P, 1998. Print.

Yaeger, Brian. "Gray Market/White Whale." *All about Beer*. 31.2. May 2010. Web.

———. "Portrait of Dead Soldiers Left in Yard #1: Bridgeport India Pale Ale. Red, White, and Brew: Peoples, Places, and Beers." *Red, White, and Brew*. Blog. 13 May 2013. Web.

———. *Red, White, and Brew: An American Beer Odyssey*. New York: St. Martin's Griffin, 2008. Print.

Zappa, Frank. "Titties and Beer." *YouTube*. 14 Mar. 2011. Music recording.

Zeschuk, Greg. "The Beer Diaries Talks Beer #4: Pliny the Elder." *TheBeerDiaries.tv*. 2 Oct. 2013. Web.

Zinczenko, David, and Leighton McClellan. "Trading Buds for Micro-Brewskis: Craft Beer's Renaissance Continues to Grow." *ABC News*. 30 Aug. 2013. Web.

INDEX

addiction, 226, 228–30
adjuncts, xi, 48, 88
aesthetic, xii–xiii, 134–40, 142–44, 147, 159–60, 168, 174, 176, 205
Against the Grain (brewery), 15, 70, 181–82, 206
aggregation, xii, 2, 17, 65–66, 71–72, 95–97, 99–126, 130–32, 140, 144, 169, 196, 202, 205, 207–8, 225, 232, 235
Alström, Jason and Todd, 37, 49, 83, 105–6, 132–33
Alworth, Jeff, 101–2
anecdotes, x, xiii, 1, 6–8, 10, 16–23, 25–28, 33–39, 42–43, 45–46, 50–72, 74–75, 95, 110, 114, 117–18, 147, 149, 158–59, 179, 185–86, 189–92, 209–10, 231–37
Arts and Crafts movement, x–xii, 18, 136, 138–40, 207
Asheville, North Carolina, 8, 14, 70, 93, 234
assumptions, x, xiii, 28, 38, 76–81, 83, 85, 92, 95, 103, 106–15, 117, 119, 122, 126, 131, 151, 177, 187, 210–11, 226, 228
authenticity, 87–89, 136, 146, 201–2, 205

"Back off, you hippies" drawing, 183–84
Barabási, Albert-László, 59–60, 220
bar mitzvah, 60–62, 64–65
Barthes, Roland, 12, 24, 28–29, 40, 46, 51, 53–54, 56, 62, 104–5, 140, 142, 176, 182–83, 200–201, 204, 207, 236
Beard, James, 22–24
Beer Advocate, 27, 30, 34, 37, 49, 74, 83, 89, 99, 105, 123, 152, 156–57, 161–63, 174, 196, 211–17, 225
beeroir, 82
Beer 3.0, 132–33, 141, 148
Belgium, 69, 93, 101–3, 111–15
Bell's Brewery, 3, 35, 37, 77, 83–84, 90, 112, 203
Benjamin, Walter, xi, 1–2, 33, 183
blogs, xi, 2, 6, 13–14, 30, 32–35, 42, 44, 48–49, 73, 87, 95, 101–2, 109, 116–18, 121–22, 124–25, 137, 151, 157, 161–62, 164, 169–72, 176–77, 179, 183–86, 193, 196, 200, 202, 211, 213, 216–17, 221, 225, 227–29
Blue Stallion Brewery, 8, 105, 236
bottle shares, 222–23
brevity, 14, 234
Brewers Association, ix, 85–88, 101, 129, 188
BrewGuide, 83
Brown, Bill, 98, 122
Brummett, Barry, 22, 27, 29
Budweiser, 9, 26–27, 39, 47, 62, 85, 90, 100–101, 103, 105–9, 112, 141, 152, 234
Burke, Kenneth, 21–22, 27–29, 52–53

Calagione, Sam, ix, 30, 92, 144, 146–47

INDEX

Canadian Breakfast Stout (CBS), 168, 173, 214, 216, 219, 222

Cantillon, 66–77, 101–2, 105, 111–14, 214, 216–17, 220, 233

carpentry, 137–43, 146–56, 168, 170, 173–78, 206

cellar, 52, 74, 172, 174, 212, 215, 221

children, 9, 236

Cicero, 134, 167, 171

circulation, 6, 27, 80, 128, 138, 147, 204

cluster, 84, 90, 92–93, 114, 218

Collaborative Consumption, 109, 199

compulsion, 186, 211–12

Connectors, 126, 135–37, 141, 149–53, 158, 160, 170, 175

contagion, xii, 17, 23–25, 27, 30, 37, 40–42, 45–47, 50–53, 59, 67, 72–75, 117–18, 123, 128, 131, 134, 140, 148, 164, 169, 185–86, 191–201, 204, 210, 218, 225, 228, 232–35

cool, 125–26, 200

Cornell, Martyn, 21, 79, 81

Cottone, Vincent, 85

Country Boy Brewing, xv, 8, 19, 105

Cowan, Jeremy, xvi, 60–64, 67, 69, 122

crafty, 85–91, 100, 136, 141, 146, 185, 218

Crouch, Andy, 47, 73, 116–20

Dark Lord, xv, 67, 155–223

de Certeau, Michel, 33

Demosthenes, 166–67

digital footprint, 95–96, 119, 145

displacement, 192, 207–12, 230–36

drink local, 105–6

Eckhardt, Fred, 48, 50

ecology, 76–79, 81–82, 91, 100, 108

Edbauer, Jenny, 77

"Edinburgh Ale, 1844"photograph, 190, 199, 207

engagement, 125–26, 135–37, 148–50, 153, 158, 160, 164, 204, 223, 228

Epiphanator, 237

equipment for living, 27, 34

Erickson, Jack, 10, 12, 43, 84

Ethereal (brewery), 8, 105

Facebook, x, 2, 13, 24, 29, 31, 33, 36, 44, 63, 95–96, 99, 151, 157, 171–72, 181, 183, 189, 192, 194–99, 203–6, 208–11, 216, 218, 221–22, 237

father-son stories, 28, 68, 231–36

Fight Club, 141–43

fizzy beer, 2, 47, 50, 131, 134

Flat Branch Brewing, 8, 20, 221

Flickr, 14, 91, 157, 161, 171, 184, 198, 203, 206, 222

fucked up, 114–15, 117

Galloway, Alex, 2

Google+, 13, 31, 44, 106–7, 183, 186, 198–99, 204, 206, 224

Goose Island Black Friday, 156, 217–20, 229–30

grand narrative, xiii, 14, 16–18, 25, 27–28, 39, 42–44, 47, 54, 117, 159, 175, 182, 189, 192, 207, 209, 229

Great American Beer Festival (GABF), 191–92, 195–97, 199–200, 231

Grossman, Ken, 48, 64

handmade, xi–xii, 136–41

Heineken, 9–10, 22–24, 26, 29, 46–47, 60, 232

Hendersonville, North Carolina, 232, 234–35

Hieronymus, Stan, xvi, 59, 63, 69, 76, 92–93, 184

hypertext, 6

270

INDEX

"I Am a Craft Brewer" video, 49, 63, 143–44, 166, 176, 199
identity, xii–xiii, 22, 38, 50–53, 56–60, 62–69, 71–72, 78, 80–83, 97, 100, 104, 106, 125, 130, 139, 148–49, 150, 158, 160, 167, 196–97, 199–200, 230
imagine, 4, 14, 20–21, 56, 58, 76, 84, 111, 117, 146, 164, 166–68, 171, 177, 181, 183, 202, 211
industrial, xi–xii, 47, 88–89, 136, 138–39, 156, 207, 209, 229
Instagram, x, 13–14, 29, 125, 181, 183, 186, 189–90, 198, 201–4, 206, 215, 219, 236

Jackson, Michael, 10, 40, 43–44, 48, 67–69, 92, 216
Jeffries, Ron, 49, 103
Jenkins, Henry, 45–46, 65, 148, 150, 158, 185, 194
juxtaposition, 5, 148, 180

Kentucky, xv, 8, 13, 68, 78–80, 97, 99, 104–6, 114, 122, 151–52, 172, 187, 209–10, 230, 233
Koch, Greg, 48–49, 74, 100, 130–31

lambic, 11, 66, 69–70, 93, 100–103, 108–9, 111–15, 187–88, 197–98, 220
Latour, Bruno, 29, 39, 46, 60, 105–7, 131, 139, 142, 144–45, 147, 159–60, 167, 175–77, 186
Lazar, Sam, 53–56, 59, 64–65, 70
link, 6, 18–19, 82, 119, 135, 151, 160, 163, 170
lists, 33, 35, 208–14, 225–28, 234
Lost Abbey, 26, 90, 108, 112, 187, 214, 220–21, 223
lupus salictarius, 76, 79
Lyotard, Jean François, 16, 25

Mad Men, 24, 46
Maffesoli, Michel, 43, 56, 153–54, 164, 166–67
Magee, Tony, 49, 150–51
Make Mine Potato, 33–34, 118, 120, 164, 172, 219
Manneken Pis, 69
Marx Brothers, 128–30
Maytag, Fritz, 150–52, 167
McAuliffe, Jack, 50, 84
McCullough, Malcolm, xii, 139, 158
McLuhan, Marshall, 44, 57, 65, 125, 135–36, 152–53, 164, 167, 199–200
message board, xi, 30, 47, 73, 78, 99, 154, 160, 174, 213, 218
MF Doom, 129–30, 132
Miami, Florida, 20, 22–24, 34, 53, 83
misrating, 43–44, 56, 186
Morris, William, x, xiii, 51, 136–38, 140–41, 143
myth, 3, 6–7, 38, 44, 51, 53–58, 60, 63–65, 68–69, 72, 74, 78, 84, 90, 104, 132, 136, 166–69, 214

nerd, 163
networks, x, 20, 29, 33, 43, 45–46, 50–51, 53, 59–60, 65, 71–98, 100, 108, 110, 115, 126, 142, 144–46, 148, 150, 156, 158, 175, 177–78, 207, 220, 222
New Glarus (brewery), 8, 49, 225, 227
now, 205–8

Odell Brewing, 90, 94–97, 112, 145
Oliver, Garrett, xvi, 26, 81, 108, 110
Ong, Walter, 152, 154
Orwell, George, 9, 21

parental beer tales, 4–5, 15, 19, 24, 231–32
participation, x, xiii, 39–40, 44–45, 51, 125, 147, 153–54, 158–59, 164–65, 173, 199–200, 223–24

INDEX

Payottenland, 101, 103–4
permission marketing, 32, 194–203, 218
Plato, 127, 134, 136, 141, 145
Pliny the Elder, xiii, xv, 33, 72–84, 95, 98, 106, 108, 117–18, 120–26, 144, 146, 184–85, 209, 213, 216, 222–25, 230
Prairie Artisan Ales, 110–15, 201
proairesis, 41–41, 146–47
Pulp Fiction, 1, 3
punctum, 207

Quintilian, 149, 154, 166

RateBeer, 13, 30–40, 45, 51, 66, 72–73, 78, 88, 96, 99, 113, 118–20, 125, 150–52, 157, 161–63, 169, 172–73, 181, 186, 206, 208, 210–30
Really Simple Syndication (RSS), 33, 36, 116, 118–19, 121, 151, 206
revolution, 8–9, 37, 41, 47–56, 72, 86, 88, 91, 114, 120, 125, 133–36, 139–48, 159, 167, 181, 204, 236
Rice, Jenny, xvi
Russian River (brewery), xiii, 8, 14–15, 72–76, 84, 100, 107–8, 112, 121–26, 143, 146, 155, 185, 187, 213–14, 225, 230

Schlafly (brewery), ix, 17, 100, 107, 203, 216, 223
secrecy, 43, 56, 153, 155, 197
selfie, 235–37
sentiment, 104, 136, 154, 158–60, 166, 189, 205
sharing, x, xiii, xvi, 3–5, 7–8, 11–17, 22, 24, 26–28, 30–33, 42–46, 64–65, 67, 71, 109, 117–18, 149–50, 154, 158, 162, 164–69, 178–206, 218–20, 223, 226–37
Shirky, Clay, 38–39, 41–42, 45, 168, 189

snapshots, 14, 159, 179, 182, 185–86, 188, 190–91, 193, 204, 209–10, 231–32, 234
spatial, 68, 83–84, 209
Spokane Style, 93–94
Stone Brewing, 37, 48–50, 77, 81, 90, 96, 130–31, 197, 203
suggestion, 7, 52, 139

taxonomy, 77, 82–90, 101–2, 106, 120–21, 125, 137, 201, 208, 218, 223
terroir, xiii, 14, 35, 71, 77, 79–126, 139, 142, 145, 149, 179, 186, 189, 192, 194, 205, 208–9, 212, 218–22, 225–26, 230, 232, 234–35, 237
Three's Company, 57, 129–30, 146
Three Stooges, 57, 127–28, 130, 132, 175
topos, 41, 47, 154, 192, 223, 229
tracings, 46, 63, 107, 117, 122, 142, 145, 147, 156, 159–60, 166–68, 174–77, 236
trades, 154, 162, 167, 178, 204–5, 213, 215–16, 220–30
transmedia, 45–47, 51, 53, 68, 159
Trillin, Calvin, 5
Trubek, Amy, 80–81, 86, 91–92, 95, 123, 191
Twitter, x, 2, 13, 24, 29, 31, 36, 44, 99, 118–19, 156–57, 162, 186, 189, 209, 218–19, 222, 224

Ulmer, Gregory, 6–7, 63, 65, 146
Untappd, 150
urination, 62–63, 68–69
user generated, 38, 43, 115, 132, 201, 221

Vered IPA, 121
vitalism, 153–54, 166

Weather Channel, 210
Weaver, Ken, ix, 226–28

weed, 191
West Coast style, 83–84
West Sixth Brewing, xv, 8, 84, 105–6, 228
Weyerbacher (brewery), 30, 35, 37, 39, 41, 43, 56, 65, 72, 115, 132, 151, 188
whales, 203, 214–17, 230, 236
Wicked Weed (brewery), 11, 70, 206, 234
wisdom of crowds, 39, 151, 188

yard work, 10, 22–23, 27–28
yeast, 57, 74, 81, 93, 101–2, 111–12, 116, 120, 128, 130, 141
YouTube, xi, 33, 117–18, 123, 163, 172, 214, 216

Zappa, Frank, 130, 150
Zoigl-Star, 56, 58–59, 63, 66–67, 190, 199
Zombie Dust, 33, 83

JEFF RICE holds the Martha B. Reynolds Endowed Professorship for Digital Media and is the chair of writing, rhetoric, and digital studies at the University of Kentucky. He is the author, editor, or coeditor of six books, including *Digital Detroit: Rhetoric and Space in the Age of the Network*; *From A to <A>: Keywords in Markup* (with Bradley Dilger); and *The Rhetoric of Cool: Composition Studies and New Media*. He blogs at *Yellow Dog* and *Make Mine Potato*.